The Crisis of Quebec, 1914-1918

The Crisis of Quebec, 1914-1918

by Elizabeth H. Armstrong

WITH AN INTRODUCTION BY
Joseph Levitt

The Carleton Library No. 74

McClelland and Stewart Limited

THE CARLETON LIBRARY

A series of Canadian reprints and new collections of source material relating to Canada, issued under the editorial supervision of the Institute of Canadian Studies of Carleton University, Ottawa.

DIRECTOR OF THE INSTITUTE
Davidson Dunton

GENERAL EDITOR
Michael Gnarowski

EXECUTIVE EDITOR
James H. Marsh

EDITORIAL BOARD
B. Carman Bickerton (*History*)
Dennis Forcese (*Sociology*)
David Knight (*Geography*)
J. George Neuspiel (*Law*)
Thomas K. Rymes (*Economics*)
Derek G. Smith (*Anthropology*)
Michael S. Whittington (*Political Science*)

The Crisis of Quebec, 1914-1918 is republished by agreement with Columbia University Press, which first published it in 1937.

© 1974, McClelland and Stewart Limited

ALL RIGHTS RESERVED
ISBN 0-7710-9774-3

The Canadian Publishers
McClelland and Stewart Limited
25 Hollinger Road, Toronto

Printed in Canada by Webcom Limited

INTRODUCTION
TO THE CARLETON LIBRARY EDITION

The Crisis of Quebec, 1914-1918 by Elizabeth H. Armstrong is a welcome addition to the Carleton Library. First published in 1937, it remains the best general treatment of one of the major turning points in the history of French Canada. *The Crisis of Quebec* would have been a valuable book simply because it dealt vividly with a period of French-Canadian history on which not much work had been done. But the book was significant in quite another way. Up to the time of its appearance, the most important work on post-Confederation French-Canadian history had been the biography of Wilfrid Laurier by Oscar Douglas Skelton. That Laurier emphasized the "common Canadianism" of English and French made him a hero to Skelton and gave the historian an opportunity to underline what the two peoples had in common. Miss Armstrong, however, was struck by the distinctness of French Canada. Its reaction to the war demonstrated to her symptoms that seemed to indicate "the rise of a definite separate French-Canadian nationality." The events of Quebec in the last decade have shown how perceptive she was and have made the *Crisis of Quebec* one of those rare books in Canadian history which grow more significant with the passage of time.

The book has faults, but they are the faults of the perspective of the age in which Miss Armstrong was studying Quebec. Her stereotyped view of French Canada resulted in inconsistencies in the explanation she offered of the conscription crisis. She rigidly equated French-Canadian nationalism with Catholicism and isolationism at a time in Quebec's history when it is essential to separate – not identify – nationalist urgings and religion. Her analysis of nationalism in Quebec is further undermined by her studied neglect of English-Canadian nationalism as a factor in the conscription crisis. Moreover, her affection for Canada and her distrust of nationalism and fear of isolationism caused her to be much too harsh to Henri Bourassa and too kind by ample measure to Wilfrid Laurier. Had the private papers of these major personages and others – such as Borden and Gouin – been made available to her, she may have seen more of the political side of Laurier and the pan-Canadianism of Bourassa's views.

Elizabeth Armstrong's generation of American liberals, horrified by the rise of a brutal and racist Naziism, was not disposed to regard any nationalist movement with favor. Yet, because she sympathised with French Canada's desire to resist assimilation by the English-speaking majority, she was forced to distinguish between two kinds of nationalist movements: an "active" one which expanded to dominate other peoples, and a "passive" one content to remain at its hearth. For her, French-Canadian nationalism provided an "extraordinary vivid illustration of the passive sense of nationality."[1]

She used the term "passive" because she believed French Canadians wished "to be left alone to the enjoyment of their peculiar form of life."[2] The French-Canadian "Nationalist," she insisted, was "not on the look out for new fields to conquer."[3] Thus she implied that the attention of French Canadians in Quebec was concentrated exclusively on life in their province. This was true of many, especially those who lived in the countryside. But by 1914 almost half the population of Quebec lived in the cities and towns, the result in part of the new industrial order. It had brought forward an urban elite of small businessmen and professionals who vigorously affirmed that all of Canada from the Atlantic to the Pacific belonged as much to French Canada as it did to English Canada.

Encouraged by the accession of a French Canadian to

[1] E. H. Armstrong, below, p. ix. Conscription raised important social issues in English Canada but because Miss Armstrong was interested in Quebec she presented it solely as a French-English question. Since this introduction is concerned with Miss Armstrong's work it deals only with this aspect of conscription.
[2] *Ibid*, p. viii
[3] *Ibid.*, p. vii

the office of Prime Minister, they agreed with Henri Bourassa that it was necessary "apporter notre pierre à l'édifice nationale, nous y ménager la place qui nous y revient de droit."[4] One reason they supported colonization was their belief that there could be built a French-Canadian rural empire stretching from St. Jerome across Northern Ontario to Winnipeg. Their conviction that the West was also their territory explains their anger over the injury to French-Canadian interests imposed by the educational arrangements in the new provinces of Saskatchewan and Alberta in 1905 and their apprehension at the influx to that area of immigrants who did not accept that Canada was an Anglo-French country.

The year 1903 saw the birth of the Nationalist League, a tiny organization of French-Canadian intellectuals. Although the League, as such, never amounted to much, the movement it represented had a considerable influence in Quebec, owing in part to the power of intellect and personality of its main spokesman, Henri Bourassa. Two important points in the Nationalist program were a bilingual Canada and a Canada that was fully autonomous within the British Empire. The Nationalists became prominent in Federal politics when sixteen of them were elected in Quebec over their claim that Laurier's naval bill would automatically turn over the Canadian navy to Great Britain in case of an Imperial war. These Nationalist members of Parliament became discredited in Quebec because they eventually drifted into the Conservative party. The term "Nationalist," as it was used during the war period, could refer either to this group of Quebec members of Parliament who all loyally supported the war, or to the French-Canadian nationalist movement which stayed loyal to Bourassa. When Miss Armstrong uses the term subsequent to Chapter I she means the followers of Bourassa. The earlier references are to Nationalist members of Parliament. Laurier, however, often used the term indiscriminantly, overlooking the split within the movement.

Meanwhile, there had been a significant French-Canadian emigration from Quebec towards Ontario. Between 1880 and 1910 much of eastern Ontario became French speaking; while in Ontario as a whole the propor-

---

[4] *Le Nationaliste*, April 3, 1904, p. 2 col. 3

tion of French Canadians rose from 5 to 10 per cent. In Ottawa in 1910, a French-Canadian Congress of Education made up of twelve hundred delegates, chosen by local nominating conventions from all over the province, proposed that French be a legal language of instruction in Ontario. Two years later, the passing of Regulation 17, imposing severe constraint on French in Ontario schools, infuriated informed French Canadians. Of course they resented the attack on their culture and the downgrading of their language to an inferior status. But they were also bitter because the new law would pen up French Canadians in a Quebec reserve; a French Canadian could not assume his rightful patrimony in Ontario without assimilating. Thus Miss Armstrong, by using the term "passive" overlooked those French Canadians who were sufficiently interested in the country beyond Quebec to be aggressive in pressing their claims to the whole of Canada.

Miss Armstrong was also influenced in her interpretation by the isolationism of the thirties which had been blind to the rise of Hitler. She believed that French Canadians in the First World War had similar isolationist attitudes. She speaks of an "instinctive French Canadian recoil from foreign involvement."[5] Elsewhere she writes, "If the German armies succeeded in reaching the channel ports what would it matter whether ... every French Canadian in Ontario enjoyed his full rights."[6] The implication here was that the French Canadians ought to have accepted their share of the responsibility of maintaining a rational and humane European community.

There may well have been a strong case for Canadian participation in the war, but French Canadians had no information on which to base any kind of judgement. Even the government at Ottawa relied on the press in England, since it had been excluded from any share in British diplomacy. What French Canadians could see was that Canada, as a British colony, had been drawn into a conflict about which hardly anyone knew anything. Separated from the fighting by three thousand miles of ocean, they simply did not believe that their country was in danger. In these circumstances they took an understandable

[5] Armstrong, *Crisis*, op. cit., p. 63
[6] *Ibid.*, p. 241.

attitude towards the war. They wished for an Allied victory; there should be no limit to the economic aid to Britain. If Canadians, including some French-speaking ones, wished to go off and fight for the Allied side: well and good. But no one had a right to force another to lay down his life in what was at bottom not a Canadian but a British war.

The author contends that French Canadians could not think intelligently about an active role for Canada in the war because they were under the sway of "passion."[7] This term, however, might be more applicable to the mood of English Canada. Anglo-Canadians had no particular knowledge of European politics either, yet more than a quarter million of them enlisted. Robert Borden, John Dafoe, Arthur Meighen and Newton Rowell were all convinced that Britain was in danger, that freedom must be saved from Prussian militarism and that through the war Canada would emerge as one of the important nations of the world. "I need hardly say to you that nothing has stirred me more deeply in all my life than the world war," wrote Rowell to Laurier.[8] The sense of taking part in the intense drama which would alter the future of the world is plainly manifest in the rhetoric of two of the leading actors of the conscription crisis:

> United around Britain (the Allies) will win and they all know that come what may, though the world may crash, Britain will stand true, undismayed unconquerable[9]

and

> A thousand years from now Canadian youths will read the story of their deeds with hearts uplifted and with kindling eyes. Safe in such immortality what matters is that they sleep, far from Canada upon the battlefields of France.[10]

---

[7] *Ibid.*, p. 172

[8] Cited by M. E. Prang, "The Political Career of Newton Wesley Rowell' unpublished Ph.D. thesis (University of Toronto, 1959), p. 331.

[9] Arthur Meighen, *Canadian Annual Review*, 1917 (Toronto, 1918) p. 618.

[10] John Dafoe, *Over the Canadian Battlefields* (Toronto, 1919) p. 82

These powerful feelings explain why the government insisted on conscription. Borden argued that "whether Canada shall continue or withdraw her effort in this war, whether our troops shall be supported or abandoned is the extreme question."[11] Certainly Canada faced the choice of either reducing the four divisions overseas or introducing conscription. Yet the supplying of adequate reserves for those four divisions was not necessarily the best way to contribute to the war effort in the spring of 1917. Though Borden had been told that there were a million more German troops on the Western Front than in 1916, he apparently did not question this report although he knew that the British Prime Minister, Lloyd George, was much more concerned with the danger of the German submarine blockade of his country than he was by a new German attack on the Western Front. In fact the war was to be won not by military blows but by economic pressures.[12] With the information then available to him, Borden could not have been expected to understand how small a role battle would play in winning the war. Yet in view of the shortage of manpower, he might have asked himself whether Canada's commitment abroad should not have been reduced to boost industrial production at home, if there was a good chance, as it then seemed that much of Canadian supplies on the way to England would be sunk by enemy U-boats.

But Borden in his speeches explaining his decision does not touch on this problem at all. For him conscription was not a strategic act to win the war, but an ideological commitment to guard Canada's honor. "Thousands of men," he told Parliament," have made the supreme sacrifice for our liberty and preservation... Common gratitude, apart from other considerations, should bring the whole force of this nation behind them. I have promised that this help shall be given."[13] This pledge could only be redeemed if the war effort were pushed to the limit. Con-

---

[11] R. L. Borden, *Canadian Annual Review*, 1917 (Toronto, 1918), p. 593

[12] Captain Sir Basil Liddell Hart, *History of the 20th Century*, A. J. P. Taylor, editor, Chapter 27, p. 735

[13] R. L. Borden, *Canada, House of Commons Debates*, May 18, 1917, p. 1542

scription had become a "test and a symbol";[14] it had become an absolute "moral necessity."[15]

The blood spilt in France made it psychologically impossible for most Anglo-Canadians to question the rhetoric which rationalized the war and the death of so many young Canadian soldiers. Their anger at Laurier in 1917 is very instructive. He hoped for an Allied victory; but he appeared to be saying that Canada ought not to give herself over, body and soul, to achieve victory. These Anglo-Canadians believed that if they tolerated any slackening of fervour, they would betray a great moral crusade. French Canadians, on the other hand, genuinely did not understand that the commitment to the war by Anglo-Canadian editorialists and politicians was an expression of their raging Canadian nationalism. To them Anglo-Canadians remained imperialists, under the skin, whose first loyalty was not to Canada but to the British Empire. The war split the two peoples because it revealed that each had a different conception of what was most important for Canada's future: the one believed that as a dynamic Britannic nation, she should help shape Europe's destiny; the other was convinced that as a small North American nation, she should cope with her own internal problems. In retrospect it would be hard to maintain that of the two, in their assessment, the French Canadians were less realistic.

A differing conception of the national interest led naturally to notable differences in the rates of recruiting among English and French. Miss Armstrong lays part of the blame for the low French-Canadian enlistment on the inept and tactless methods of the Conservatives. However, the most important reason, in her opinion, was the bitterness French Canadians felt over Regulation 17; it was "responsible more than anything else for the gradual slowing up of the war effort of French Canada."[16] In this development she suggests Bourassa played a role of "great significance."[17]

[14] J. W. Dafoe, *Laurier: A Study in Canadian Politics* (Toronto, 1963), p. 104
[15] H. B. Neatby, *Laurier and a Liberal Quebec, A Study in Political Management* (Toronto: The Carleton Library No. 63, 1973), p.
[16] Armstrong, *Crisis, op. cit.*, p. 91
[17] *Ibid.*, p. 112

How many French-Canadian recruits would have been enough? The answer is presumably as many as would have obviated the introduction of conscription. In May 1917 to keep four Canadian divisions at full strength in France, Prime Minister Borden needed at least 70,000 replacements. The previous year the enlistments had averaged some 6000 a month. Since most of the men who wished to join had already gone, the government would have been lucky, if for the rest of the year, an average of 5000 a month had volunteered, giving a total of 35,000 recruits. The only condition under which conscription could have been avoided while maintaining Canadian strength in France was the availability of another 35,000 soldiers. These might have been expected to come from French Canada. Now according to Miss Armstrong only 14,000 French Canadians enlisted, of whom 50 per cent came from outside Quebec. Her argument boils down to the dubious assertion that it was mainly the Nationlist agitation that prevented more than two and a half times that number joining. She asserts accurately that the "high watermark of French-Canadian enthusiasm for active participation in the war"[18] was a giant recruiting meeting on October 15, 1914, well before the beginning of the Nationalist war-time campaign on Regulation 17. Leading politicians from both parties, led by Laurier, urged young French Canadians to join, but the net result was a paltry 575 men. Young French Canadians simply did not believe that Canada had any great stake in the war. They continued to be sceptical despite the exhortations of not only politicans but also most of the French-Canadian press and the Roman Catholic hierarchy. Certainly, without Regulation 17 more French Canadians might have joined, but not in numbers enough to prevent conscription.

The author described Bourassa as a "mixture of sincere patriotism and demagoguery."[19] The agitation over restrictions on French in the Ontario school system, she hinted, might have been deliberately fomented to undermine Canadian participation in the war overseas. But

[18] *Ibid.*, p. 85
[19] *Ibid.*, p. 96

there is no reason to question his commitment to the rights of Franco-Ontarians; his whole career testifies to the depth of his conviction that Canada must become a truly bi-cultural country. Had there been no war he would have protested against Regulation 17. Had there been no French language question in Ontario, he would have opposed Canadian participation in the war as vehemently as he did. At the same time it was only natural for him to consider the continued restriction of French rights in Ontario as evidence of the hypocrisy of the Anglo-Canadian politicians who maintained that the war was a crusade for freedom.

Although the author defined Bourassa's attitude towards the war as one of "isolationism,"[20] the main reason he rejected Canadian participation in the war was that he was convinced that its inspiration was imperalist, and not that it was taking place in Europe. Canada was in the conflict not to defend her national interests but to save the British Empire. He had always hated empires which he believed crushed human liberty and prevented intellectual and moral progress. These great empires, inspired by the greed for gold, were smashing up small nationalities in their struggle to dominate Europe. These intellectual convictions of Bourassa are re-inforced by the sadness at the slaughter on the battlefields:

> The sun of the year 1915 rose in a cloud of fire. It is setting in a sea of blood. The most civilized peoples in the world persist in tearing each other apart with a foolish rage. Five million men, it is said, are dead or mutilated for life. Frightful miseries accumulate. And the massacre continues.[21]

These are not the words of a man who is indifferent to what is going on in Europe. Nor was he without what he considered to be a positive solution. He wished the great powers on either side to accept the advice of Pope Benoit XV and negotiate a peace in which neither side would be victorious. In this view he was, no doubt, visionary but not isolationist.

[20] *Ibid.*, p. 152
[21] H. Bourassa, *Le Pape arbitre de la paix* (Montreal, 1918), p. 40. (Translation by J. Levitt)

"A good deal may be said for Bourassa's thesis on the value of French" wrote Miss Armstrong, "but it was hardly a popular theory in the English-speaking Canada of 1915 and it only helped to disturb racial feeling."[22] Here she was criticizing Bourassa not because what he says was wrong, but because it was the wrong time to say it. Bourassa had an extraordinary talent for getting under peoples' skin. Anyone with a deep affection for the Mother Country would have been deeply wounded had he read the following sentence in a Bourassa editorial: "Les flots de sang français feront germer des moissons d'or anglais."[23] Still, it was not so much his stinging words but what he stood for which aroused his opponents' fury.

Laurier, who was always tactful, stirred up no little racial animosity himself because he opposed conscription. The cleavage between the two peoples was such that any vigorous defence of the majority position of the one was bound to rouse anger amongst the other. Yet this was no reason to expect men of character like Bourassa and Laurier to keep quiet on matters about which they felt very deeply.

Though Miss Armstrong regarded Bourassa with a certain amount of distaste, she displayed nothing but admiration for Laurier who, according to her, "was born to be an apostle of tolerance and peace and to him the great goal of racial understanding transcended any petty partisanship."[24] Be that as it may, it was around the head of Laurier along with that of Borden that the whole conscription crisis swirled. It began when Borden returned from overseas in May 1917 determined to introduce conscription. He asked Laurier to join him in a coalition government to carry the bill. Laurier's refusal was an act of great significance because it meant that conscription became an issue of partisan party politics.

Laurier's motives in rejecting Borden's offer have become a subject of considerable controversy among Canadian historians. Miss Armstrong argued that he had turned down the invitation because of its condition that

---

[22] Armstrong, *Crisis, op. cit.*, p. 97
[23] *Le Devoir*, May 1st, 1917, p. 1
[24] Armstrong, *Crisis, op. cit.*, p. 21

such a government must accept conscription and that conscription would result in "racial cleavage."[25] Many contemporary writers continue to believe this interpretation that Laurier's actions in this crisis were based on high principle.[26] This view had been challenged very early by John Dafoe, one of the architects of the Union government. He claimed that Laurier had been motivated by two definite reasons: "to win back, if he could, the prime ministership of Canada; but in any event to establish his position forever as the unquestioned, unchallenged leader of his own people."[27] Dafoe's premise that Laurier might have had political and personal reasons was not widely accepted for many years, but recently important historians have shown more sympathy for this point of view.[28]

Certainly Laurier's political inducements were much stronger than Miss Armstrong allows. When the offer was made to Laurier in May 1917, the Liberal party was on the upswing and his acceptance would have been of considerable benefit to Borden. At that time he had no reason to believe that conscription would split away the entire Anglo-Canadian wing of his party. Then too as a man of pride it was only natural for him to be concerned about his image in Quebec. For many years in dueling with Bourassa he had hammered away at the idea that although in certain circumstances Canada as a free country might fight for Great Britain, he was unalterably opposed to conscription. How could he go back on his word in any honorable way? As he wrote to Rowell, in accepting conscription he would have lost his own "self-respect" as well.[29]

[25] *Ibid.*, p. 176
[26] J. M. S. Careless, *Canada: A Story of Challenge* (Toronto, 1963) p. 336; E. McInnis, *Canada: A Political and Social History* (New York, 1962) p. 411; H. B. Neatby, *Laurier, op. cit.*, p. 384.
[27] J. Dafoe, *Laurier, op. cit.* p. 96
[28] D. G. Creighton, *Canada's First Century* (Toronto 1970), p. 148; G. R. Cook, "Dafoe, Laurier and the Formation of Union Government," in C. Berger, ed., *Conscription, 1917* (Toronto, n.d.), p. 27.
[29] O. D. Skelton, *Life and Letters of Sir Wilfrid Laurier*, vol. 2, (Toronto, 1965), p. 191

Still, there is no reason to doubt that Laurier believed he was acting to save national unity. He feared that the coercion of the French by the English-speaking majority would only envenom the relations between the two groups. He was convinced that if he accepted conscription he would hand Quebec over to Bourassa, the consequence of which could only be the further polarization of political opinion in Canada. Nor was a rejection of conscription inconsistent with his often proclaimed insistence on the necessity of Allied victory. His speeches showed an understanding of the importance of food and ammunition to Britain. His policy would entail a more judicious use of manpower, taking into account the twin needs of more recruits and increased supplies. The mixture of expediency and principle which underlay Laurier's actions during the crisis is best exemplified by his proposal of a referendum on conscription. A referendum would take the issue out of party politics, and that would have been advantageous to the Liberals. But there might be enough resistance in English Canada to block the measure; even a substantial show of opposition to conscription outside Quebec would prevent it from becoming the occasion of a French-English confrontation.

Laurier's modern critics make a valid point when they suggest that the country might have escaped disruption if he had joined the coalition.[30] Party ties were very strong and there was a great personal affection for him among Liberals. In the summer of 1917, Western and Ontario Liberals remained loyal to him despite his stand against conscription; it might well have been that most of the Quebec party would have remained faithful if he had gone conscriptionist.[31] In that case the election of 1917 would not have taken on the nature of a contest between English and French. Nor did it necessarily follow that Bourassa would have swept Quebec; in 1911, even supported by Conservative money, the Nationalists managed to win only 16 seats from Laurier.

[30] Creighton, *Canada's First Century, op. cit.*, p. 148, R. Graham, *Arthur Meighen: The Door of Opportunity* (Toronto, 1960), p. 124
[31] Armstrong, *Crisis: op. cit.*, p. 176

Another issue which flows from the controversy over Laurier's motives is whether in view of the exacerbation of the relations between the two peoples, conscription was worthwhile. Miss Armstrong suggested that whether by voluntary means or conscription Canada simply could not produce the number of men for which Borden was asking. It has been shown that this was not so.[32] The Military Service Act did result in the sending of 47,000 men overseas and there is no doubt that had the war continued, the quota of 100,000 men, sought by the government, would have been fulfilled.

At the conclusion of her book, the author posed an important question: why did not French Canada rebel? Her answer was that French-Canadian nationalism was passive. Had it been active, it might not have shrunk from the "ultimate test of armed resistance."[33] For some the Quebec riots of Easter 1918 was a try. But the great majority of French Canadians, like Bourassa himself, were pledged to law and order. On the other hand if the war had lasted longer, there might have been sufficient casualties among French-Canadian conscripts for there to have been an even more serious political crisis.

With the ending of the war, tensions between the two peoples eased; yet the baneful effects of the conscription crisis for Canadian unity persisted. Ever since the time of Lafontaine and Baldwin, the French Canadians had assumed that Canada was a partnership between the two peoples. After Confederation the bi-ethnic nature of both the Liberal and Conservative parties had prevented a direct confrontation between English and French. Even when Riel was hanged, most French-Canadian Conservative members stayed loyal to Macdonald. During the crises over the Boer War in 1899, the Autonomy School Bill in 1905 and the Naval Bill in 1910 the great majority of Quebec members along with their English-speaking counterparts continued to support Laurier. In 1917 this system broke down because "party, race and issue coin-

[32] See A. M. Willaims, "Conscription 1917: A Brief for the Defence," *Canadian Historical Review*, xxxvii (4), December, 1959.

[33] Armstrong, *Crisis, op. cit.*, p. 244

cided."[34] The great harm wrought in 1917 was not that English and French became angry with each other but that many French Canadians came to believe that Canada was not governed by two concurrent majorities.

One lesson which some French Canadians drew was that they had little influence over events in English Canada; gone was the tumult and shouting over the inferior status of French in schools outside Quebec. Bourassa, it is true, continued to believe that Canada was as much the homeland of French Canadians as of the English. But the Nationalist movement had fragmented. One important faction, led by Abbé Groulx, had lost all genuine interest in the rest of Canada and had certainly ceased to believe that Ottawa could protect French Canada's legitimate interests. Thus, a significant number of French-Canadian intellectuals had begun, for the first time since Confederation, to view Quebec as their true political homeland. The great value of Miss Armstrong's book is that it is the best account of the events which gave rise to this Canadian tragedy.

Joseph Levitt
University of Ottawa

[34] A. M. Lower, *Colony to Nation: A History of Canada* (Toronto, 1957), p. 466.

The Crisis of Quebec
1914-18

I

The Roots of French Canadianism

WHEN by a stroke of the pen the French king ceded Canada to the British in 1763, French Canadian nationality was born. The habitant who was so suddenly deprived of the government to which he had always been accustomed was compelled to adjust himself to an alien allegiance and found himself sorely bewildered. It is not true, as was formerly believed, that all the officials and nobility returned to France leaving only the ignorant peasantry. The fact remains, however, that most of the officials did depart from Canada, leaving the seigneurs or feudal landowners as sole leaders of a sorely tried and puzzled people. Some of the seigneurs went to London and played a part in the framing of the Quebec Act of 1774, while those who remained at home tried to arouse the people to stand up for their rights. The Church, for her part, while not battling for the civil rights of the population, did all she could to maintain the strength of her own position. The Church, with her extraordinary power to bend with the storm rather than break, realized with uncanny foresight that the day of France on the American continent was done and that the only means of saving the religion and nationality of 60,000 faithful French Canadians was to accept the British régime wholeheartedly. By that acceptance there was born a new nationality on the soil of French Canada.

The position of the French Canadian habitant under the French régime was much more independent and happy than has been generally supposed. French Canadianism had indeed asserted itself as early as the beginning of the eighteenth century. It had forced on a reluctant home government the appointment of the Canadian-born Vaudreuil as governor. French-born priests and even officers met opposition from their comrades born in Canada. Though the French régime was essentially a paternalistic one, the relation of the habitant to the government was not without its compensations. The captain of militia in each parish was the main link between the authorities and the population. He acted as liaison officer who transmitted the commands of the government to the habitants, and if they were disobeyed, reported the delinquents to the intendant or to the governor.[1] Although the habitants were undoubtedly poor, they were far less oppressed by social and economic distinctions than were their brethren in the old country. Montcalm himself said that the Canadian habitant lived better than the rural noblesse of France. There were no taxes, and even the seigneurial duties and church tithes were comparatively light. The early French Canadian's relation with the Church was a happy and intimate one, and the lower ranks of the clergy had been habitually recruited from the habitants themselves. The relation of the habitant to the seigneur was a similarly easy one, for the social and economic condition of the two classes differed very little. The French Canadian's feeling about the mother country was at the conquest already of mixed character. New France had been developing along different lines from the old country. There was more freedom and less class distinction than in Europe, and the "Canadien" was beginning to think of himself as different from the Frenchman. If anything had been needed to emphasize the growing feeling of regret at French policy, it was the French King's lighthearted abandonment of the colony at the Treaty of Paris, in 1763.

When the colony was taken over by the British, it was much more willing to accept the new régime than might have been expected. Many of the habitants were dissatisfied with French rule, and the mass of the people was thoroughly tired of the endless

[1] A. L. Burt, *The Old Province of Quebec*, pp. 3-5.

wars of the past generation. Nevertheless, they found themselves puzzled and hesitant at the change in allegiance. Discontented as they had sometimes been, separation from France had never been seriously contemplated. It was after all a rude shock to the habitant to find that he had lost his country at one stroke of the pen so suddenly and completely and was in the future to be governed by a Protestant and English-speaking power. In this dark moment the *Canadien* sought help and guidance from the seigneurs who remained the real leaders of the people for the first twenty years of the British régime, when they were replaced by the *avocats* and the *hommes de profession*. The captains of militia practically disappeared, and the rôle of the Church was still a small one.

By the Treaty of Paris of 1763 the king of France ceded all his rights in Canada to the king of Great Britain. The new sovereign of Canada promised in return that his new subjects should be granted "the liberty of the Catholic religion" and added, that "they may profess the worship of their religion according to the rites of the Romish Church as far as the laws of Great Britain permit." [2] For barely ten years after the conquest the French Canadians were governed by governors under the royal proclamation of October, 1763.[3] Under letters patent issued just before the proclamation the governor was empowered to set up a government for the province, to establish courts, and to legislate by means of a Council and Assembly. The immediate results of the conquest for the habitant were a general worsening of the status he had previously known. This naturally did not increase the friendly relations between the habitant and the new government. The habitant found that his laws were to be prescribed and his religion jeopardized by the avowed intention of the British to Protestantize the new province. The French Canadian's ability to hold office was removed by requiring him to subscribe to the

[2] Treaty of Paris, 1763, Article 4, in W. P. M. Kennedy, *Statutes, Treaties and Documents of the Canadian Constitution*, pp. 32-35.
[3] A. L. Burt, *op. cit.*, pp. 27-57.

Test Act, which no Roman Catholic could do. As a result the habitant would have been ineligible even for the Assembly which was contemplated for the province.

Fortunately for the survival of the French Canadians the British governors were extremely friendly to their nationality. Governor Murray tacitly ignored the instructions for the Anglicization and Protestantization of the new province. He allowed French Canadians to act as jurors in spite of the fact that as Roman Catholics they were disqualified from office, and he refused to call an Assembly in which the representatives of the English minority, the merchants of Montreal and Quebec, would have been the only members. Murray's conciliatory policy was partly owing to his genuine liking and respect for the French Canadians but even more largely to his desire to win their allegiance by impressing them with the power, justice, and fairness of British rule. Murray and his successors were also well aware of the growing discontent with British rule in the New England colonies, and they hoped that if the French Canadians could be made into loyal subjects they would constitute a formidable threat to any attempts at rebellion in the south. The conciliatory policy of the first British governors was largely successful. The French Canadian's faith in British justice received its firm foundation, and the help given by Murray in preventing Protestantization by the appointment of a bishop to the vacant see of Quebec rallied the whole body of the clergy to the support of Britain. The era of peace after the long period of wars was very welcome to the weary habitant, and his former martial qualities began to grow stale with disuse. The fact that the cession of Canada had been so lightheartedly undertaken by France made any hope that the colony might revert to the mother country seem impossible to the habitants and strengthened their desire to make the best of the new régime.

Government by proclamations, which were in effect a dead letter, could not continue, and in 1774 Parliament passed the Quebec

The Roots of French Canadianism

Act for the governance of the colony.[4] The Quebec Act, by its affirmation of the right of non-English peoples in the Empire to keep their own customs and privileges,[5] saved Canada from joining the rebels in the southern colonies in the Revolution which was so soon to break out. With this affirmation of rights the French Canadian nationality received its formal consecration. By the terms of the Quebec Act the feudal tenure of land was maintained, and the loyalty of the seigneurial class to the new régime was thereby guaranteed. The right of the Church to collect tithes was confirmed and supported by law, whereby the loyalty to Britain of that influential body was secured. In order to please the French Canadians the promise to establish an Assembly for which they would not have been eligible was revoked. The dominance of the French language in the province was maintained, and, not least important, a simple oath of allegiance was substituted for the oath of allegiance to which Roman Catholics could not subscribe. As a result of the Quebec Act French Canada was given the mold to which it was to conform for many generations, while the power of the Church was given an enormous impetus by the firm establishment of tithes. But it must not be supposed that because the Quebec Act established a form for a French Canadian state all classes of the population were satisfied. There was a good deal of dissatisfaction among the poorer classes with the domination of the seigneurs and the clergy, and there was distinct resentment at the interference with the influence of the captains of militia. The results of this dissatisfaction among the habitants were to be made evident in the course of the American Revolution.

It might have seemed logical that a new possession, such as the Province of Quebec, which was not yet firm in its allegiance to Britain would have immediately joined the cause of the American rebels.[6] There was in fact a good deal of sympathy among the hab-

[4] Kennedy, *op. cit.*, pp. 137-40.
[5] Burt, *op. cit.*, pp. 177-202.
[6] Burt, *op. cit.*, pp. 202-48.

itants for the cause of the Revolution, and in some cases active aid was given to the invaders when they came to Quebec. But on the whole the French Canadians remained on the fence and were apt to favor the cause of the victor of the moment or the party which could pay for their services in hard cash. The revolutionaries had entirely forfeited the support of the clergy by their denunciation of the establishment of the Roman Catholic Church by the Quebec Act. In spite of the habitant's latent dissatisfaction with these very provisions of the Quebec Act the clergy maintained great influence over him, and the Pastoral Mandement of Bishop Briand enjoining him to strict loyalty to Britain, while it did not stir him to active help for the British, checked much latent treason. The American leaders were surprised at their inability to raise Quebec against the King, but the French Canadians' habit of obeying constituted authority even when it was not popular with them was as compelling then as it undoubtedly is today.

The closing phases of the American Revolution brought to Canada the immigration of the Loyalists who in time were to prove a more serious menace to the maintenance of French Canadian nationality than the actual British conquest had been. The Loyalists who immigrated to the western portion of the Province of Quebec were less numerous and of lower social status than those who went to the maritime colonies.[7] Nevertheless they brought with them the demand for the English representative institutions and English law that they had enjoyed in the southern colonies from which their loyalty to Great Britain had forcibly expelled them. From the very beginning of the Loyalist immigration there was bad feeling between the Loyalists and the earlier inhabitants of Canada, who felt that this was but a new attempt to drive out their nationality and their rights from the country where they had existed for more than one hundred and fifty years. The Loyalists for their part had no intention of living under a régime where a

[7] Burt, *op. cit.*, pp. 357-400.

The Roots of French Canadianism

dominant Catholic Church, an unrepresentative Council, and French law were the order of the day. The French Canadians were quick to see the menace to them contained in the Loyalists' demands for a representative Assembly, the establishment of English law, and the right of habeas corpus. The menace of absorption and assimilation contained in the Loyalist demands united the French Canadians at the very outset of their life as a separate nationality, as nothing else could have done. It was obvious that some form of compromise would have to be found. The crux of the problem was the inability of the government to get the French Canadians to abandon the French civil law and their equal inability to make the English Loyalists give up the English civil and commercial law to which they were accustomed. In the conflict between the French Canadians and the Loyalists lay the beginning of that racial struggle which has played so prominent a part in Canadian life ever since.

In 1786 Sir Guy Carleton, who had recently been created Lord Dorchester, was sent out to Canada as governor for the second time in an attempt to reconcile the difficulties between the two nationalities. But it was five years before the Constitutional Act of 1791, which was to become the keystone of government in Canada, was passed by Parliament.[8] The Constitutional Act of 1791 established the principle of dual Anglo-French control of Canada. It was in fact the first of the compromises which attempted to keep the two Canadian peoples living together on an amicable basis. The French Canadians secured the confirmation of all their rights and privileges including the maintenance of French civil law and feudal tenure. The Roman Catholic Church was left in unimpaired control of the tithes. The English were granted the promise of representative institutions and the establishment of English law and free land tenure. In order to make it possible for the two systems of government to exist the Act provided for the

[8] Constitutional Act of 1791 in Kennedy, *op. cit.*, pp. 194-205.

division of Canada into two parts. Lower Canada which was the oldest settled portion of the province along the St. Lawrence was allotted to the French, while the Loyalists secured the western districts henceforth to be known as Upper Canada. With the confirmation of the French Canadians in their rights and privileges and their acceptance of them French Canada definitely cast off even the semblance of a connection with France and started on a new course as a loyal British possession, grateful for the benefits conferred upon her. Possessed of new weapons for the preservation of her distinct nationality, such as a representative Assembly, and blessed with liberties France had never dreamed of conferring, the French Canadian was henceforth to be neither French nor English but essentially a Canadian of French speech and British allegiance.

The reaction of French Canada to the events of the French Revolution was to prove that here was indeed a separate nationality. Canada had naturally remained untouched by the current of rationalist or revolutionary thought which had been sweeping France in the late eighteenth century. It is indeed doubtful whether such a simple and religious people would have been much affected by a Rousseau or a Voltaire. But there could be no doubt that French Canada was horrified at the news of the excesses of the French Revolution. The persecution of the Church and the execution of the anointed King of France seemed acts of unspeakable sacrilege to the simple habitant, an attitude of mind which the Canadian clergy were glad to encourage. The wars of the Revolution and of Napoleon scarcely affected the French Canadian. Except for the short-lived American invasion of 1812 in which he bore a valiant part in the defense of the province the great current of world events hardly touched him. While his brethren of old France were undergoing revolution and war for a generation, the French Canadian was at peace. No French Canadian churches were defiled and burned, no Revolutionary Tri-

The Roots of French Canadianism

bunal interfered with the peace of his Majesty's French Canadian subjects, and no French Canadian peasants were conscripted to feed a Corsican's ambitions. The French Canadian is a traditionalist. The Napoleonic wars, which affected him so little, accustomed him to the idea that no matter what was at stake for the British Empire as a whole he would not be called upon to play an active part in wars, unless they were for the defense of Canadian territory. The Church impressed upon the people the duty they owed by praying for the success of British arms.[9] When the armies of Napoleon carried the name and the glory of France to the uttermost corners of Europe there was indeed a stirring of emotional sympathy for the old country in French Canadian hearts, but it went no farther. For the French Canadian was learning that he had a new nationality which was neither French nor British but Canadian, in whose shelter he could remain at home and cultivate his land safe from the alarms of European wars. It was this tradition of the safe isolation of Quebec that was to bear fruit in Quebec's reluctance to take an active part in the Great War of 1914-18.

With the close of the Napoleonic wars began the period of an "active" rather than "passive" French Canadian nationalism which was to last only until the rebellion of 1837. The period between 1815 and 1837 was one of political apprenticeship for the young French Canadian "nation." From the outset, the French Canadians had taken to representative institutions with a zeal and an aptitude that had surprised the British. As early as 1793 the French Canadians had elected one of their own number as Speaker of the assembly and had defeated all attempts to oust French as the dominant language of the province. By 1815 men springing from the lower classes, of which the lawyers, or "avocats," were the most prominent, had supplanted the older representatives of the noblesse in control of the assembly. The seigneurs

[9] *Mandements des évêques de Quebec*, II, 472.

in the assembly had been accustomed to side with the government and because of their social status were often part of the so-called "Château Clique" by means of which the British governor from his residence in the Château St. Louis ruled the province, often in defiance of the wishes of the majority of the assembly.

The main grievances of the assembly were the control by the governor and council of the public purse and the system whereby all the administrative officers, including the governor, the provincial judges, and the members of the executive council, were appointed by the crown and were totally independent of control by the assembly. When Louis Joseph Papineau was elected speaker of the assembly, in 1815, the party that wished to secure popular control of the government and the public revenue obtained a real leader. Papineau was impregnated with the ideas of the American and French Revolutions, was widely read in the eighteenth-century Rationalist thinkers, and had a strong anticlerical bias. He realized that the quarrel between the British governor and the French Canadian assembly for the control of appointments and the revenues was essentially a nationalistic rather than a constitutional one, for it was based on the injured self-esteem of the French Canadians, who felt themselves treated as inferiors. It was evident that in the course of the 1830's national consciousness and racial identity had become a creed with the French Canadians. Papineau, like the anticlerical rationalistic Liberal of European type that he was, gave French Canadian nationalism the "active" character that it possessed during this period.

In 1822 the British government attempted to dominate the French Canadians by a proposal for the reunion of Upper and Lower Canada, the limitation of the rights of the French language, the vesting of clerical appointments in the governor, and the complete control of the revenues by the crown.[10] It proved impossible, however, to fasten any such scheme on an awakened race-conscious

[10] Kennedy, *op. cit.*, p. 243.

The Roots of French Canadianism

Lower Canada, and the weary struggle for control between the government and the assembly continued year after year. In 1834 the assembly, under Papineau's leadership, passed the famous Ninety-two Resolutions which constituted a sort of grand remonstrance of the French Canadian's complaints against the British government. In essence the Ninety-two Resolutions demanded the control of the revenues by the assembly, an elective legislative council, and a judiciary dependent on the assembly.[11] The agitation for reform came to a head in the years between the passage of the Ninety-two Resolutions and 1837. Although the French Canadian agitation was largely a political one, the economic depression of 1837 lent fuel to the fires of resentment against the government. The British government sent out a Commission of Inquiry, but it took the firm stand in 1837 that responsible government was impossible of realization, while it offered the assembly control of the revenues if in return the representatives of the people would guarantee the salaries of the appointive officers. The decision of the home government added considerably to the resentment of the Canadians over the fact that self-government was an appearance rather than a reality. Responsible cabinet government seemed to them and was in fact too logical a conclusion of representative government to be ultimately denied. By 1837 there was practically a paralysis of government. Supply was refused to the government, a boycott of British goods was introduced, and Papineau's followers, known as the *Patriotes,* held enthusiastic meetings at which incitements to violence, to independence, or to annexation to the United States were all wildly applauded.

In the autumn of 1837 the popular discontent broke into open revolt.[12] But from the beginning the rebellion seemed foredoomed to failure, and it proved to be nothing more than a series of blunders with fighting on a miniature scale. Papineau fled at the

[11] *Ibid.,* pp. 270-90.
[12] A. De Celles, *The Patriotes of 1837,* pp. 106-13, "Chronicles of Canada," Vol. XXV. C. Wittke, *A History of Canada,* pp. 106-12.

very beginning of the outbreak and by so doing took all the heart out of his followers. The Church in taking a very firm stand against the rebellion believed that it had not saved French Canada from the dangers of racial absorption and of loss of religion at the conquest only to let it be sucked into the vortex of rebellion and social revolution at the bidding of the anticlerical Papineau. There was never any danger that Papineau's anticlericalism would carry away the mass of the French Canadian people, but there can be little doubt that it was the deciding factor in prejudicing the Church against him. In the course of the autumn there were some minor "battles," but the rebels could not stand against the British regulars and with their disastrous defeat at Lacolle in December the rebellion was at an end. Although the Church's influence may have counted somewhat against the rebellion, the real cause of its failure may be sought in the total military unpreparedness of the people.

The French Canadian national idea had been defeated in 1837, and with it the possibility that an active Liberal nation on the European model would arise on the banks of the St. Lawrence. In managing to save the French Canadian nationality at all, the French Canadian political leaders actually deprived it of its "active" nationalistic character. Henceforth, French Canadian nationalism was to be a controlled force which was to seek development of its rights and privileges within the bounds of reason but which was to avoid excess and interference with the rights of others at all costs. Passionate aggression in behalf of French Canadian nationalism was to be succeeded by a passive reasoned conviction of the advantages of French Canadian nationality. Deriving a great advantage from the fact that rebellion against constituted authority was instinctively abhorrent to the French Canadians, the Church was able to swing Quebec back into the path of loyal submission to the crown. By suavity and persuasion much might be gained that never could be gained by force. All through the struggles of the confederation period of the 1860's, the troubles of the Red River and Northwest rebellions, the vexatious school questions of the 1890's, the bitter controversies over Canadian participation in the Boer War, and in the Great War itself, there was never any real doubt that Quebec would remain loyal and submissive though ever steadfast in the full assertion of her rights.

When Lord Durham published his famous report on the affairs of British North America in 1839, it seemed indeed as if he had sounded the doom of the French Canadian nationality's chances of survival.[13] But as a matter of fact Durham's opposition to the maintenance of two nationalities in Canada served to quicken the determination of French Canadians to preserve their status as a distinct nationality with its own language, religion, and laws. Inspired by a dream of the North American union of all the British provinces, Lord Durham saw in the French Canadians, whose culture he despised, the chief obstacle for his cherished ideal. He believed that the French Canadians were a backward race with antiquated laws and a low form of civilization. Unconsciously, Lord Durham had provided the French Canadians with the very stimulus they needed. If French Canada was to endure at all, it was vitally necessary to defend her religion, her language, and her institutions against absorption and assimilation. Lord Durham added to French Canadian nationalism a strong defensive, rather than an active, flavor.

With the reunion of Upper and Lower Canada in 1841 the scheme of Lord Durham for the gradual control of French Canada began to take shape. However, responsible government with its increased popular control over the revenues and the administration proved to be the very lever by which the French Canadians attained the provincial and racial autonomy which Lord Durham had dreaded. In the first years after the reunion of the two Canadas an attempt was made, especially on the part of

[13] Earl of Durham, *Report of,* 4th ed., 3 vols., edited by Sir C. Lucas.

the executive, to make the system work. But by the time Lord Elgin became governor, in 1847, it was apparent that the attempt would have to be abandoned, and the period until confederation, in 1867, was devoted to finding a substitute for what had proved to be an unworkable system of government.[14] Lord Durham believed that French Canadians and Anglo-Canadians would divide into parties on strictly "racial" lines and that as a result of the English being in the majority the French could be easily dominated. Instead, both racial groups divided on party lines, and the French Canadian party groups had to be considered by government and opposition alike whenever a majority vote was necessary. This principle of the "double majority" not only made government impracticable but also so greatly increased the power of the French Canadians to make or mar legislation that they became the very keystone of government. As government without the consent of the French Canadians became impossible, resentment in the English provinces grew steadily. This was especially so because although French and English Canadians had an equal number of seats in the parliament of United Canada the population of Upper Canada was rapidly outstripping that of Lower Canada. It was generally felt that the only way out was a federal form of government in which each part of the province would obtain practical control over its own affairs, but the attainment of such a federation was slow.

Though based principally on the paralysis of government under the Union system, the movement for a federation of the Canadas, which came to a head in the 1860's, had other and powerful motivations. The British maritime provinces were anxious for better communications and trading conditions with their Canadian neighbors. They hoped that this might be brought about by some form of general federation between themselves and the province of Canada, though at that time they were giving practical con-

[14] O. D. Skelton, *Life and Letters of Sir Wilfrid Laurier*, I, 104-44.

sideration to an exclusively legislative union. The termination of the Reciprocity Treaty with the United States, in 1866, made intercolonial trade especially desirable. The exigencies of the American Civil War and the threat of imminent war between England and the United States made the necessity for a tightening of the defenses of the British North American provinces seem imperative. In September, 1864, there met at Charlottetown, Prince Edward Island, the first conference between the political leaders of the maritime provinces and of Canada. Its avowed purpose was to consider a maritime union, but it actually discussed the possibility of creating a British North American federation. The Canadian delegation included English-speaking leaders, such as John A. Macdonald, George Brown, and A. T. Galt, while the French Canadians were represented by George Cartier and Etienne Taché.[15] The French Canadians, as a whole, were divided on the federation schemes; Cartier led those who believed it was the best solution whereby Quebec would obtain control of her own affairs, while another faction, led by Antoine Dorion and comprising many of the clergy, believed that Quebec as a mere unit of a Canadian federation would be swamped in the sea of Anglo-Saxonism. The Canadian delegates were enthusiastically welcomed at Charlottetown, and a tentative agreement was made, providing for a federal union, representation by population in the lower House (a demand which was deemed essential by the English-speaking majority), and equal representation of the three regions of Upper Canada, Lower Canada, and the maritimes in the upper House.

A few weeks later a conference took place between a delegation from the Maritimes and the entire cabinet of United Canada at Quebec. In record time the Quebec conference arrived at the solution of a federal union. The opposition to the measure among the French Canadians was strong, but it was appreciated by all

[15] W. M. Whitelaw, *The Maritimes and Canada before Confederation*, pp. 204 *et seq.*

parties that some way out of the existing chaos had to be found, and all were willing to give the scheme a trial. The essential duality of the races was recognized in the creation of a federal rather than a legislative union with responsible government. The lower House was organized under the system of representation by population as agreed upon at Charlottetown, while the upper House was made appointive and especially representative of the various sections of the new nation. While the proposed federal government was invested with large powers over taxation, trade and commerce, money and finance, and so forth, the administration of each province was to be left entirely within the control of its electors represented in their respective provincial parliaments. Every precaution was taken to preserve the special rights which French Canadians felt were peculiarly necessary to any scheme of union. In the guarantee of provincial autonomy it was specifically provided that Quebec, while sharing the system of English criminal law with the other provinces, should be allowed to keep her own French civil law.[16] Most important of all, the control of education was placed entirely within the jurisdiction of the several provinces, a provision which clearly safeguarded the rights of the Catholic Church to control education in Quebec. Furthermore, Quebec was guaranteed against any attempt to swamp her, by the provisions that she should have a fixed number of members in the federal House of Commons and that every other province was to calculate its representation in the same proportion to its population as the Quebec delegation of sixty-five members was to the population of that province.

As the result of the decisions of the Quebec conference, which were embodied in the British North America Act and passed by the Imperial Parliament in 1867, the province of Quebec became the pivot of the new Dominion. French Canadian nationality had been made secure against any attempt to interfere with its growth.

[16] For British North America Act, see Kennedy, *op. cit.*, pp. 617-33.

The Roots of French Canadianism

In the national field Quebec had to be consulted before any vital decision could be taken. Safe behind the Chinese wall of her security French Canada was free to develop as she pleased.

Quebec has not changed very much under Confederation, which in itself made slow development possible. The innate French passion for security was indulged in. Old methods of commerce and trade, of agriculture and education were encouraged merely because they were old and traditional. Innovation was frowned upon not least by churchmen who wanted to keep the faithful safe from the contamination of modern freethinking materialism. The safety and security which the British North America Act had provided for Quebec were to prove a doubtful boon when she came face to face with the cold realism of world politics, first in the South African War and to a far greater extent in 1914-18.

II

The Trials of French Canadian Nationality
1867-1914

ONCE the problem of confederation had been settled and Quebec had become mistress within her own domain, the new Dominion of Canada turned to other and wider interests. The course of empire was sweeping its westward way in Canada, as well as in the United States. In the thirty years that succeeded Confederation Canada was occupied with opening up her wide western territory. By 1885 the railway to the Pacific was completed in spite of many obstacles. The great new province of Manitoba was carved out of the Northwest territory which had been acquired by the Dominion from the Hudson's Bay Company in 1869-70. New industries were being founded, and the great wheat fields of the western prairies began to figure in world markets.

During most of this period, Canada was controlled by the political genius of John A. Macdonald. The master politician survived not only the scandals that accompanied the opening up of the West and the building of the Canadian Pacific Railway but the far more difficult business of keeping the French Canadians reasonably content and satisfied. From the outset Macdonald's policy was to play off one French Canadian politician against another and one faction in Quebec against the other in order to keep the situation in hand. He laid down an unwritten rule that all regional and religious elements should be represented in the federal cabinet, and as a result there were always French Canadian ministers in the government of Canada.

Macdonald's policy of conciliation toward the French Canadians was put to a severe test when the half-breeds of both French and English stock in the Red River district in Manitoba rose in revolt against the Dominion's taking over the territory from the Hudson's Bay Company in 1869-70. Under the leadership of Louis Riel, who was himself half Indian and half French Canadian, the half-breeds, fearing that their rights and privileges would be interfered with, raised the standard of revolt. Macdonald was successful in ending the rebellion by means of an armed expedition; and then he proceeded to please the French Canadians, who were sympathetic to their half-breed brethren, by conniving at the escape of Riel to the United States. Fifteen years later, in 1885, however, Riel returned at the call of the Indians of the territory and once more attempted to stir the half-breeds to revolt. This time there was no possibility of compromise for the government, and Riel was tried for treason, convicted, and hanged at Regina, in spite of the passionate and unanimous protest of Quebec. Macdonald's firm stand for the execution of Riel lost him the support of the French Canadians. In 1887 he attempted to regain it by giving his support to the law passed by the Quebec legislature returning to the Church the Jesuit estates confiscated after the conquest. This measure aroused the anger of the more fanatical anti-Catholics, and a cry for federal disallowance of the Quebec law was raised in Ontario. But Macdonald was firmly against this interference with provincial autonomy and, as a result, recovered much of his former popularity in Quebec.

The Conservative Party, or "Bleus," who followed John A. Macdonald, had its inception at the middle of the century and soon became a dominant factor in Quebec. The Liberal Party was the inheritor of the "Patriote" or "Rouge" tradition of Papineau and as such was discredited as being contaminated with revolutionary principles. The Church was especially vehement in its opposition to the Liberal Party in Quebec, in which it saw the ally of European revolutionary liberalism and of the Catholic Liberal movement of Acton and Döllinger which with its critical attitude toward papal infallibility and its anti-Jesuit bias was causing so much distress to conservative Catholics in the 1870's. The Canadian Church went to considerable lengths to save its flock from the contagion of such ideas. In 1871 there appeared the so-called "Catholic Program" which condemned liberalism in general and Catholic liberalism in particular and urged the voters of Canada to support only those candidates who could be counted on to safeguard the religious, political, and social doctrines of the Church. Actual clerical interference with voting and open instructions from the pulpit to the voters to support the Conservatives became so flagrant at this time that an appeal to the courts became necessary. After the Supreme Court of Canada in 1876 had ruled that there had been undue interference on the part of the clergy in a particular election, the tone of the clerical fanatics was slightly moderated, and the advice from the Holy See that the Canadian Church must beware of going too far was influential in restoring a modicum of objectivity in the Church's attitude toward the Liberal Party.[1]

The reconciliation of Quebec to the Liberal Party was, however, the accomplishment of a French Canadian, Wilfrid Laurier. His was the influence that turned the French Canadians' prejudice against the Liberals into wholehearted support. At the outset of his career the young Laurier firmly repudiated the idea that Canadian liberalism was allied to the European form of that doctrine which he branded as frankly revolutionary and liberal only in name.[2] In Laurier's opinion Canadian liberalism was to be based rather on the great English liberal idea, the liberalism of the great Whig tradition, the liberalism of John Bright and Gladstone. By the master stroke of making liberalism respectable Laurier opened the gate for the adherence of many good Catholics

[1] O. D. Skelton, *Life and Letters of Sir Wilfrid Laurier*, I, 118-46.
[2] *Ibid.*, I, 146-53.

to his party, and as early as 1877 even the Church, seeing that it had gone too far, openly stated that no political party as such was to be condemned.[3] Despite the fact that the young French Canadian had fought clerical influence where he believed it was wrong, he was then and always remained a faithful son of the Church in which he had been born. Laurier was never a fanatic, and he was always anxious to avert any semblance of racial or religious cleavage in Canada. His highest ideal was the gradual development of a common unhyphenated Canadian nationality and the conciliation of the two Canadian peoples. He was born to be an apostle of tolerance and peace, and to him the great goal of racial understanding transcended any petty partisanship. He was never able to succeed fully, perhaps because he had trained himself so completely to see both sides of the racial question that in times of crisis such as the Great War, he was unable to understand the extreme partisanship which had persisted in spite of all his efforts.

When Laurier was chosen as leader of the opposition, in 1887, there were many men who believed that the country would never stand being ruled by a French Canadian, for the leader of her Majesty's opposition might very conceivably in time become the prime minister of Canada. Laurier himself had grave misgivings lest he should seem too good a Catholic to please Ontario and not submissive enough to please his own province of Quebec.[4] Some Liberals feared that in choosing a French Canadian the party had doomed itself to extinction, but there were wiser heads who saw in Laurier the very means of delivering a solid Quebec vote into the Liberal column. Time was to prove the optimists right, for what French Canadian, faced with the choice between the English-speaking standard bearer of his regular party and a man of his own race and religion, would not want the latter to become the prime minister of Canada? It was a shrewd calculation, and, as a result, for nearly thirty years the province voted proudly

[3] *Ibid.*, I, 146.   [4] *Ibid.*, I, 475.

for the greatest man the French Canadian race had produced.

Shortly after Laurier had assumed the leadership of the Liberal Party the country was plunged into bitter dispute over the rights of the French language in the schools of Manitoba. When the province was set up in 1870 the English-speaking inhabitants were far fewer than the half-breed population of French speech and Catholic religion. In fact, at that time there was considerable doubt whether the West would be English or French, as many French Canadians were emigrating from Quebec to the fertile lands in the West. Liberal provisions for the religious and language rights of the French-speaking population were made in the early years. But by 1890 it was apparent that Manitoba was to be predominantly English speaking, and the province was no longer content to leave the control of the separate Roman Catholic schools in the hands of the Church. The province, which according to the educational clauses of the British North America Act had complete control of the situation, proceeded to establish school regulations that in Quebec were considered to be a decided interference with the rights and privileges accorded to French Canadians at confederation. The Dominion divided on clearly racial lines. The French Canadians as a whole, with the Catholic clergy at their head, wanted to safeguard the separate Roman Catholic schools in Manitoba, while English-speaking Canadians were vehemently opposed to what they considered the erection of special privileges for French Canadians and Roman Catholics in a predominantly English-speaking and Protestant province. Between 1890 and the eventual settlement of the Manitoba school dispute seven years later, the country as a whole was torn by racial strife. The Manitoba school law of 1890, so obnoxious to Roman Catholics, was challenged by every legal means. Appeals for federal disallowance fell on deaf ears at Ottawa where the government of the aged John A. Macdonald was anxious to avoid entanglement in the controversy. On a final appeal to the judicial committee of the

The Trials of French Canadian Nationality 23

Privy Council in London, a decision favorable to the Manitoba law had been given. Even that did not discourage the champions of separate schools, and pressure on the federal government became so great that in 1896 it consented to introduce a so-called Remedial Bill which should force Manitoba to set up a separate school system for Roman Catholics under denominational supervision and with a share in the provincial educational grant.

Facing the situation squarely Laurier took the bold step of firmly opposing the Remedial Bill as a sham relief which provided a maximum of provincial coercion and a minimum of help to the minority. In spite of the horrified disapproval of the Church authorities who saw in Laurier the avowed enemy of his own race and religion and their vehement opposition to him in the general election of 1896, fought on the schools issue, he was triumphantly victorious. Laurier was a man of principle, and he was convinced that he should stand up for what he considered right regardless of the fact that he was a Catholic and naturally sympathetic with his own people in Manitoba. Even the openly expressed opposition of the bishops could not prevent Laurier from being elected. While the Liberals won a decisive victory throughout the Dominion, the most amazing fact was that Quebec, the stronghold of religious and political conservatism, gave the Liberals forty-nine out of the province's sixty-five seats in the federal Parliament. Quebec, which had been opposed to Laurier on religious grounds, had proved in her support of her great son that national sentiment transcended religious devotion. The Laurier-Greenway Agreement of 1897 which kept the Manitoba school system intact but guaranteed religious teaching to the French Canadian minority was by no means acceptable to the Church, which continued to fight Laurier at every step. But Laurier, strong in his victory and the support of the rank and file of his coreligionists, dared to appeal to Rome for help in bringing the question to a peaceful conclusion. The Holy See sent a Mission over to Canada

24 The Trials of French Canadian Nationality

to study the question, and in December, 1897, the Papal Encyclical, which was its result, urged the faithful to accept the Laurier-Greenway Agreement in the interests of peace and moderation. The approval of Rome made Laurier's triumph complete and consecrated him the undoubted leader of all the French Canadians in the Dominion.

In the closing years of the nineteenth century Canada, hitherto secure in her North American isolation, was swept into the current of imperial and world affairs that was to bear her far from her original position as a young and struggling colony whose interests were confined to her own borders. Her membership in the British Empire was to involve her in the great imperialistic struggle for new territories and new fields of economic endeavor in which England and all other European countries were engaged in the quarter century that preceded 1914. Before it ended Canada's isolation was over, and her sons were to give up their lives for the Empire on the sands of South Africa and the bloody plains of France and Flanders. As the great wave of commercial and territorial expansion swept over England there was an ever-growing demand that the self-governing colonies should at last assume a share in the burden of defense of the Empire from which they derived so many benefits. The least that they could do was to provide for their own defense, and going but a step further there came the suggestion from imperialistically-minded Britons that the self-governing colonies should make contributions in men and money to the defense of the Empire. Almost before she was aware of it Canada found herself involved in this controversy, for the South African War brought the question actively into the view of the Canadian people, and the years between 1899 and 1914 were filled with agitation and counter-agitation regarding Canada's possible participation in imperial wars.

With the proposals for participation of the self-governing colonies in imperial defense went the suggestion for the centralization

The Trials of French Canadian Nationality

of imperial authority of which that great imperialist Joseph Chamberlain was the sponsor. Chamberlain would have welcomed the creation of an imperial council to which the self-governing colonies would send representatives. These projects were first suggested at the initial Colonial Conference of 1887 and in an ampler form at the Diamond Jubilee Conference of 1897 which Laurier attended with the prime ministers of the other Dominions. The presence of Laurier, a French Canadian and a Catholic, the first minister of the crown in the greatest of her Majesty's colonies, seemed to many the symbol of the success of Britain's policy which had kept the colonies bound to her in loyalty by the grant of the fullest local autonomy. Laurier, though occasionally dazzled by the vision of an imperial council in which he, the descendant of the conquered race of 1763, should represent both Canadian races, was careful to make no promises, pointing out that Canada was satisfied with her existent relationship to the mother country and that no scheme of imperial representation must interfere with her own legislative autonomy.[5]

The South African War, which broke out in 1899, proved that Canada could no longer dissociate herself entirely from the wars of the Empire. The country was divided along racial lines on the question of whether Canada should take part. English-speaking Canada, moved for the first time by an imperial patriotism, insisted that Canadian volunteers should be sent to the aid of the mother country at bay in South Africa. French Canada was on the whole uninterested, and saw no reason to involve Canada in a quarrel that in no way concerned her. Nevertheless, it is noteworthy that when the temporal power of the Pope was menaced in 1870, scores of French Canadians rushed overseas to enlist in the ranks of the papal Zouaves for the defense of Rome against the forces of the new Italy. As far back as 1882 French Canadians had been willing to send a contingent to serve as boatmen in the

[5] Sir Wilfrid Laurier, *Discours*, p. 35.

British force ordered to subdue the Soudan. It had then afforded them satisfaction to see their countrymen called upon by England for important service. But that pride had passed. Canada was no longer the small country that liked to be noticed. She was conscious of her own powers, and there was no need to send her sons to die in South Africa to prove her valor.

Laurier was in a difficult position between the indifference, not to say hostility, of his own people toward any Canadian participation and the growing war fever among English-speaking Canadians. He sought refuge in a compromise which he hoped would satisfy the war party and at the same time please the more pacifically minded French Canadians. By an Order-in-Council of October, 1899, the government offered to equip and transport to South Africa a body of volunteers who on arrival should be maintained at the expense of the mother country.[6] Laurier hoped that this compromise measure would not be considered official participation and hence would avoid the difficulty of creating a precedent for the automatic involvement of Canada in all the wars of the Empire. His hope was vain. There was an immediate outcry of protest from Quebec. A considerable number of French Canadians, led by a former supporter of Laurier, Henri Bourassa, protested against the government war policy as being contrary to the tradition of Canadian autonomy. The eloquent Bourassa obtained considerable support, and, when he resigned his seat in protest, he was returned without a contest by his constituents.

Bourassa was not alone in his opposition to Canadian participation. Many of the large newspapers were wholeheartedly critical of the government's course, and there was considerable passive hostility to it throughout the province of Quebec. It was held in check by Laurier's immense popularity which enabled him to gain a respectful hearing for his argument that he had hoped that brotherhood in arms might contribute to racial good feeling.[7] In

[6] Skelton, *op. cit.*, II, 97.   [7] Laurier, *op. cit.*, pp. 257-58.

spite of Bourassa's active opposition Quebec returned an almost solid Laurier delegation at the general election of 1900. Nevertheless, Bourassa's "nationalistic" reaction against Canadian participation in the wars of the Empire and the support given to his protest had shown that the French Canadian instinctively desired to avoid foreign entanglements and felt that he was in no way obliged to defend any country but his own. Furthermore, the abuse heaped on Quebec for her lukewarm attitude by English-speaking Canada was symptomatic of the fact that racial peace was only skin deep and that whenever a really vital issue appeared the cleavage between French and English Canadians was all but unbridgeable.

For some years after the South African War the question of Canada's place in the Empire was less acute. But with the intensification of the rivalry between Germany and England and the armament race that it involved, Canada was inexorably swept into that "militaristic vortex" that Laurier had always dreaded. Once more, as the "German scare" became more acute, Canada was divided into two opposing tendencies on racial lines. Imperial "patriotism" was opposed by Canadian "nationalism." The growing imperial demand for active help in the defense of the Empire, especially the suggestion that Canada build her own navy, met with more and more opposition in French Canada. At this time was born the "Nationalist" movement under the guidance of Henri Bourassa.

One of Bourassa's brilliant young followers, Olivar Asselin, founded the Ligue Nationaliste in 1903 and a year later a weekly newspaper called *Le Nationaliste,* but it was not until Bourassa's establishment of the daily *Devoir* in Montreal, in 1909, that the Nationalist movement became a real issue in Canadian political life. The Nationalist program of the *Devoir* called for the complete autonomy of Canada, coupled with loyalty to Britain, provincial autonomy, respect for minority rights in the matter of religious and ethical teaching, and full duality of language in the public service and laws.[8] Well edited and written with a degree of literary style rather rare in French Canadian journalism, the *Devoir* proved an excellent means of propaganda for the Nationalist cause. Trenchant editorials attacked Laurier's handling of the problem of imperial defense and his school policy which was displeasing to extremists like the Nationalists. The prime minister was accused of being willing to plunge Canada into war at the bidding of Britain. Bourassa ridiculed the "German peril" but aroused the deepest fears and prejudices of his French Canadian readers by the prediction that any participation in a major war would inevitably bring in its train the conscription of all Canadians for military service. A mixture of demagoguery and shrewd common sense, the *Devoir* fast became a power to be reckoned with in French Canada.

The controversy in 1910-11 over the bill for a Canadian navy brought the quarrel between those favoring Canadian participation in imperial wars and those who were bitterly opposed to it to a head and afforded the Nationalists a great opportunity of putting their ideas before the Canadian public. Public opinion in English-speaking Canada was pushing Laurier inevitably toward some step that would show Canadian solidarity with Britain. Laurier had always believed in deferring to the wishes of the parliamentary majority and had made this the keystone of his policy, and so he felt he must now take heed of public opinion.[9] The large industrial and financial interests of Montreal and Toronto, all English-speaking Canadians, were strongly in favor of helping the mother country to the utmost. Quebec, however, instinctively recoiled from any measure which might involve Canada in any war not strictly in defense of her own borders. In consequence, he introduced the Naval Service Bill of 1910 which called for a

---
[8] H. Bourassa, *Le "Devoir": son origine, son passé, son avenir.*
[9] Skelton, *op. cit.*, I, 322.

Canadian contribution of five cruisers and six destroyers that were to form a Canadian navy, which in time of peace was to be under Canadian control but which in time of war might be placed at the disposal of the British naval authorities. The Laurier naval bill was a compromise. By bringing in the measure and giving it his full support Laurier tried to please the imperially-minded Canadians who were clamoring for help for Britain; and by insisting that the navy should be Canadian and not a purely British organization he hoped to please his own race. He disclaimed the accusation of being an imperialist which the Nationalists were hurling at him but did not deny that if Britain became involved in war Canada, as a part of her Empire, would automatically be involved, though he reserved for the Parliament of Canada the decision as to whether the Dominion should take an active part.[10] The Laurier naval bill was passed through Parliament, although the Conservatives protested that it did not do enough and many French Canadians of both parties believed that it involved Canada too much.

The passage of the Laurier naval bill by no means brought the controversy between Anglo-Canadian imperialists and French Canadian anti-imperialists to an end. Bourassa saw an opportunity to weaken Laurier in his own province, for he realized how deep and instinctive was the French Canadian's aversion to involvement in foreign entanglements. In the columns of the newly founded *Devoir* and on lecture platforms throughout Quebec Bourassa and his lieutenants attacked the Laurier naval policy as presaging the end of Canadian antonomy with automatic participation in all imperial wars. The Nationalist leader succeeded in rallying many of the younger clergy to his standard by an appeal to the ultramontane spirit and to the distrust of Laurier who was still believed by many earnest churchmen to have sacrificed their interests in the Manitoba school question of the 1890's and again in

[10] *Ibid.*, II, 327-28.

1905 in Alberta. Laurier was not unconscious of the rising tide of opposition to his naval policy in Quebec nor did he underestimate the force of Bourassa's appeal. He did all he could in vigorous speeches to ridicule the idea that the new navy would ever be anything but Canadian and asserted that its only purpose was to defend Canadian territory.

When in the autumn of 1910 Laurier's old seat in Drummond-Arthabaska became vacant, the Nationalists were quick to seize the opportunity to fight Laurier on his own ground. It seemed impossible that any candidate who did not support Laurier could be elected in this Liberal stronghold, but under Bourassa's direction the Nationalists put up a candidate of their own in opposition to the official Liberal nominee. Time was to prove that Bourassa had chosen the right moment. Taking an active part in the campaign himself he made the Laurier naval bill the main issue. The Nationalist speakers on every platform asserted that the bill meant that Canada would be tied hand and foot to participation in every imperial war and added their vehement opposition to any new policy which would involve Canada in wars with which she had no connection, especially while she had no voice in controlling the foreign policy of Britain.[11]

Though the Nationalists were constantly repeating *l'Impérialisme, voilà l'ennemi,* they lost no chance of heaping abuse on England. Responsible politicians, for example, P. E. Blondin and Alfred Sevigny, who in 1914 were to be ministers of the crown urging French Canadians to enlist to fight for England, in 1910 were telling French Canadians that they owed nothing to England and that Canada had had enough of England.[12] The Conservatives were naturally delighted to see this split in the Liberal ranks in Quebec, and the leader of the Quebec opposition, Mr. Monk, helped considerably in the electoral campaign. Every trick

[11] H. Bourassa, *op. cit.*, p. 9, for Resolution passed at St. Eustache, July, 1910.
[12] P. E. Blondin, speaking at St. Louis de Blanford, October 25, 1910, quoted by R. Lemieux in Hansard, *Commons,* 1917, p. 144.

The Trials of French Canadian Nationality

was resorted to that might turn French Canadian sentiment against Laurier. Men dressed in uniform were sent through the countryside ostensibly making lists of all males for eventual service in what the Nationalists called the "Laurier navy." Bourassa himself warned his compatriots that the naval policy would involve the conscription of Canadians for overseas service at England's beck and call. Armand Lavergne asserted loudly that England was in debt to Canada rather than the reverse. Every change was rung on the instinctive dislike of the French Canadian for foreign adventure, and, on November 3, the Nationalists returned their candidate by a majority of 207 votes in a poll of 6,695.[13]

The sensation throughout Canada was immense. It was a body blow to the dominance of Laurier and his ideas of racial conciliation in Quebec. The Drummond-Arthabaska election was won by the Nationalists because they appealed to the essential *Canadienisme* of French Canadians. They had not invented the French Canadian's innate conservatism and his passionate desire to be left alone to the enjoyment of his patrimony but had merely used these feelings for their own ends. The Nationalists had raised the bogey of fear that the peace and contentment of the French Canadians would be disturbed in the interests of that distant England with which at heart they had little in common and little sympathy. The French Canadian's anxiety over the possibility of entanglement in the wars of the Empire was not only an indication of his desire for isolation and his satisfaction in his own nationality but a warning that he could not be expected to show the enthusiasm for England's cause that his fellow Canadians of English speech felt was so necessary in the current crisis.

A year after the Drummond-Arthabaska bye-election Laurier and the Liberals were unexpectedly swept out of power. The issue in the rest of Canada was reciprocity with the United States, but in Quebec it was the Laurier naval bill. The Quebec Conservatives

[13] *Sessional Paper No. 18*, 1911, in Library of Parliament, Ottawa.

formed a tacit alliance with the Nationalists, which permitted the latter group to nominate candidates favorable to their ideas. Although the Conservatives and their leader, Sir Robert Borden, undoubtedly favored some form of naval aid for the Empire, they soft-pedaled this issue in Quebec and allowed the Nationalists *carte blanche* for their attack on the Laurier naval bill. Laurier was caught between two fires and felt that he was being branded as a traitor to England in Ontario and a traitor to his own people in Quebec. He insisted that the inspiration of his life had been a policy of true Canadianism, of moderation and conciliation.[14] All the efforts of the Liberals to escape from the pincers of the Conservatives and their Nationalist allies proved vain. The Conservatives won a great victory, but the most significant part of that victory lay in the fact that the Nationalists succeeded in electing twenty-seven of their candidates in Quebec and in reducing the Liberal majority in Laurier's own province from forty-three to eleven seats.

When the new Conservative government took power, Sir Robert Borden naturally offered places in the cabinet to the Nationalist allies who had been so instrumental in reducing the Liberal majority in Quebec. It was persistently rumored that portfolios had been offered to Bourassa and his principal lieutenant, Armand Lavergne. In any case, two minor Nationalist leaders, Messrs. Pelletier and Nantel, were made members of the Cabinet, while P. E. Blondin became deputy speaker.[15] When Sir Robert Borden introduced as a substitute for the Naval Act of 1910, which had never been enforced, a bill proposing an emergency contribution of thirty-five million dollars to the British navy, there was consternation among his Nationalist followers. They had been elected on a platform which branded the Laurier navy as a betrayal of Canadian autonomy, and now their Conservative allies were proposing to pay a huge contribution for the sole interests of Britain. Bor-

[14] Skelton, *op. cit.*, II, 380.   [15] *Ibid.*, II, 388.

den attempted to satisfy the Nationalists by promising that no permanent naval policy (the contribution of $35,000,000 was held to be an emergency measure) should be decided upon without a popular consultation. He added the proposal that a Canadian resident minister in London should attend all the meetings of the Committee of Imperial Defense and that the British government must consult the minister before embarking on any important step in foreign policy. While attending the meetings of the Committee of Imperial Defense in London in 1912, the new prime minister had become much impressed with the naval needs of the Empire. The British government had taken Canada into its full confidence for the first time, had explained the most secret circumstances of its international relations to the Canadian prime minister, and had even put before him the "War Book" which laid down the method by which the resources of the Empire were to be mobilized immediately on the outbreak of war.

In spite of his initiation into these weighty secrets Sir Robert Borden did not find passage of his naval measure an easy problem. The debate on the Borden naval bill was a very long one, and the government only succeeded in ramming it through the Commons by enforcing closure. But the Senate, which still had a Liberal majority, defeated the bill in spite of the "emergency" that government had so often stressed and its threats to dissolve the Parliament if it did not pass the naval bill. Sir Robert Borden allowed the measure to be shelved. The solid opposition of the Liberals coupled with the hardly lukewarm support from the Nationalists made any other course impossible in the excited state of public opinion. Local difficulties were greater than imperial needs. It was obvious that Quebec was opposed to a naval bill whether it was proposed by Laurier or by anyone else. The debates on the Borden bill had revealed the deep racial cleavage on the subject. The French Canadians had stood together regardless of their political affiliations. The passive nationalism of Quebec, which brooked no interference with its splendid isolationism, had won another victory with the abandonment of the bill. For fear of worse conflict the government allowed the matter to drift, and the outbreak of hostilities in 1914 found Canada in a large measure unprepared for war.

III

French Canadian Nationalism at the Outbreak of the War

"Notre foi, notre langue et nos institutions"

WITH the indefinite postponement of the Borden naval bill, the passive sense of nationality which the French Canadian people had gradually evolved seemed to have won a distinct victory. French Canada had stood firm against involvement in the naval policies of the mother country because she wished, as always, to concentrate her efforts on developing her own interests at home. If the passionate adherence of the French Canadian people to their own particular form of nationalism is to be understood, especially during the bitter conflicts of 1914-18, it is necessary to pause for a moment to analyze the essential elements of which French Canadian particularism is made up.

The evolution of the spirit of French Canadian nationalism has been a gradual one, but by the outbreak of the World War the French Canadian's deep allegiance to his faith, his language, and his institutions had become a sacred code to which the vast majority of the inhabitants of Quebec adhered. The intensity of the French Canadian's nationalistic faith has made Quebec a state within a state, as the foreign visitor soon realizes. Montreal is indeed a cosmopolitan city, but even here it is very evident that the French element is the strongest and that French Canadian interests come first. Once outside the city limits of Montreal, whether the visitor goes north to the countryside near St. Lin, where Wilfrid Laurier was born, or south to the thriving towns along the Richelieu, there can be no doubt in his mind that he is in a land where the Roman Catholic faith, the French language, the administration of justice, the public press, in fact every aspect of life, is neither British nor English Canadian but is essentially and completely French Canadian.

Perhaps the most important element in the French Canadian's particular sense of nationality is his devotion to the Roman Catholic faith. The Church has been immensely successful in having itself accepted as the guardian and almost the very expression of French Canadian civilization. In the 175 years since the conquest it has become more and more closely identified with the interests and aspirations of the French Canadian people until it almost seems that the Church is French Canada. In other countries the Church seems to be only one part of the national life, but in Quebec it embraces all facets of the French Canadians' existence as a people. The French Canadian's life is passed within its orbit, and for the most part he is content to have it so. He is convinced that to the Church he owes the survival of his race and language, and he is not ungrateful. In return, he is glad to acknowledge that there is hardly a field of endeavor in which the Church is not concerned. The omnipresence of the ecclesiastical buildings, of the huge hospitals and educational institutions, and of the magnificent churches and convents is a living testimony of the French Canadian's devotion to his Church. Perhaps this devotion is due more than anything else to the intense religious feeling of French Canada which has been an historical fact ever since the days of the French régime.

The original population of New France crossed the seas in the midst of the Counter Reformation which was sweeping Catholic Europe in the seventeenth century. The explorers of New France felt themselves to be apostles of Christ, the soldiers had the spirit of crusaders to a large extent, and all life in the colony took on a religious tenor. In France this spirit of religiosity withered after the middle of the seventeenth century, but in

Nationalism at the Outbreak of the War 37

Canada it remained a living force. While France concentrated on the glories of the "Roi Soleil" and the troubles of his successors, her sons overseas were busy exploring the wilderness and holding fast to the rock of Quebec. In the primitive community of New France the Church naturally played an important part and kept its faith pure and shining, in striking contrast to the low level, morally and intellectually, to which the French Church had sunk under the blight of the material glory of Versailles. The vigor of the Canadian Church has been maintained ever since.

The immense strength of the Catholic Church in Canada has been based not only on its historical rôle as the apostle of Christ in the wilderness and as the protector of a conquered race but even more on the essential oneness between itself and its flock. The close association of the common people with the clergy works to mutual advantage. The priest and the bishop understand the rank and file from which they have sprung themselves. Although the average French Canadian respects the priest in his sacred character, he also knows him as a boy with whom he went to school or worked in the fields and in consequence feels that he may take his everyday problems to his spiritual pastor without risk of being misunderstood. Naturally, the association of the clergy with the people is closer on the part of the lower ranks of the parish priests than with the hierarchy. The prelates have been more highly educated and through their position and the opportunities for travel are more inclined to be tolerant of the ideas and aspirations of other races than are the French Canadians generally. The lower clergy, on the other hand, are often as intolerant and as fanatical as the poorest peasant in a remote Quebec village. This division between higher and lower ranks of the clergy has occasionally led to jealousy and even public criticism, but on the whole the Church has managed to preserve a united front.

The oneness of leaders and led accounts perhaps for the fact that a definite anticlerical movement has never made much headway in French Canada in spite of sporadic outbursts. Doubtless there are many people who do not accept the teaching of the Church, but they are apt to go to mass and to keep their opinions to themselves. The average French Canadian's preoccupation with the Church has further served to identify the latter with all his struggles for the protection of his peculiar rights and privileges, and the Church for her part has always served as leader in the defense and protection of French Canadian institutions.

If the French Canadian dislike for anticlericalism needed any impetus, it was supplied by the considerable influx of members of French religious orders who came to Canada as a result of the expulsion of the congregations in 1905-6. In the districts where they settled these exiled religious played a considerable part in further prejudicing French Canadians against atheistical and freethinking France. It has even been stated in competent quarters that French Canadian enlistments during the World War were definitely less in such districts than in those where the native Canadian clergy kept their flocks within the bounds of strict loyalty to Britain and friendliness to her French ally.[1]

The organization of the Roman Catholic Church in Canada is a very independent one. As far as the state is concerned, the Church occupies a position which allows it complete freedom of administration.[2] The main resources of the Church—the tithes—are legally sanctioned by the civil code of the province of Quebec. Church property is exempt from taxation, but the Church is allowed to own real property and to derive revenue from investments. The bishops are even permitted to request their flocks to petition the provincial legislature to authorize new taxes for the erection of church schools or hospitals. The relation of the Cana-

---

[1] The authority for this statement is a well-known officer attached, during the war, to Recruiting Missions and a long time resident of a district where French religious exiles had settled.

[2] For the organization of the church, see A. Siegfried, *Les Deux Races au Canada*, pp. 15 *et seq.*

dian Church to Rome is also a very free one. Theoretically the Canadian bishops are chosen by the Vatican, but actually the names to be considered by the Pope are presented by the Canadian hierarchy, and it is seldom that the wishes of the men on the spot are disregarded.

In the great influence of education by the Church in Quebec lies the real secret of the clerical dominance over the hearts and minds of the French Canadian people. The Quebec educational system is supervised by a Superior Council of Public Instruction with two subcommittees, one Catholic and one Protestant, which control the administration of the schools of their respective denominations. The Catholic committee consists of the archbishops, bishops, and a certain number of Catholic laymen. A school commission elected by the inhabitants of each community manages the school and chooses the teacher, but especially in rural districts it is generally the candidate selected by the parish priest that is selected.

The secondary schools are no less subject to clerical dominance. The teachers are largely members of the religious orders, and there is a distinct preference for the traditional classical curriculum which will lead to the favorite French Canadian careers of medicine and law. The oldest French Canadian university is Laval at Quebec, but its branch in Montreal has greatly expanded in recent years and is now independent as the Université de Montréal. This great institution under the leadership of forward-looking men has made an earnest attempt to turn French Canadians away from their predilection for the old-fashioned classical program toward an interest in the commercial and economic subjects in which they have hitherto lagged behind their Anglo-Canadian fellow citizens. There can be no doubt that the movement gained considerable impetus from the rapid urbanization and industrialization of Montreal, which taught the younger generation of French Canadians the imperative need of training for technical and commercial positions if they were not to be left behind their Anglo-Canadian rivals. The establishment of the Ecole des Hautes Etudes Commerciales in the Université de Montréal has doubtless given momentum to the present-day movement among the younger French Canadians for the ownership and control of Quebec's immense natural resources by her own citizens rather than by foreign or English Canadian capitalists.

Nevertheless, education in the province of Quebec has kept its strong religious flavor in spite of the exigencies of modern materialistic life. Its object has been to form good men who shall also be good Catholics. The universities were conceived as being the means of preserving the best traditions of the past rather than a laboratory for new ones. The emphasis on training in the classics, philosophy, and metaphysics rather than on commerce and industry until a few years ago served to differentiate the graduate of French Canadian schools and colleges from his fellow Canadians of English speech. The formative years of his life were spent in an isolation from the current of ideas that are actuating thousands of his countrymen. The Church has believed that it was acting wisely in protecting him during those crucial years from contamination with the ideas of Canadians of English speech and Protestant faith. It is not surprising that the French Canadian has emerged from this training not only a good Catholic but also a man who firmly believes himself to be a member of a favored race, whose only country is Quebec, where his fathers lived and died and where alone he can find the faith, the language, and the institutions he has been taught to believe are the only good ones. It is in the schools, the seminaries, and the universities of Quebec that the French Canadian acquires that overwhelming sense of belonging to a separate and superior nationality that is at the bottom of so much of the racial conflict in Canada.

The observer of things French Canadian is immediately struck with the large part played by the clergy in almost every aspect of life in Quebec. The French Canadian, accustomed to accepting the authority of the Church since childhood, is perfectly willing to permit its admixture in affairs such as politics and the press, art and the theater, which in other countries are considered the sole concern of the individual. On the other hand, the complete independence accorded the clergy by the state has accustomed them to believe that they have a right to interfere in any matter that concerns the spiritual and moral welfare of their people. This attitude is willingly accepted by the laymen, many of whom believe with Bourassa that the clergy are and should remain the leading class in French Canadian society.[3] As a result, the press has been carefully watched by the clergy and successfully controlled by means of private advice and even occasional public remonstrance. Censorship of the theater and of the movies has been exercised through clerical admonitions to the faithful to avoid such plays as for moral or other reasons do not meet with the approval of the Church. There still exists a rather comprehensive index of forbidden books on which modern French authors figure conspicuously.

Most striking of all, the Church has never hesitated to interfere in politics whenever it felt that the spiritual welfare of its flock was concerned. So intense has this clerical interference become at times, as in the anti-Liberal campaigns of the 1870's and the dispute over the Manitoba school laws between 1890 and 1897, that the Vatican itself has had to call the clergy to account and urge them to moderate their zeal. There is naturally no clerical activity that has more greatly prejudiced Anglo-Canadians against their French Canadian fellow citizens than this interference with politics. Clerical interference obviously has given momentum to the fanatical battle cries of "No popery," "No clerical domination," and "Down with priest-ridden Quebec" that have been so fertile a source of misunderstanding between the two Canadian races.

[3] H. Bourassa, *Le Patriotisme canadien-français*, p. 20.

From the standpoint of the Church, however, clerical interference has been intended as no more and no less than the mission confided to it from God to preserve the faith, the language, and the institutions of the French Canadian people in order that it may remain the standard bearer of French Catholicism on this continent.

If the faith of Rome is the primary element in the French Canadian's national feeling, his passionate devotion to his language and his institutions is hardly less strong. The French Canadian passion for politics is well known, and it has been his genius to use politics as a means of preserving his particular institutions. In French Canada politics dominates the front page. Political speeches in and out of Parliament are frequently reported in full and are chiefly noteworthy for the violence of their tone. In spite of the extreme partisanship of French Canadian politics and the scurrilous personalities that are often bandied between political opponents, there can be no doubt that the essential requisite of French Canadian political life is compromise.[4]

Obviously, elections in the province of Quebec are more easily won by an emphasis on the necessity for preserving the virtues and glories of French Canadian institutions. But once a French Canadian politician reaches Ottawa he realizes that the particular form of civilization that he represents covers only one-third of the Dominion at best and that the only chance of its preservation lies in the age-old policy which so many of his compatriots and coreligionists have so brilliantly followed of *Suaviter in modo sed fortiter in re*. The main result of this spirit of political compromise has been that no attempts to found a separate French Canadian party on strictly national lines have ever got very far. Even the Nationalists at the height of their ascendancy between 1911 and 1918 disclaimed any desire to form a separate party. French Canadians have usually been shrewd enough to

---

[4] G. Vattier, *La Mentalité canadienne française*, pp. 238 *et seq.*

realize that their greatest safety lay in having friends at court in both the Liberal and Conservative parties. As a result, political opportunism and intense loyalty to a party rather than to a political principle have been the outstanding characteristics of French Canadian political life. Arguments on the ticklish questions of race and religion were avoided whenever possible, but, when there arose any major dispute in which the vital interests of the French Canadians were at stake, their representatives, whether Liberal or Conservative, could be counted on to vote solidly for the party that promised the most for French Canada.

The French Canadian press has naturally reflected its readers' intense preoccupation with politics. Each of the large daily newspapers of Montreal and Quebec has had a definite political loyalty and affiliation. These newspapers are usually owned or controlled by the political leaders themselves or their principal backers. Even in rural communities the local weekly newspapers usually serve as the mouthpiece of some small political boss or of a rising politician anxious to make a name for himself. The result of this preoccupation with provincial politics is that the newspapers subordinate news of a more general character to the narrower political developments of the day and have played an important part in keeping the interests of French Canadians focused on matters of narrow and provincial rather than on national or even imperial interests. Papers like the English *Gazette*, of Montreal, with its affiliation with the leading international news services and its special correspondents abroad, are, naturally, read by many cultivated French Canadians, but the mass of the population can scarcely be said to be affected by them. The average French Canadian lacks even the news of England and the Empire in general to which the English language newspapers devote considerable space. Besides the larger French Canadian newspapers, there are some like the *Action catholique* with its specialized religious emphasis, but the newspapers with a wide circulation throughout the provinces are primarily and narrowly partisan political organs.

In the economic field there can be little doubt that the French Canadian's progress has been retarded not only by his early lack of training in commerce and industry but also by the Anglo-Canadian's control of capital and business administration. As has been seen, the modern trend of industrialization has drawn many a French Canadian to the factories in spite of the fact that he is still primarily an agriculturist, but taken in the large he has remained an employee rather than an employer of labor. In the past one hundred years many thousands of French Canadians have crossed the border into New England in search of economic betterment, where in many states they form a very large proportion of the industrial population, numbering more than one million in all, and they are well thought of, not only for their industry and frugality, but also for their qualities of order and good citizenship.[5]

But if until the present the French Canadian has had little opportunity of shining in the world of big finance and industry, he has nevertheless distinguished himself in the liberal professions, especially in that of the law, where his natural gift for oratory and his delight in litigation have been most noticeable. As far as literature and art are concerned the French Canadian has not yet attracted any widespread attention. There can be no doubt that there is little originality in form and idea in French Canadian literature, but it should be borne in mind that it represents the writings of a young and still most uncomplicated people, who have never been forced to seek a means of expression in literature. Everything the French Canadian writes, from the "national" poetry of Frechette to the historical treatises of Garneau, is apt to be serious and grave and possessed of a distinctly

[5] For an interesting study of the Franco-Americans, see, G. T. Prior, *The French Canadians in New England*, 1932. See p. 109, for statistics of Franco-Americans in New England.

moral tone. The Church's hostility to modern French literature as being impregnated with freethinking and atheism has not been without influence on French Canadian literary expression. One need only talk to any cultivated French Canadian, however, to realize that he is French enough to be deeply impregnated with that country's love of artistic expression. The French Canadian's passion for oratory is an indication of this tendency, and, after all, love for the spoken word is a symptom that with the advent of a greater cultural experience the French Canadian may well produce a strong indigenous literature of his own. Meanwhile he has been content to express his nationality through religion and politics rather than through the more usual forms of literature and art. Nevertheless, the French Canadians should not be thought of as a nation of rude peasants utterly devoid of culture. There seems little reason to doubt that in time the eloquence of the priest or the lawyer, the statesmanship of prelate or politician will not be French Canada's only claims to intellectual and artistic eminence. It is naturally impossible to conclude this inquiry into the framework of French Canadian life without some consideration of the reaction of the French Canadian to his political status. The curious, not to say the anomalous, position of a French-speaking people in a state based on British principles of government, the majority of whose inhabitants speak English, calls for some comment if the position is to be understood.

The French Canadian's feelings about France are rather confused. There is sentimental love for the country of his ancestors. There is horror at the regicide and revolutionary France of 1793, mixed with a certain pride in that glorious Corsican adventurer who subdued the kings of Europe to the will of France. Finally, there is a deep-rooted dislike and fear of the anticlericalism of the Third Republic. In fact, the French Canadian's feeling about France is an incalculable emotion, as the Anglo-Canadians who counted on their wholehearted enthusiasm for the cause of France in 1914 were to find to their cost. Even French observers have been puzzled to find out what is really at the heart of French Canadian feeling for the old motherland.[6] The contradictory nature of French Canadian sentiment for France was shown in 1870, when a wave of sympathy for the stricken mother country swept through Quebec but did not prevent the enlistment of Papal Zouaves who were to defend Rome from all her enemies even if they should prove to be French.[7] Bourassa, as typical a French Canadian as any, has said that while his compatriots' love for France was both natural and legitimate, deep and enduring, it must remain platonic.[8] There can be little doubt that an instinctive love for France still exists among French Canadians, but it is not unmixed with bitterness; and the old deep sense of humiliation that French Canadians felt at France's lighthearted cession of the colony in 1763 persists in their hearts. They still have not forgotten the public manifestations of joy that took place to mark the loss of a troublesome colony, the court fêtes given to celebrate the event, and Voltaire's scornful description of Canada as "a few acres of snow." The best known of French Canadian poets summed up the people's bitterness when he said:

> Nous t'avons pardonné ton abandon, O France
> Mais s'il nous vient encore parfois quelques rancœurs
> C'est que, vois tu, toujours blessure héréditaire
> Tant que le sang Gaulois battra dans notre artère
> Ces vieux souvenirs-là saigneront dans nos cœurs.[9]

The young French Canadian in the church schools is taught to honor the French origins of his race, but it is obvious that the sentiments inculcated are not very deep.[10] As a result, the

---
[6] Vattier, *La Mentalité canadienne française*, p. 248.
[7] For French sympathies in 1870, see Faucher de St. Maurice, *Le Canada et les Canadiens-français pendant la guerre franco-prussienne*.
[8] Bourassa, *Le Patriotisme canadien-français*, p. 11.
[9] L. Frechette, *Légende d'un peuple*, p. 167.
[10] Rutché and Forget, *Précis d'histoire du Canada*, p. 125.

Nationalism at the Outbreak of the War 47

feelings of the average French Canadian toward France are, as Bourassa wished them to be, platonic and reasonable. This state of affairs is not alone due to the old wounds engendered by the cession of 1763 nor to the natural recoil from the events of the French Revolution. The fear and dislike engendered by modern anticlerical freethinking France in the hearts and minds of the French Canadian clergy, and by them implanted in the hearts of their flock, are largely responsible. Even before the separation of Church and State in France, in 1905, the ecclesiastical authorities of French Canada had been watching developments anxiously for some time. Students had been discouraged from going to France, and even clerical visits to the old motherland had been frowned on. On the other hand, French lecturers and teachers coming to Quebec had been subjected to a severe censorship of their opinions before being allowed to come in contact with the people.[11]

Summing up the feeling of French Canadians for France, confused and contradictory as it is, one may safely assert that it rests upon a basis of real affection. There is resentment; there is fear; there is suspicion. But affection is greater than all of these. Many years ago Bourassa told his compatriots that they should be French in the way that Americans were English.[12] Here also French Canadians have taken Bourassa's advice. Just as Americans often dislike England, resent her, and sometimes even combat her, so do French Canadians dislike and resent France. But when all is said and done, the original mother country is the only European land that either Americans or French Canadians come near understanding or for which they have any sentimental feeling at all. The mistake made by many earnest people in Canada in 1914-18 was in not realizing that the inhabitants of Quebec were not Frenchmen but French Canadians and that their

[11] Siegfried, *Les Deux Races au Canada*, pp. 29-39.
[12] Bourassa, *op. cit.*, p. 13.

deepest interests and affections were centered on this continent.

If it is difficult to discover the true feeling of the French Canadian for France, the analysis of his attitude toward Britain presents even more complexity. The often-quoted *Albion notre foi, la France notre cœur* of the poet Cremazié's picturesque description of the French Canadian's divided loyalty is by no means the whole story. The essence of the French Canadian relation to Britain is an absolutely correct and reasonable, even if unenthusiastic, loyalty. The union between the French Canadian and Britain is a *mariage de raison,* but like other arrangements of the same kind, it has proved an enduring one. As a matter of fact, the French Canadian's full and loyal acceptance of the British connection, based on reason, logic, and self-interest as it is, is thoroughly French. The French Canadian knows perfectly well that he owes to Britain, first and foremost, the protection and the constitutional liberty under which he has been free to keep and develop his own peculiar institutions. Not that these liberties were attained without a struggle, but once they had been granted by Britain she loyally kept her promise to preserve them. To the wisdom of great British statesmen, as well as to their own efforts, the French Canadians feel they owe escape from the attempted anglicization and absorption which their Anglo-Canadian brethren, and even some British leaders, such as Durham, would like to have brought about. Political liberty enabled them to more than hold their own in this bitter struggle, until their peculiar institutions, rights, and privileges were enshrined in the Canadian Constitution by the British North America Act of 1867. The British connection definitely saved French Canada from that annexation to the United States which would have meant the death knell of all their hope of survival as a separate racial and religious entity.

A study of French Canadian feeling toward Britain leads one to believe that though loyalty as we have shown is perhaps the basic constituent involved, actually there are other and more complex reactions of which the French Canadian's feeling about his English-speaking fellow citizens is the most important. As a matter of fact, there is the official and the unofficial attitude toward everything English. The official one, sponsored by the Church, adopted by all French Canadian political leaders, and universally accepted by all representatives of French Canadian opinion, is based on absolute loyalty to the British connection and gratitude for the protection it has involved.

This official attitude is none the less sincere because it does not happen to be the whole of the picture. Underneath this cult of loyalism is a mistrust, a suspiciousness, bordering at times on dislike, which seems perfectly natural. Mistrust, suspicion, and even dislike have been part of the instinctive reactions of Englishmen and Frenchmen toward each other since the days of the Norman French Conquest of England, in 1066. It would take more than the one hundred and fifty years that the two races have lived together in the closest juxtaposition in Canada to wipe out that deep racial antipathy. The wonder of the matter is that they have got on as well as they have. The instinctive racial antipathy has been carried over to all English-speaking Canadians whether they happen to be born in Great Britain or whether they are native sons of the Dominion like the French Canadians themselves. To the man of Quebec, his fellow citizens from Toronto or Winnipeg are just as much *les Anglas* as the British officials whom Papineau opposed. For this simple reason he is inclined to dislike and resent them. He believes that the Anglo-Canadians despise his religion, ridicule his language as a *patois*, treat him as an inferior, a mere "hewer of wood and drawer of water," and do all in their power to undermine his position in the Dominion. The French Canadian very much dislikes the assumption prevalent in the English-speaking provinces that Canada is essentially an English-speaking country, which leaves out of the picture the fact that the French Canadians were the first settlers in the country and even today constitute a third of its population. The French Canadian is convinced that his fellow citizens of English speech want to keep him out of the best places in the civil service, in industry, even in public life. He has a deep-rooted antipathy for the Anglo-Canadian insistence on "progress" and wishes himself to make haste slowly according to the tradition and customs of his ancestors. These unofficial feelings of distrust and resentment toward the English-speaking Canadians are always smoldering under the surface of interracial relationships. It needs only a political crisis, and they burst into open flame; the stock arguments against anything English are trotted out immediately and repeated on countless public platforms, in the press, and even in the Parliament of the Dominion.

Nevertheless, in studying the difficulties between the two Canadian nationalities it should be borne in mind that the modern French Canadian is apt to differentiate between England and English-speaking Canadians. His principal distrust is of the latter, for he feels that he is likely to get much more justice and appreciation from Britain herself than from his fellow citizens of English speech in the Dominion. It is they, nowadays, not the British government, who are accused of wanting to submerge the French Canadian nationality, and it is for this reason that the French Canadian feels that there is safety in a maintenance of the British connection. He may and often does dislike Britain's imperial policy and feel that it involves a danger to Canada, but on the whole he feels safer within the British Empire than in an independent Canada controlled by an Anglo-Canadian majority at Ottawa. French Canada's loyalty to Britain is essentially based on self-interest, but it is none-the-less real. French Canada's attitude toward English-speaking Canada is one of suspicious watchfulness with occasional outbursts of active dislike.

As far as the French Canadian attitude toward the United States

Nationalism at the Outbreak of the War 51

is concerned, it has often been said to be compounded of antipathy and fascination.[18] The bugaboo of annexation has never seriously troubled the French Canadian, for he is convinced that God who has preserved French Canada from so many calamities will avert this one also. The frequency of intercourse between the French Canadians of Quebec and their relatives who have emigrated to the United States has familiarized them with American manners and customs but has not taken away their dislike for American materialism or the wide prevalence of Protestantism in that country. Nevertheless, the French Canadian thinks of the United States as a place of marvels and is immensely impressed by the grand scale of its universities, its hospitals, its public libraries, and its museums. There has naturally been a great pride in French Canada for the widely extended missionary enterprise of the Canadian Church in the United States which now numbers nearly one thousand parishes in New England alone.[14] It is astonishing that the original French Canadian settlers in New England and their descendants have perpetuated their ancestors' intense preoccupation with the preservation of their own language, religion, and institutions. The French Catholic communities in the United States are as well known for their antipathy to their Irish coreligionists as are the French Canadians of the Ontario parishes. The French Canadians, both in the United States and in Canada, have always resisted the attempts of the Irish Catholics to control them. As a result there have been bitter quarrels between the two nationalities who profess the same religious faith. The essence of this quarrel lay in the French Canadians' fear that the Irish would tend to absorb them and to interfere with the preservation of their language and customs. But although there has been considerable intercourse between the French Canadians in the Dominion and their brethren of the United States, the mass of the people of

[18] Vattier, *La Mentalité canadienne française*, p. 332.
[14] Prior, *French Canadians in New England*, p. 315.

French Canada have remained indifferent to the attraction of the form of civilization peculiar to the United States.

Finally, there is undoubtedly a distinct if somewhat vague French Canadian "patriotism." Perhaps it would be better to call it an instinct or feeling of nationality. There is deep and passionate devotion in the French Canadian for his native province of Quebec which to him is always "Canada." There is pride in her history, in her struggle to preserve her religion and language, in her institutions and traditions, and a firm determination to guard that priceless heritage. There is sometimes an almost naïve sense of Quebec's perfection. The most fundamental characteristic of the French Canadian's feeling for his country is the conviction that to her alone does he owe an absolute and undivided allegiance. There is probably not a French Canadian alive who does not feel this fundamental allegiance to Quebec deep within his heart.

The second great characteristic of French Canadian national feeling is the intense desire to be left undisturbed to the enjoyment of his own peculiar institutions and customs, which above all must remain changeless. With all the tenacity, all the stubbornness of his peasant blood he clings to the old traditions, the old language, and the old faith of his fathers. It is this enormously strong passive force that lies at the very source of the French Canadian's nationalism, and which, up until now, has resisted all attempts at change. The French Canadian does not want his peculiar status within the Dominion or his relation to the Empire to be changed. He has developed and maintained his institutions within clearly defined lines, and he is content that they should remain what they are. He does not crave independence for the province of Quebec, and reunion to France would be utterly abhorrent to him. He does not wish to impose his ways of life and thought on his fellow Canadians of English speech, as any thorough-going active nationalist in other countries would do. This does not mean that some French Canadians, Bourassa among them, have not dreamed

Nationalism at the Outbreak of the War 53

dreams of French Canada as a proselytizing force which shall eventually bring the American continent back to the arms of Rome and to the glories of French civilization. But it has always remained a vague and almost mystical dream that has never really affected the main current of French Canadian thought regarding their national mission. It is obviously possible that at some date in the future this passive sense of nationality will turn into an active and aggressive nationalism, but it remains to be recorded that so far there is little sign of such a possibility.

It was this passive, but intensely held, sense of nationality that the war policies of the Canadian government were to encounter in 1914-18. The defensive attitude which any criticism of French Canadian institutions and customs always engenders was aroused to the full by the blunders of the government's recruiting policy in Quebec, by the veiled hints that French Canada was not doing her full part in the war, and by the ill-timed attempts to enforce a larger degree of provincial control over the church schools in Ontario. The isolation of Quebec was never more poignantly apparent than during these war years. The profound ignorance of the rest of Canada about Quebec was perhaps largely responsible, but one cannot overlook the tendency of French Canada to live within its Chinese wall, where indeed, "Naught shall suffer change." [15]

[15] L. Hémon, *Maria Chapdelaine*, p. 294.

IV

The United Canada of 1914

IN SPITE of the sense of bewilderment and shock with which the Canadian people met the advent of war in the August days of 1914, it did not find the Dominion government completely unprepared for the emergency. Under the stress of the growing sense that a general war was imminent in Europe the British government had drawn up a plan for meeting the crisis when it should arise. When the Canadian government was informed of this plan, it prepared a "War Book" of its own in co-operation with the Committee of Imperial Defense, providing for special handling of the needs which it was expected war would bring in its train.

The Canadian War Book, analogous to the British one, provided not only for the eventual raising of troops but also for the issuance of orders-in-council and proclamations dealing with such war-time measures as the censorship of cables and the prohibition of certain exports. The emergency measures taken at this time provided the basis for the war statutes later passed by the Canadian Parliament which gave immense though vaguely defined powers to the Dominion government for the prosecution of the war.

In accordance with the War Book plan, even before the outbreak of hostilities Canadian naval training ships were placed at the disposal of the British government and Canadian naval volunteers were summoned to report for active service. Furthermore, at a special meeting of the Militia Council, summoned on July 30, by Colonel Sam Hughes, the Minister of Militia, the dispatch of a contingent of about 20,000 men to the seat of war was definitely decided upon, should Britain become involved in the threatening

The United Canada of 1914

conflict. On August 1, three days before the British declaration of war, the Canadian government, through the medium of a dispatch sent by the Governor General, H.R.H., the Duke of Connaught, asked the British government for suggestions as to how Canada could best aid the mother country and spoke confidently of Canada's desire to offer an adequate force.

On August 3 the Canadian government took occasion, by means of orders-in-council, to protect the financial stability of the country. Britain entered the war on August 4, and Canada, as part of the Empire, became *ipso facto* a belligerent also. On the same day the Governor General telegraphed the King that "Canada stands united from the Pacific to the Atlantic in her determination to uphold the honor and traditions of our Empire."[1] A day later, the British government accepted the Canadian offer of a military contingent, and on August 6 suggested that it be made up of a division of about 22,500 men. A century of peace had ended. Canada was involved in the greatest of modern wars.

The most striking phenomenon in the first months of the war was the practical unanimity of all shades of Canadian opinion. There was no doubt in Canadian minds that Britain's cause was just and that it was the duty of the dominions to support the mother country with every means at their hands. As the months lengthened into years this unanimity split along the party and racial and even religious lines that are the curse of Canadian politics. But in 1914 Canadians of both races and all religions were bound in a sort of *union sacrée*.

Enthusiasm was not limited to the cities and the towns where men of English speech predominated and where loyalty to the old country in her hour of need might naturally have been expected. Throughout the length and breadth of the province of Quebec there were demonstrations of popular acclaim for the cause of Britain and her allies. The streets of Montreal were filled nightly

[1] Sir Charles Lucas, *The Empire at War*, II, 7-9.

during these early days of August with milling crowds who alternately shouted *Vive le Roi* and *Vive la France,* and who cheered the consuls of the allied powers and the Canadian militia regiments which had already offered their services. The leading French Canadian newspapers carried the intertwined flags of Britain and France at the head of their columns, and one of them, the *Patrie,* bore the huge headline, *Vivent la France et l'Angleterre et Dieu sauve le Roi.* In Quebec, the old capital of Canada, there were enthusiastic pro-war demonstrations in which English, Irish, and French Canadians joined. Even in the small towns of the province there were parades and cheers for the war. It was obvious from the provincial press that the body of the province, as well as the metropolitan centers, rejoiced at what seemed, at the time, to be the coming of the long-desired peace between the two Canadian races.

In this crisis of national life the French Canadians turned naturally to their leaders in Church and State for advice and counsel. With a unanimity that is all the more striking when the bitter divisions of the later years of the war are considered, the representatives of every shade of French Canadian political opinion, Liberals, Conservatives, and even Nationalists seemed to vie with each other in expressions of enthusiasm for the Allied cause and for Canadian participation. The greatest of living French Canadians, Sir Wilfrid Laurier, had no doubt that the time had come for the adjournment of all party strife in this hour of the mother country's dire need. From the very beginning of the European conflict, the official leader of French-Canadian thought ranged himself on the side of an active Canadian participation in the war. He believed that the French Canadian people had a great opportunity of proving their loyalty to the utmost in this great imperial and national emergency. It was his wish that friend and foe alike should know that there was but one mind and heart in Canada and that all Canadians, regardless of race, stood behind

The United Canada of 1914

the mother country. Laurier appealed to his own countrymen in eloquent terms to enlist and to remember that in fighting for Britain and for France the very cause for which they were called upon to fight was to them doubly sacred. There can be little doubt that it was Laurier's fervent wish that the conflict between the two nationalities in Canada would be wiped out by the common brotherhood of arms. He urged his fellow Liberals to adhere strictly to a truce of parties for the period of the emergency and promised that he and his followers would raise no question and offer no criticism so long as there was danger at the front.[2]

If Laurier was the most eloquent advocate of full Canadian participation among the French Canadians, he was by no means the only one. Prominent Liberal senators expressed the opinion that everything that could possibly be done for the mother country should be accomplished. One of Laurier's chief lieutenants in the House of Commons, Rodolphe Lemieux, as early as August 3 urged his countrymen to rally to the defense of the Canadian coasts and to the defense of the great Empire to which they belonged.[3] Leading French Canadian business men, such as Sir Rodolphe Forget, of Montreal, asserted that their people would show their deep appreciation of the civil and religious liberty accorded them within the British Empire by fighting in her defense.[4] Even some of the Nationalists were swept into the maelstrom of patriotic enthusiasm. P. E. Lamarche, a Nationalist M. P. from Quebec, asserted that it was every Canadian's duty to defend the Empire; and Alfred Sevigny, later to be rewarded with a seat in the Borden cabinet, insisted that Canada was entering the war with a united front.[5]

It is noteworthy that in the early days of the war, the Church

[2] O. D. Skelton, *Life and Letters of Sir Wilfrid Laurier*, II, 428. Also *Debates, House of Commons*, Canada, *Fourth Session, George V*, pp. 8-9, hereinafter cited as *Hansard*.
[3] *Canadian Annual Review*, 1914, p. 142.
[4] *Gazette*, August 6, 1914.
[5] J. F. Hopkins, *Canada at War*, p. 34.

added its powerful voice to the great chorus of approval of Canadian participation in the conflict. True to their own conception of their rôle in the state, the Catholic leaders of the French Canadians did not hesitate once again to express their unfaltering loyalty to Britain. A few days after the declaration of war the Archbishop of Montreal, Monseigneur Bruchesi, declared that Great Britain had been dragged in in spite of herself and that it was the duty of the faithful to give the mother country loyal and hearty support, for both religion and patriotism demanded it of them.[6]

That the Catholic leaders did not at this time shrink from envisaging a wholehearted Canadian co-operation in the Empire's war effort is proved by Archbishop Bruchesi's supplementary statement that:

> If troops have to be sent to the other side, our brave young men will not hesitate to face the ordeal, and I know that we will find in them the same heroism which characterized their forefathers so many years ago.[7]

A few weeks later, when the first of the Canadian troops were leaving for the training camp at Valcartier near Quebec, the Archbishop in blessing them took care not only to point out that if England was at war Canada was naturally involved, as Laurier had already stated, but also admonished the French Canadians among the soldiers to remember that:

> England has protected our liberties and our faith. Under her flag we have found peace, and now in appreciation of what England has done, you go as French Canadians to do your utmost to keep the Union Jack flying in honor to the breeze.[8]

Although Archbishop Bruchesi was undoubtedly expressing the considered opinion of the Catholic hierarchy on the issues involved

---

[6] *Canadian Annual Review*, 1914, p. 287. [7] *Gazette*, August 8, 1914.
[8] *Ibid.*, August 25, 1914.

in Canadian participation, the seal of official approval of Canadian policy was definitely fixed by the joint Pastoral of the Canadian bishops published at the end of September, 1914.[9] The pronouncements of the Catholic hierarchy in the form of Pastoral Letters and *Mandements* on matters not only of faith and doctrine but also of national and imperial interest have been of the greatest importance in French Canada since the very foundation of the colony. In fact, they have been at times of great influence in keeping the French Canadians in the path of obedience and loyalty to the mother country. It appears only natural, in consequence, that in a country where the Catholic Church plays a leading, if not a dominant, part in every relation of daily life the official opinion of the spiritual pastors of the people on so important an issue as Canada's part in the World War on one hand should be listened to with the greatest respect on the part of the faithful and on the other should be carefully analyzed as an indication of the real attitude of the French Canadians by the public opinion of Canada. The bishops did not hesitate to assert that because England was engaged in the war, it was clear that the fate of all parts of the Empire was linked to the success of her arms. The essence of the episcopal position was that England "counts on our help with perfect right and this help we are happy to say has been generously offered her in men and in money."[10] It is noteworthy that the Pastoral Letter, aside from this expression of fundamental principle of loyalty to the mother country, was devoted for the greater part to exhorting the faithful to contribute to the various War Relief funds and to aid in the bringing about of a righteous peace by assiduity in prayers and by frequent attendance at mass. This Pastoral Letter later in the war became the center of an acrimo-

---

[9] *Lettre pastorale de NN. SS. les archévêques et évêques des provinces ecclésiastiques de Québec, Montréal et Ottawa, sur les devoirs des Catholiques dans la guerre actuelle,* 1914, No. 86. Official copy of this Pastoral was supplied to writer by Archivist of the Bishopric of Quebec.
[10] *Ibid.*

nious controversy as to whether it was actually a sincere enthusiastic endorsement of Canadian participation or a mere lip service to the traditional Catholic ideal of loyalty to the sovereign power. Some even maintained that in admitting the justice of England's claim to active Canadian aid the Church had gone too far.

What was the real meaning of the Pastoral behind its rather florid ecclesiastical verbiage? Essentially, in saying that when England was engaged in war she counted rightfully on Canadian help, the Church in Canada carried out the traditional view of the duties of the French Canadian as a British subject, a view which the Church has held since 1763. In return for the protection of the rights of religion and language and customs the French Canadian was bound, in the opinion of the Church, to be utterly loyal to Great Britain. By means of that attitude the Church believed, and with considerable truth, that it had managed to preserve French and Catholic civilization on the continent of America. In consequence the Pastoral Letter of September 23, 1914, expressed the official loyal attitude of the Roman Catholic Church in Canada. But was its approbation of Canadian intervention with men and money anything more than official? Are we to read in the short sentences announcing the fact that Canadians have volunteered and in the long paragraphs dealing with the devotional measures of prayer for the re-establishment of peace and charity for the victims of war an indication that the Church, through its hierarchy, was giving only faint-hearted approval to the cause espoused by the responsible government of Canada? It is a question whether the bishops would have been enthusiastic about Canadian intervention had they known how widely it was to extend. In the early months of the war there were few people who had any appreciation of what it involved or who could foresee that hundreds of thousands of young Canadians would be needed at the front and that other thousands would be absorbed in the new industries of war, in short, that every activity of daily life would be invaded

The United Canada of 1914

and subordinated to the demands of a world war. It is not impossible that the Catholic leaders made the mistake so common in 1914 of underestimating the extent of the war and believed that by expressing cordial if rather *pro-forma* approval of Canadian participation they were doing quite enough. If the hierarchy had been able to foresee not only how deeply involved Canada was to become in the World War but also how the conflict between the two races was to reach unprecedented proportions, until it actually seemed that open-armed rebellion was within the bounds of possibility, surely they would have closed their Pastoral Letter with something more than pious exhortation to the faithful to pray for peace. But the duty incumbent on French Canadians as British subjects had been recognized, and, as a result, from that time forward the clergy, or the great majority of them, loyally observed the recommendations to loyalty and co-operation expressed in the Pastoral. There were admittedly some divergent ideas of French Canada's duty within the ranks of the clergy, but the attitude of the Canadian hierarchy remained throughout the war not only scrupulously correct but also sincerely loyal.

In the Catholic press the Church possessed another potent means of influencing the public opinion of Quebec which it used extensively throughout the war. There were a number of periodicals reaching a wide circle throughout the province, of which the *Revue dominicaine,* published by that order at St. Hyacinthe, the *Revue canadienne,* edited by the faculty of Laval University, and the *Petit canadien,* organ of the powerful St. Jean Baptiste Society, were the most important. All heartily endorsed Canadian participation. The daily *Action sociale,* published in Quebec, was the most influential of the church publications, especially since it was generally supposed to possess the unqualified approval of, if its policy was not actually controlled by, the highest members of the Quebec hierarchy. It is noteworthy that from the very outset of the war the *Action sociale* did not hesitate to assert that it was the absolute obligation of Canadians to defend the Empire of which their country was an integral part and that, furthermore, England was entirely justified in demanding such help of them.[11]

The *Action sociale* followed the lead of the Pastoral Mandement by taking the traditional stand of the Canadian Church that "loyalty to the crown of England rests on the imperative duty of obeying those powers established by God to govern society," [12] and asserted that this loyalty should not be diminished by the memory of the mistakes or even the injustices which had been committed against the French Canadian people.[13] It called upon the faithful to realize that this duty to the legitimate sovereign of Canada was mandatory upon them, and that they possessed no power of deciding whether or not they were called upon to lend him aid as the exponents of popular sovereignty erroneously asserted.[14] This ultraloyalism of the hierarchy as expressed in the *Action sociale* later came in for considerable criticism from many French Canadians and especially from the Nationalists who thought it contrary to that other great tradition, the respect for Canadian autonomy. When party strife reasserted itself in the course of the war, Bourassa and the Nationalists did not hesitate to attack openly this attitude of the *Action sociale* as being opposed to the best interests of Canada.[15] The ensuing controversy was of considerable importance in further dissipating French Canadian enthusiasm for the war.

It seems obvious that when the hierarchy, through the *Action sociale,* deemed it wise to take the high ground of traditional com-

[11] *Action sociale*, September 11, 1914.
[12] *Ibid.*
[13] *Ibid.*, October 14, 1914.
[14] *Ibid.*
[15] The editor of the *Action sociale*, the Abbé D'Amours, was to come in for a good deal of the Nationalistic condemnation. He was an able Jesuit, who had studied extensively both in Canada and in Rome and had been Superior of the Jesuit Seminary at Rimouski for three years prior to his joining the staff of the *Action sociale* in 1908-9. In consequence of the controversy over the attitude of the paper he was practically forced into retirement in 1918.

plete loyalty to Great Britain in return for the protection she had afforded the French Canadian nationality, it was not anticipating these later conflicts of opinion but was simply reasserting a policy which it had successfully followed since the conquest. Perhaps the leaders of the church saw, like Laurier, an opportunity for an assuagement of the race conflict in the enthusiastic loyalty for the cause of Britain displayed by all Canadians regardless of race in the early days of the war. To the close observer there was only one discordant note in the French Canadian chorus of approval for Canada's war effort. Here and there, especially in the provincial press, voices were raised urging Canada to look first to her own defense before rushing to the aid of Britain overseas.[16] This reservation about Canadian war policy is not without significance. It was probably based largely on the assumption very generally held at the time, which arose from a complete lack of appreciation of the magnitude of the war, that Britain would never need Canadian assistance. Looking into it more deeply, however, it should have sounded a warning note, for it went back to the traditional Liberal tenet that Canada alone was responsible as to whether she should take part in a war outside her own territory and to the even more fundamental and instinctive belief of the French Canadian that his first duty was to his own country and that his only real obligation was the defense of Canadian soil. In the rest of Canada little attention was paid to this hesitation in certain French Canadian circles, especially in the rural press at the time, but as the war progressed the instinctive French Canadian recoil from foreign involvement was appreciated at its true importance.

The Parliament of Canada, which met in special session on August 18 to consider the government's war measures, reflected the extraordinary unity of the Canadian people. It is noteworthy that in the short four days of the session every one of the government bills dealing with the war was passed without a dissenting

[16] *Avenir du nord*, August 7, 21, 1914; *Bien public*, August 6, 1914.

voice. In fact Sir Wilfrid Laurier, the leader of the Liberal opposition, had to insist at one time that the government measures be at least read and not merely passed without any discussion whatsoever. On the Liberal as much as on the Conservative side of the House of Commons it seemed to be the consensus of opinion that the government should be given *carte blanche* to help win the war. If those Liberals who so heartily approved of the government measures could have foreseen how long the war would last, they might have sung a different tune. But in August, 1914, there were few people who could conceive that the war would last for more than a very short time.

The unanimity of sentiment prevalent in the House of Commons was echoed to an even greater extent in the Senate, a fact not without significance, as the Liberals still had a majority in the upper House, and only a year previously had thrown out the Borden government's naval proposals.[17] But in August, 1914, the Senate confined itself to a swift approval of the war measures proposed by the government and to enthusiastic paeans of patriotism. Not only the government leader, Senator Lougheed, spoke on the benefits of the party truce and on the manifest destiny of Canada in contributing men and money to the Allied cause, but Liberals, such as Senator Dandurand, let loose vials of wrath upon the Germans; and the French Canadian Senator Bolduc declared that "when we behold the English standard floating next to the French colors, there is an irresistible feeling which stirs the hearts of those who are the children of France as well as those of England."[18]

As a result of the unanimity of feeling regarding Canada's war effort, eight measures of far-reaching importance were given the approval of Parliament in short order. Of the fifty million dollars appropriated for the defense of Canada the Prime Minister esti-

[17] Hansard, *Senate*, 1914, pp. 1 *et seq.*
[18] Hansard, *Commons and Senate* (*passim*), 1914.

The United Canada of 1914 65

mated that at least thirty million dollars would be expended for the Canadian Expeditionary Forces already in process of organization. Another act provided for the financing of the extraordinary war expenditures by raising seven million dollars in war taxes, and still another was designed to protect the currency. The financial proposals of the government aroused some slight opposition on the grounds that they jeopardized provincial rights, but there was never any likelihood that they would not be passed. The War Measures Act gave retroactive authority for the steps which had already been taken by the Governor General-in-Council under the War Book, and provided for censorship, suspension of habeas corpus in certain cases, control of immigration and trade, and wide powers with regard to arrest.[19] The Act so passed was based on the provisions of the British Defense of the Realm Act which itself temporarily converted Britain from a democracy controlled by Parliament to an oligarchy run by the cabinet for the duration of the war. It is noteworthy that Canada followed British precedent in her war measures from her initial participation in the Committee of Imperial Defense, through the establishment of the War Book and the passage of the War Measures Act. This Act, which to a great extent transferred the function of the legislature to the executive, was to have far-reaching consequences in the course of the war.[20] In practice the Governor General-in-Council was the cabinet, and by the wide use of the order-in-council a committee representing the majority party was empowered to govern by ordinance. What came to be known in 1918 as order-in-council government, comprising such unpopular measures as the wholesale cancellation of draft exemptions by a mere decree of the Governor General-in-Council, was legalized by the wide powers granted under the War Measures Act of 1914. At that time it met with

[19] *Acts of Parliament of the Dominion of Canada, 4th Session, 12th Parliament*, Ottawa, 1914, p. 2.
[20] Lucas, *The Empire at War*, II, 11-12.

scarcely any opposition. Minor bills, such as the measure establishing a Canadian Patriotic Fund, were enthusiastically approved by both houses of Parliament and showed the evident desire of Canadians of both races to be represented in organized war relief. The short session of August, 1914, was a striking manifestation of the united determination of all Canada to come to the aid of the mother country.

Not only were the political and religious leaders of the French Canadian people almost unanimous in their enthusiastic approval of Canadian intervention for the defense of the Empire, but the French Canadian press in the cities and throughout the countryside also added its voice to the swelling chorus of patriotism. Canada is very distinctly a North American country, and it is consequently most natural that the press should play a large part in the daily life of the people. In its general form the French Canadian press resembles that of the United States. There are glaring headlines in huge type, numerous photographs, and the immense amount of advertising matter that is, perhaps, the salient characteristic which differentiates the American from the European newspaper. In spite of this external similarity the French Canadian press is much more quiet in tone and in content than its prototype. It is much less sensational and places a great deal more emphasis on questions of religion and public decency. The larger metropolitan dailies, such as the *Presse, Patrie, L'Evénement, Le Canada,* and *Le Soleil,* are chiefly organs of political opinion managed in the interests of one of the two major political parties and controlled by some of the leading supporters of those parties. The Montreal *Devoir,* founded by Henri Bourassa, in 1910, in the interests of the Nationalist idea, continued to be a widely circulated organ of propaganda for the Nationalist movement throughout the war. The *Action sociale* (renamed *Action catholique* in 1915) was the largest of the newspapers edited from the strictly clerical point of view, of which *La Croix* was another example. At the outbreak

The United Canada of 1914

of the World War the Montreal *Presse* was the evening newspaper of the largest circulation and perhaps the widest influence among the French Canadians. Its politics had a slight Liberal tinge, though in general it attempted to preserve political impartiality. The *Patrie,* which had long been owned by the Tarte family, former supporters and later bitter opponents of Laurier, was more tolerant of ideas other than French Canadian ones than were some of its smaller contemporaries. In fact it is noteworthy that the large Montreal newspapers were far more apt to be tolerant of the opinions of their Anglo-Canadian fellow citizens, with whom they lived in the closest proximity, than the press of Quebec city (where the French Canadians were the dominant factor in the population) or the press of some overwhelmingly French-speaking rural community. The Quebec *Evénement* for its part was as decidedly Conservative in its politics and general editorial attitude as the *Canada* was Liberal.

The French Canadian press did not differ from that of the rest of Canada or of the United States in taking considerable time to appreciate the importance and significance of the European crisis of July, 1914. Up to the outbreak of hostilities, there was far more news about the Caillaux trial in Paris or the impending rebellion in Ireland, than about the course of events that swiftly and relentlessly was dragging Canada into that very "militaristic vortex" which statesmen like Laurier had regarded as imminent for a decade previously.

In view of the fact that the French Canadian press was so distinctly divided on partisan political lines, it is especially striking that, with the exception of the *Devoir,* there was absolutely no difference of opinion on the righteousness of the cause of the Allies or of the necessity of Canada's coming to the help of the mother country in the great emergency.[21] It was generally conceded that, in the event of war, there would be only one voice

[21] *Presse,* August 4, 6, 1914.

when the safety of the British Empire was at stake, for "the entire Canadian people will approve what the federal Government shall decide to do for the defense of the federal flag."[22] The Liberal papers could not resist pointing out that the logic of events had justified Sir Wilfrid Laurier's much discussed assertion that when Britain is at war, Canada is at war also.[23] This slight reversion to type on the part of partisan Liberals was countered by the assertion, in the Conservative ranks, that their opponents were chiefly to blame for Canada's lack of military preparation.[24] But these echoes of pre-war dissensions were quite lost in the joyful paeans that greeted the union of the two Canadian races in the common cause. The *Patrie* hailed the spirit of the Entente Cordiale in Canada by declaring: "There are no longer French Canadians and English Canadians. Only one race now exists, united by the closest bonds in a common cause."[25]

There was much insistence in August, 1914, that this newly acquired racial unity must be preserved, and the opinions expressed in some Nationalist quarters that French Canada should insist on certain concessions as to the rights of the French language in the English provinces before giving wholehearted support to the war effort of the Dominion aroused condemnation.[26] The entire metropolitan press of French Canada, with the obvious exception of the *Devoir,* resounded with the praises of the French Canadians who were enlisting for overseas service. As early as August 7 the *Presse* called for volunteers, and four days later it initiated the publication of a daily column called "The Rôle of Our Country," which regaled its readers with gossipy news of the militia regiments and recruiting stations, the number of men who had enlisted, the horse presented to a popular colonel, and descriptions of how the soldiers told the rosary together. All the newspapers united in eloquent praise of the French Canadian

[22] *Patrie,* August 3, 1914.
[23] *Presse,* August 6, 1914.
[24] *Evénement,* August 5, 1914.
[25] *Patrie,* August 5, 1914.
[26] *Ibid.,* August 6, 1914.

The United Canada of 1914

militia regiments that took occasion to show their warlike enthusiasm by parading through the streets of Montreal and Quebec in the warm summer evenings of early August.[27]

The atmosphere of these early days of the war reflected the joy of the French Canadians at being part of a great movement in which they, as well as their fellow Canadians of English speech, were called upon to play a great and worthy part. Gone was the feeling of inferiority which they had often had; gone, too, was the feeling, so prevalent in the South African War, that this was an alien cause in which they felt no call to bear a part. Their old mother land of France, to whom they owed a filial affection, was in mortal danger. Britain, to whom they owed a deep debt of gratitude for their political and religious liberty, was menaced as never before. Their leaders in Church and State were convinced that Canada's part was to rush to the aid of Britain and the Allies, and the heart of French Canada approved.

Though the newspapers of rural Quebec were less swift to appreciate the issues involved in the war than were their associates in the cities, they were none-the-less enthusiastic for the cause of Britain and France. The study of some of the representative newspapers published in the provincial towns of Quebec makes it apparent how very far away a European war seemed to the average French Canadian.

Only fifty miles north of Montreal, on reaching the thriving town of Joliette, one already feels far away from anything that does not narrowly concern Quebec. The local newspaper, the *Etoile du nord,* bears as its subtitle the words: *Agriculture, Colonisation, Commerce, Industrie,* and looking out of the window of the tiny editorial office to the busy market square and the lazy smoke from a few factory chimneys, one can well believe it. Like most of the rural Quebec newspapers the *Etoile du nord* devotes most of its space to local news. Up to July 31 there was not

[27] *Presse,* August 6; *Patrie,* August 6, 10; *Evénement,* August 9, 1914.

a single mention of the threatening war in Europe. By August 6 the whole front page was full of the usual crop of wild rumors regarding the happenings of the previous week in Europe. On August 13 the visit of the Minister of Militia to the camp at Valcartier was noted, but the war news was still quite overshadowed by the notices of births and deaths, the announcements of entrance examinations for the Normal School and of a large sale of land at the neighboring town of St. Jacques de l'Achigan. In spite of the fact that by early September the war news had crowded out the local happenings from the front page, the thought that Canada was involved in a life and death struggle that would drain her dry of men and money was very far from the mind of the rural Quebec newspaper editor of 1914.

The average French Canadian realized that Canada was part of the Empire and that many Canadians would feel impelled to volunteer for active service abroad as others had done in the South African War. But it was with a sense of cordial appreciation for a cause which could only casually concern Canada that papers such as the *Etoile du nord* gave their hearty approval to Dr. Arthur Mignault's appeal for a French Canadian regiment on October 15, adding complacently that French Canadians would soon take their places on European battlefields and prove that the blood of heroes still ran in their veins.

In spite of the approval given by leaders of rural opinion such as the *Etoile du nord* not only to the cause of the Allies but also to Canadian participation in the war, it seems obvious that the interest of the rural population in events so far from their ken soon dwindled. By the close of 1914 it is particularly striking to note that in the columns of the *Etoile du nord* war news in general and of Canadian participation in particular had been considerably reduced in space. In analyzing the meagerness of war news it should, however, be recalled that, owing to the strictness of the censorship between August 1914 and the early summer of

The United Canada of 1914

1915, it was exceedingly hard for the Canadian and even for the British press to get adequate military news. The usual long columns on local happenings and more especially personal notes about leading ecclesiastics of the district resumed their apparently rightful place on the front page.

Forty miles northeast from Joliette, across rough, barren country broken only by poor-looking villages, such as St. Lin, where Wilfrid Laurier was born, and New Glasgow, where he went to school, the smiling town of St. Jerome lies in the Laurentian foothills. There are numerous factories in St. Jerome, but the wide streets and the spacious houses under the great old shade trees give the town an air of comfortable old-fashioned well-being. The local newspaper, the *Avenir du nord,* was widely known as a well-edited, well-written, and soundly Liberal organ. It is noteworthy that from the very beginning of the war the *Avenir du nord* was asserting that Canada was heart and soul for the cause of the Allies and that as Canadians and as British subjects their countrymen would know their duty first in protecting Canada and then in rushing to the aid of Britain should the need arise.[28]

Turning south from the semi-agricultural, semi-industrial towns of St. Jerome and Joliette to St. Hyacinthe on the Richelieu River, the observer encounters a different atmosphere. In spite of the huge billboard at the railway station that today announces to the traveler that he will find in St. Hyacinthe paved streets, excellent labor conditions, unlimited water power, and three railways, it is not by these acquisitions of modern civilization but by the old-world religious setting of the town that the visitor is struck. Religious of all kinds, secular clergy in long soutanes and with rolled hats, and regular clergy in the sober brown of the Franciscans or in the white of the Dominicans, to the stranger's eye seem to fill the streets. There is a magnificently large Dominican church, a huge hospital conducted by the religious, and many

[28] *Avenir du nord,* August 7, 1914.

smaller church edifices, among which stand a large seminary for priests and the offices of the influential *Revue dominicaine*. In this ecclesiastical atmosphere the visitor is not surprised to find a large picture of Christ in the dusty little office of the *Courrier de St. Hyacinthe* and a crucifix over the young editor's desk. The timehonored slogan *nos institutions, notre langue, et nos lois* adorns each title page of the weekly, which is distinctly Conservative in its political allegiance. The most startling thing about its columns during the year 1914 was the extraordinarily small amount of comment on the war in general and on Canadian participation in particular. The impending crisis in Europe was never mentioned in July, and the war was almost a week old before the *Courrier de St. Hyacinthe* commented on its satisfaction that the unity of the two Canadian races was perfect and that there was no Canadian that would avoid doing his duty in the great emergency.[29] Being a Conservative organ the *Courrier de St. Hyacinthe* was not troubled with any doubts that Canada should first look to her own protection, but it did not hesitate to urge on the French Canadians the necessity of putting not only the material resources of Canada but also "the support of our strong arms"[30] at the disposal of Canada's two mother countries. Like other rural newspapers of Quebec, the *Courrier de St. Hyacinthe,* having taken a high stand of approval for Canadian participation, concerned itself very little during the rest of 1914 with the details of Canada's war effort but returned to a consideration of local happenings and the fascination of local politics.

Turning from that part of the province which looks to the great city of Montreal as its metropolitan center to the districts around Quebec city, we find that the rural press reflected a very similar attitude of loyalty to Britain and a decided, if sometimes limited, enthusiasm for Canada's active participation in the war. It was

[29] *Courrier de St. Hyacinthe,* August 8, 1914.
[30] *Courrier de St. Hyacinthe,* August 15, 1914.

noticeable here, too, that the newspapers with Conservative affiliations were naturally more interested in the war issues than the Liberal organs. In the town of Montmagny, some forty miles to the east of Quebec, the weekly *Le Peuple* is a well-edited and well-written paper with Conservative affiliations. Montmagny numbered among its prominent citizens the fiery Nationalist, Armand Lavergne, who in the course of the war was to become one of the most influential partisans in the interest of stopping Canada's war effort. The little town was also the headquarters of the 61st Militia Regiment, which Lavergne commanded and which he later refused to recruit for active service. In spite of this potent Nationalist influence in the town from the very beginning of the war the *Peuple* was firm in its loyal approval of Canada's war participation. The columns of the paper abounded with news of the war and of how Canadians were everywhere enlisting for overseas service. On August 14 the *Peuple* reported with approval that the Hon. Mr. Pelletier, Postmaster General, had addressed a large meeting in the town, which had been honored with the presence of Cardinal Begin, in which the ex-Nationalist member of the federal cabinet had told his fellow countrymen that it was the duty of French Canadians not only to observe the truce of political parties but also to answer the call of their country, for it was Canada as an integral part of the Empire that was to be defended. The *Peuple* published considerable recruiting news in the summer and autumn of 1914 and did not tire of repeating that French Canadians would be the foremost to answer the call of King and country.

The enthusiasm of the *Peuple* may be measured by its statement on August 14 that there was a decided possibility that a well-known French Canadian militia officer, Colonel Lessard, might be appointed to the command of the Canadian Expeditionary Forces. French Canadians were advised on September 4 that in order to preserve the *status quo* of their race, it was to their interest to contribute with all their power to the preservation of the British

Empire. The columns of the *Peuple* carried frequent poems of the most unimpeachable patriotism, and an article in favor of the French Canadian schools in Ontario was introduced with apologies for intruding on the more important issue of the war. The bishops' Pastoral Letter favoring Canadian participation met with the unqualified approval of the *Peuple* on October 2, and the editor did not hesitate to characterize as fanatics and demagogues any who opposed the verdict of the bishops. Evidently the *Peuple* referred to Bourassa and the Nationalists when it remarked at the same time that the Church which blessed patriots did not love demagogues, for a month later, in the issue of November 5, the Nationalist leader was attacked by name for having mentioned the mere possibility of some future conflict between Britain and France. All through the closing months of 1914 the Montmagny newspaper brought enthusiastic reports of the progress of recruiting. It is not without significance that this attitude of fervent loyalty was displayed in a typical Quebec community, which had been subjected on the spot to the brilliant anti-imperialist argumentation of a Lavergne.

Turning from Montmagny to the much larger industrial city of Three Rivers, half way between Montreal and Quebec, there is quite a different picture. Three Rivers as the site of some of the largest paper mills in the world has in consequence an essentially industrialized population. The French Canadians, while forming a majority of the population, have close contact with a considerable number of English-speaking Canadians. Nevertheless the town itself is essentially French Canadian in its atmosphere. The great pile of the Séminaire St. Joseph dominates the countryside for miles around. There are sixteen Roman Catholic churches. The spacious dignity of the Bishop's residence adorns the very heart of the city. Down by the swift-flowing St. Lawrence the old houses which date back to the French régime remind the visitor that he is standing on the historic soil of one of the earliest settlements of

New France. In spite of the fact that Three Rivers is on the main railway line between Montreal and Quebec, there is a curious sense of being out of the world in this town, which one does not feel in those nearer Montreal itself. The lumberjacks from the St. Maurice Valley may be seen shopping on any street; the Laurentian Mountains are not far away; and the very water of the rivers looks as if it had been fed by cold, wild mountain torrents not so long before. There is a feeling that one is on a frontier, and in consequence the isolationism of the local newspaper, *Le Bien public,* comes with little shock. On August 6 there was approval in a general way, of Canadian war participation, but it was immediately qualified by the curious statement that the first duty of the government was the defense of Canadian soil, which might easily be invaded by German sympathizers from the United States. As early as August 13 *Le Bien public* pointed out that Britain would need food as well as men, and by October 22 it was not only insisting on the necessity of keeping an adequate military force in Canada for her defense but also was pointing out that enlistments being purely voluntary, only those who really wished to do so should enlist. *Le Bien public* maintained that it had no political affiliation with either Liberals or Conservatives or Nationalists, but it did not disguise that it considered itself a semi-religious newspaper. It is, therefore, perhaps not surprising that its columns were devoted in large part to articles in vehement defense of the Ontario minority in the school controversy, while news of recruiting occupied a poor second place. Finding its readers obviously among the rural more than the industrial population of the Three Rivers district, *Le Bien public* was an evidence that in this very circle interest in the war was very limited at the outbreak of hostilities. Rural Quebec was often more isolated and less interested in affairs outside itself than the rest of Canada realized. It must be remembered that the rural press was but an addition to the daily newspapers of Montreal and Quebec, which had a wide circulation. In consequence the rural press could confine itself to mere summaries of the war news. There can be little doubt that any isolationist or anti-war sentiment was temporarily obscured by the general enthusiasm for Canadian participation at the outbreak of hostilities, but that it existed as an undercurrent *Le Bien public* shows.

The reaction of the rural press of the province of Quebec is important in so far as it reflects the feeling of the large masses of the population living outside the cities of Montreal and Quebec. It is extremely significant that with the exception of the reservation of the St. Jerome *Avenir du nord* and that of the Three Rivers *Le Bien public* on the necessity of sending Canadian soldiers overseas, all these representative provincial newspapers heartily approved a policy of active Canadian participation in the war. They go far to prove that Canada was united in this attitude. If the government, especially those in charge of the recruiting campaign, had taken advantage of this extraordinary unity of sentiment among the French Canadians, the later Nationalist campaign, which fed on the mistaken policy of the government in the Ontario language question and on the mismanagement of French Canadian enlistments, never would have attained the proportions that it did. The initial unity of the two Canadian races was undermined by the stupid way in which French Canadians were almost discouraged from enlisting and by the renewal of the campaign to restrict the use of the French language in Ontario at a time when Britain and France were Allies on the battlefields of Europe.

But in 1914 that unity was very deep and far-reaching. Nothing could prove the essential unity of sentiment of Canada for the cause of Britain and her Allies more convincingly than the fact that the *Devoir,* organ of Henri Bourassa and the extreme Nationalists, who for years had been preaching that Canada should abstain from involvement in imperial wars, should actually approve not only of the essential justice of Britain's cause but also of Canadian participation on the side of the mother country.

The United Canada of 1914

It is true that at the outbreak of the war the attitude of the *Devoir* was somewhat ambiguous. Bourassa was in Europe, and the editors in charge took some pains to avoid committing themselves on the issue of Canadian participation, pending their chief's definite pronouncement on the subject. Nevertheless, they did not think it necessary to refrain from the criticism of government which the Nationalists were wont to employ. The *Devoir* did not hesitate to point out that the liberty of small nations should be as sacred in Canada as in Europe or to suggest in this connection that Ontario might repeal the language restrictions so obnoxious to all French Canadians now that France and Britain were allies.[31] At the time of the opening of the war session of Parliament the *Devoir* remarked in rather guarded fashion that if it were admitted that Canada's duty was to intervene in the conflict, a precedent for her automatic inclusion in any and every future British war would thereby be created.[32]

In spite of the slightly tendentious attitude of the *Devoir*, it remained for Bourassa's first editorial, of August 29, to define the Nationalist position. To the surprise of many Bourassa not only wholeheartedly endorsed Britain's entry into the war on the side of the Allies but also declared that "without a doubt, it is natural for any Canadian to wish ardently for the triumph of the Anglo-French arms." [33] On September 8 Bourassa amplified his thought on Canada's duty in the crisis by the assertion that it necessitated co-operation with the Allies and an adjournment of internal party strife. The Nationalist leader was careful to assure his friends that in spite of his feeling that Canada should lend her aid to Britain he had not changed his opinion that Canada should not participate in British wars with which she had no connection. He denied that Canada as an irresponsible dependency of Great Britain had a moral or a constitutional interest or even an immediate interest in

[31] *Devoir*, August 7, 1914.
[32] *Ibid.*, August 18, 1914.
[33] *Ibid.*, August 29, 1914.

intervention, but he asserted that Canada, as an Anglo-French nation bound to both her motherlands by a thousand ethnical, social, intellectual, and economic ties, had a vital interest in the maintenance of their prestige and power in the world. "It is, therefore," Bourassa declared, "Canada's national duty to contribute, within the bounds of her strength and by the means which are proper to herself, to the triumph, and especially to the endurance, of the combined efforts of France and England." [34]

In January, 1916, when Bourassa's attitude had undergone such a change that he was openly opposing much of Canada's war effort and was not hesitating to attack Britain wherever possible, he felt called upon to explain his advocacy of Canadian intervention in the autumn of 1914. The leader of the Nationalists explained that he had then returned from France immensely impressed with the way in which the French had sunk all their internal quarrels, intent only on one object, the driving of the invader from the soil of their country. It seemed natural to him to suppose that a similar *union sacrée* existed in Canada and that the offer of an Expeditionary Force of 20,000 men was the voluntary offer of a united nation that had forgotten its racial quarrels. Realizing that his approval of Canadian intervention would be interpreted as a reversal of his former attitude of opposition to Canadian involvement in British wars beyond the borders of Canada, he had been sure, nevertheless, that in the present case participation had been decided upon by the unanimous vote of the peoples' representatives in Parliament and that there was no question of having to prevent Parliament from creating a dangerous precedent for future Canadian involvement, as had been the case in 1899. Given these circumstances, and especially since France and England to which Canada was so closely bound had been dragged into the war against their will, the Nationalist leader had believed that he could conscientiously acquiesce in a *national* intervention which should

[34] *Ibid.*, September 8, 1914.

The United Canada of 1914 79

reserve all settlements of constitutional changes and political status. Events had proved that he had been mistaken, Bourassa asserted in 1916, for these very reservations about the constitutional status of Canada and her legal or moral obligation to intervene in the war as a part of the British Empire had been honored in the breach rather than in the observance by the imperialists who, in the words of Mr. Meighen, Solicitor-General in the Borden government, had been willing to bankrupt Canada to save the Empire.[35] Bourassa's change of attitude was to have important reactions in the future, but his qualified acceptance of Canadian participation showed that the wave of approval for Canadian intervention on the side of Great Britain and her Allies was so strong at the beginning of the war that even Bourassa and the Nationalists were almost swept away by the current of enthusiasm.

In the press and in Parliament, on the political platform and from the pulpits of the churches, there had arisen a mighty chorus of approval for Canada's war effort. Recruiting stations had been opened. Money was being raised for the Red Cross, for the relief of France, and for the newly formed Canadian Patriotic Fund. What was true of the Dominion as a whole was equally true of the province of Quebec. The provincial government had offered four million pounds of cheese as a freewill offering to the imperial authorities. The French Canadian militia regiments were receiving recruits daily. There were proposals that a French Canadian hospital staffed by French Canadian doctors be established in France. There could be little doubt but that French Canada stood shoulder to shoulder with the rest of the Dominion in a patriotic desire to lend every possible aid to the cause of the Allies. The pity of it is that the government never took full advantage of this French Canadian ardor of 1914.

[35] For Bourassa's explanation of his pro-intervention attitude of August-September, 1914, see *Le Devoir et la guerre: Discours prononcé au banquet des amis du 'Devoir' 12 Janvier, 1916*, pp. 16-20.

The Canadian military effort was from the very beginning a remarkable one. A sparsely settled country of scarcely eight million inhabitants provided almost three quarters of a million soldiers to the cause of the Allies. Before the war a scheme of mobilization for the Canadian militia had been worked out under the orders of the active Minister of Militia, Colonel Sam Hughes, but the exigencies of the war made it apparent to the authorities that this plan, which was based on the use of the very inadequately trained militia, would have to be abandoned. There can be little doubt that the Minister of Militia was actuated by a desire for greater efficiency in abandoning the original war plan which had been based on the existing militia regiments. An element of this change in plan was the doubt as to whether under the Act of 1904 the militia could actually be placed on active service outside Canada.[36] There were at that time many military authorities who believed that it would have been far wiser, while keeping to the system of voluntary enlistment, to retain the old militia units for which there was much sentimental attachment as definite *cadres* for recruiting, and there are many who still believe that it would have been better. To a certain extent this was done. Members of well-known militia units enlisted as a body and in some cases were allowed to retain certain regimental badges. The new plan for organizing the Canadian Expeditionary Force was based on an appeal for volunteers regardless of whether they had seen militia service or not. The militia regiments served as recruiting centers, but the soldiers who were grouped in new battalions soon lost any connection with the original militia unit.

Contrary to the practice followed in the South African War, when Canada had merely raised and transported her troops to the seat of war, where their maintenance and control was taken over by the imperial government, the Canadian Army of 1914-18 was always a national force, paid, administered, and controlled by the

[36] J. G. Hopkins, *Canada at War*, pp. 40-41.

The United Canada of 1914

government of the Dominion. It was a separate body of men co-operating on equal terms with the British army. Until the creation of the Ministry of Overseas Forces of Canada in 1916 the Canadian troops, once they had left Canadian soil, were under the control of the British war office. In spite of this fact they maintained a very distinct separate entity which came to be universally recognized. The establishment of the Ministry of Overseas Forces of Canada, which was virtually a separate Canadian war office in London, gave it official recognition. The independent status of the Canadian forces was further emphasized by the establishment in 1916 of a Canadian section of the British General Headquarters in France. This section served as a liaison between the Canadian troops and the British High Command but was solely responsible to the Minister of Overseas Forces.

The first call for volunteers for overseas service was issued on August 3, 1914. By August 20 the first drafts of volunteers moved into the great new camp at Valcartier near Quebec, and within a week the full 20,000 men that had been asked for were under canvas. Scarcely a month later, on September 30, the first Canadian contingent, comprising a division of more than 30,000 men, sailed for Europe.[37] The defects inherent in the new plan of organization were not apparent in the first contingent. The speed with which units were equipped and trained, the general excitement prevalent at the time, all tended to make the shortcomings of the plan seem insignificant. The entire lack of a scheme for supplying reinforcements was overlooked simply because by the time the first contingent was ready to sail there were almost enough recruits on hand to form a second contingent. It must not be forgotten that this first contingent of Canadian troops was largely composed of men born not in Canada but in the British Isles and who naturally had been the first to respond to the call for the defense of the mother country. The famous Princess Patricia's Canadian Light

[37] Lucas, *The Empire at War*, II, 83.

Infantry was composed almost exclusively of men who had actually seen service in the British army, and in consequence was the first Canadian unit to be used at the front. It does not seem surprising that the first fervor of patriotism should make its greatest appeal to those born in the old country, whose brothers and friends were enlisting in Kitchener's armies. The great majority of the British-born recruits in the first contingent hailed from the western provinces, while the Canadian-born were for the most part from Ontario and Quebec. The number of native-born in the First Division was estimated by a competent observer as about 12,500.[38] Of the number of French Canadians many estimates were subsequently made. The general impression at the time was that there were between 2,500 and 3,000. An official statement in 1917 estimated the number of French Canadians in the first contingent as a little over 1,200.[39]

Once the first contingent was out of the way the thousands of new recruits ready to take their places in the training camps were organized into the Second Division. With the advent of the winter months the open camp at Valcartier was abandoned and recruits were trained at various local centers throughout the Dominion. When the raising of a Second Division was announced in October, 1914, it was added that further contingents would be raised as required. In November the government was able to state that while 8,000 men would be kept in Canada for home defense 30,000 would thenceforth be continuously under arms in training for overseas service.[40] The men of the second contingent were much more carefully assembled and trained than those of the first. While many of them were British-born, there were far fewer who had previous military experience. In consequence it was necessary

---

[38] General Mason in Hansard, *Senate*, 1916, p. 164.

[39] *Sessional Paper 143 B, June 14, 1917*, Department of Secretary of State, in Library of Parliament, Ottawa.

[40] Lucas, *op. cit.*, II, 13 *et seq.*

to spend the winter months in intensive training before sending the division overseas in April, 1915.

It was only natural that there arose at that time a widely supported movement for the formation of a battalion to be exclusively composed of French Canadians. The fervent desire of French Canadians to prove that their province was as enthusiastic for Canadian participation as the rest of the Dominion was the underlying cause for this demand for a French Canadian unit. There was, moreover, some discontent that in the confusion and hurry of the organization of the new army French Canadians were sometimes assigned to units predominantly English-speaking and Protestant, where the atmosphere was decidedly uncongenial to them. Many people in Quebec felt at the time that French Canadians were being openly discouraged from enlisting by the Anglo-Canadian officers at Valcartier. They were further annoyed by the lack of French Canadian instructors and by the refusal of the authorities to allow more than one French Canadian company under French Canadian officers in the first contingent. It was felt in Quebec that the disappointed recruits of 1914 helped later on to influence the French Canadians against participation when enlistments were eagerly demanded by the government. The consequent desire for a unit in which French Canadians would be assured of a sympathetic *milieu* for the free exercise of their religion and customs was very strong. Meanwhile French Canadian leaders of both parties had given their support to the scheme for a French Canadian unit. Men such as Rodolphe Lemieux, J. M. Tellier, leader of the Quebec Conservatives, Senator Belcourt, a noted Liberal in the upper House, Captain Hercule Barré, a prominent militia officer, and the well-known Montreal physician, Dr. Arthur Mignealt, were actively associated with the project. Sir Wilfrid Laurier put the final seal of approval on the matter by writing the Prime Minister that it would be well to recognize the fact that Canada was composed of various ethnic elements and to take advantage of racial sentiment by forming distinct units from the several elements of the population.[41] The movement came to a head when, on September 29, the Prime Minister received a delegation of prominent French Canadians who asked that the government should consent to the formation of a battalion of their compatriots. The consequent authorization on September 30 for the formation of a battalion to be known as the Royal 22d French Canadians was hailed with patriotic satisfaction throughout the province of Quebec. Conservative and Liberal editors of rural and city newspapers alike united in cordial approval of the scheme. The news of the battalion was given every possible prominence in the press of Montreal and Quebec. The *Presse* devoted a daily column to news of the 22d, and the happenings at the barracks, and by mid-October, ventured an estimate of sixty-five officers and 1,100 men in its ranks.[42] Enthusiastic interest in the battalion was general throughout the French Canadian press. Visits to the regimental quarters were chronicled in detail, and, almost daily, photographs of the officers and men of the 22d adorned the front page. When the 22d took its departure for its training quarters at St. Jean, there was universal praise for the success of the recruiting effort.

There could be little doubt that the project for a strictly French Canadian unit had given a great stimulus to recruiting in Quebec and had revived the feeling of racial peace and unity which had shown some signs of fading. The *Presse,* in an editorial of October 15, stressed the existence of several races but only one nation in Canada and warned its compatriots against posing as French Canadians before calling themselves and feeling themselves British subjects, concerned with everything that affected the welfare of Great Britain. The great Montreal newspaper urged French Canadians to keep the local political struggles within bounds dur-

---
[41] Skelton, *Life and Letters of Sir Wilfrid Laurier,* II, 436.
[42] The strength of a wartime battalion was 1,002 men.

ing the emergency, to be faithful to the rôle of racial collaboration that providence had conferred upon them, and in consequence to be British, especially because they were French.

The high watermark of French Canadian enthusiasm for active participation in the war seems to have been reached at a monster recruiting meeting held at the Parc Sohmer, in Montreal, on the evening of October 15, 1914. Leaders of both parties addressed a crowd estimated by the *Presse* to number twenty thousand. Sir Wilfrid Laurier spoke with extraordinary eloquence on the duty that French Canadians owed to both their mother countries and urged his compatriots to enlist by invoking the example of Dollard and his sixteen companions, the immortal heroes of their race. Sent to save the young colony of Montreal they had known that they would not come back, and their courage had grown with the certainty of a triumphant death. "If," said the old Liberal leader, "there are still a few drops of the blood of Dollard and his companions in the veins of the Canadians who are present at this meeting, you will enlist in a body, for this cause is just as sacred as the one for which they gave their lives." [43]

At the Parc Sohmer meeting Laurier was assisted in his plea for French Canadian enlistments by outstanding men of every political persuasion; Sir Lomer Gouin, the Liberal Prime Minister of Quebec, sat beside Mr. Tellier, the leader of the Conservative opposition in the provincial Parliament. Mr. Lemieux was flanked by Chase Casgrain, a Conservative who was soon to be given a seat in the Borden Cabinet. The Montreal *Gazette,* in its comment on the meeting next morning, remarked that "even more signal than the appearance of the crowd, was the unanimity of the sentiment expressed by men who in politics are accustomed to express divergent views." [44]

With the formation of a French Canadian battalion and the recruiting campaign, of which the Parc Sohmer meeting was an

[43] Skelton, *op. cit.*, II, 436-37.   [44] *Gazette*, October 16, 1914.

outstanding event, it seemed that French Canada's war effort had been given exactly the proper impetus and that it would only be necessary to keep it going. Unfortunately, the government and particularly the recruiting authorities failed to do just that. The Conservative government of Sir Robert Borden was severely handicapped throughout the war by the fact that its French Canadian members represented a minority instead of a majority of their compatriots. Since the inception of the Dominion, in 1867, it had been customary to allot a certain number of cabinet seats to representatives of French Canada. Normally, when Sir Robert Borden came into power after the defeat of Laurier in 1911, he would have assigned a certain number of cabinet posts to orthodox Quebec Conservatives. But the large Conservative gain in the Liberal stronghold of Quebec was due less to old-school Conservatives than to their Nationalist allies under Bourassa, who had fought the election on the issue that Laurier's naval bill would mean conscription and the involvement of Canada in all British wars. Sir Robert Borden naturally wished to show his gratitude to the Nationalists who had reduced a Liberal majority of forty-three seats in the Quebec provincial Parliament to one of merely eleven.[45] The Prime Minister, with the approval of Bourassa, who would not take office himself, appointed some of his leading followers, such as L. J. Pelletier and W. P. Nantel, to the cabinet, while P. E. Blondin, who had taken a very prominent part in the 1911 election and the Arthabaska bye-election which preceded it, was appointed deputy speaker of the Commons. In October, 1914, the Prime Minister did appoint an old-school Conservative in the person of T. C. Casgrain to the cabinet, but in the course of the following year two more Nationalists, E. L. Patenaude and A. Sevigny, were added. With the exception of Casgrain and Pelletier all these ministers had actively opposed the Laurier naval policy and the assumption of any imperial military burdens on the part

[45] Skelton, *op. cit.*, II, 388.

of Canada.[46] Nevertheless, the responsibilities and possibly the advantages of office had changed their opinions sufficiently to allow them to support the Borden emergency naval proposal of 1913. In 1914 no French Canadians were more enthusiastic for active participation in the war than these "ex-Nationalist" ministers, as they were popularly called. The sudden change in their convictions unfortunately did not ring true to many of their compatriots, and there can be little doubt that this lack of faith in the complete sincerity of the ex-Nationalist ministers brought with it a lurking hesitancy to believe in the entire sincerity of the government as a whole. An honest change of mind, even if it is practiced by a politician, eventually is apt to win the approval of public opinion. Given the extraordinary amount of partisan political feeling in Canada, to which was added the tension of interracial feeling, it was only natural that such a change of heart as the ex-Nationalist ministers in the Borden government apparently underwent should have been received with much skepticism in Quebec.

It is impossible to estimate how much the gradual cooling off of the French Canadians' war ardor can be attributed to the actions and the speeches of men like Blondin and Patenaude. Nevertheless, the question arises whether it would not have been much better if representatives not only of an enthusiastic, if somewhat noisy, minority in Quebec but also of the tried and trusted leaders of the Liberal majority had been included in the war government of Sir Robert Borden. Had the Prime Minister been able to foresee the length and extent of the war, it seems highly probable that he would have taken advantage of the unanimity of sentiment that prevailed in August, 1914, to make the proposals of coalition to Sir Wilfrid Laurier and the Liberal leaders which came nearly three years too late, in 1917, when partisan animosity had once again returned to normal. A coalition of the two parties would

[46] Hopkins, *op. cit.*, pp. 70-71.

have given the government enormously increased strength in Quebec. For in spite of the Nationalist minority the Liberals still not only had a majority of the representatives of Quebec in the federal Parliament but also were actually in control of the provincial Parliament and government of the province, a control which they were to maintain throughout the war. If to the sincere and eloquent appeals of men like Laurier, Lemieux, and Dandurand had been added the weight of their prestige as members of the government of Canada and their responsibility for Canadian policy, it seems scarcely doubtful that French Canada's war effort would have been very different from what it was. Certain it is, in any case, that Bourassa's later campaign for nonparticipation in the war would never have attained the proportions it did attain had the Liberal leaders among the French Canadians not been fatally handicapped by being at one and the same time leaders of the opposition in the federal Parliament and men pledged to approve the government's policy for active participation in the war, a policy for which they had no iota of responsibility and over which they could exercise no control.

By the end of the year Canada was in course of transformation from a peaceful Dominion, unused to and uninterested in war, to a nation stirred by all the currents of nationalistic patriotism. In contrast to the hundreds of thousands of dollars which had been spent for the development of the country, untold millions were now being borrowed that they might be poured out in the defense of the Empire on the battlefields of France and Flanders. A peaceful, almost pacifistic people was preparing a great army to be sent overseas. All former values were overthrown. Is it great wonder that a people like the French Canadians, used to stability, loving tradition and permanence, should be distressed and a little uncertain as to where their duty lay in a situation that had no precedent in their experience? Instinctive emotional enthusiasm for the cause of France and Britain, menaced with invasion, sufficed to arouse a century-and-a-half-old habit of loyalty during the stirring autumn days of 1914. It was soon painfully clear that these sentiments, admirable in themselves, were not sufficiently strong to stand the strain of a long war overseas and the added difficulty of a bitter renewal of the struggle over the rights of the French language at home. For the moment all was well. Bourassa alone struck an alarmist note when he suggested in the *Devoir* on December 9 that if the government did not succeed in raising the 300,000 volunteers it asked for it would undoubtedly resort to compulsory enrollment. Nevertheless, the Nationalist leader supplied the only jarring tone in the general chorus of patriotism that at the end of 1914 was still ringing clear. In Quebec, in October, the Duke of Connaught expressed his admiration for the aid rendered by the Church in securing contributions for the Canadian Patriotic Fund, and loud murmurs of pleasure at the compliment arose from the French Canadian press. In November the ranks of the Royal French Canadian 22d Battalion were completely filled, to the universal satisfaction of Quebec. The English-speaking press was prodigal of cordial references to the patriotism and loyalty shown by the French Canadian people. There can be little doubt that at the end of 1914 the desire of both Canadian nationalities for mutual good will was being maintained at a high level.

V

The Revival of National Conflict

THE YEAR 1915 was marked not only by a magnificent expansion of Canada's war effort but also by the revival of racial conflict and a decided break in the unanimity of French- and English-speaking Canadians for the successful prosecution of the war. On the surface Canada's war effort went well. In the course of the year a steady stream of reinforcements went overseas to swell the ranks of the Canadian Expeditionary Forces. New industries based on the needs of war sprang into being at home and great factories employing many thousands of Canadians were erected all over the Dominion. Canadian soldiers distinguished themselves at the front, and a unanimous chorus of acclaim for their exploits at Ypres and Langemarck swept from one end of the Dominion to the other.

Underneath this seeming unanimity, however, there were forces, currents of emotion and counter-emotion, that were destined seriously to impede Canada's war effort and practically to destroy the 1914 enthusiasm of French Canadians for active participation in the European war. The reasons for this recoil of French Canada are various. Perhaps the most essential, if not the most apparent, was the instinct of French Canadians to be more interested in the problems and issues of their own communities than in those of Canada as a whole, let alone those of the British Empire. It did not come naturally to them to put winning the war overseas above all considerations of local interest. French Canada had no standards by which to judge the danger in which the British Empire stood during those momentous years. To the average man in Quebec the war remained a faraway, almost unreal matter; but

The Revival of National Conflict

the controversies at home were still of real and absorbing interest. In the emotion at the outbreak of the war French Canadians were stirred by the deep if platonic attachment to France that the dire necessity of that country had evoked in their hearts. It had seemed only natural to come to the aid of their old mother country, especially when England, to which they were attached by bonds of real loyalty, was doing the same thing. By 1915 this spontaneous feeling had worn off, and it was only natural that French Canadians should return to the narrower interests of their province and nationality.

It was most unfortunate for the cause of national solidarity that the controversy over the teaching of French in the Ontario schools should have come to a head at this moment to strengthen those forces of disunion which have so often been the bane of Canadian history.[1] The agitation over the Ontario bilingual schools, which began to flood the country in 1915, filled every newspaper with polemics and resulted in growing bitterness between the races, until the average French Canadian lost a good deal of his enthusiasm for fighting England's battles, while the average English Canadian began to credit the whisper that his French-speaking fellow citizens were not enlisting and had turned against the war. It may seem strange to the outsider that the French Canadian saw in the dispute between himself and the Anglo-Canadians of Ontario over the school question a reason for slackening his efforts to help the cause of England herself. But it is a well-known phenomenon in French Canada that in times of racial conflict the animosity displayed toward English-speaking Canada is extended to Britain as well. To the mind of the average French Canadian,

[1] The Ontario school system provided for a provincial Department of Education, which controlled and inspected all schools. The Roman Catholics of Ontario were permitted to set up schools supported by their own taxes and were exempt from the payment of taxes for the public schools of the province. This tax exemption, however, applied only to elementary schools, for all rate-payers were taxed for the public secondary schools. As a result the Roman Catholic minority had to pay double school taxes if they wished to set up secondary schools.

especially to that of the rural habitant, there is little choice between the Anglo-Canadian of Ontario and his brethren in the mother country—they are all "les Anglas." As a result of this instinctive feeling, it was not surprising to see French Canada's war effort become less enthusiastic as the Ontario schools controversy progressed. It is difficult to judge whether the agitation over the Ontario school question was wholly spontaneous or whether it was deliberately used by those elements definitely opposed to Canadian participation in any overseas war as a means of propaganda. The controversy had not arisen over night but had originated in the Merchant Report of 1912, which found many French-English schools inadequate and the English language taught with varying efficiency. As a result the Ontario Department of Education issued the famous Regulation Seventeen, in 1913, which while continuing to permit the use of French as the language of instruction and communication in the first two years decreed that it should only be used in the higher forms when the pupils did not understand English. In any case, Bourassa's well-known views against any Canadian participation in imperial wars, which he had consistently held since the South African War, lent color to the accusation that he was stirring up the bilingual school controversy in order to hinder Canada's war effort.

There can be little doubt but that the bitterness aroused by the dispute over the Ontario bilingual schools was responsible more than anything else for the gradual slowing up of the war effort of French Canada. The revival of partisan politics and the misgivings aroused by the growing involvement of Canada in the wars of the Empire played their part in dampening the French Canadian's war enthusiasm, but the Ontario school dispute touched him on the raw and aroused all his deepest misgivings and racial sensitiveness. Any alteration of the *status quo* of the language regulations seemed to the French Canadian an infringement of his essential constitutional rights. The whole history of the interrelationship

The Revival of National Conflict 93

of the two Canadian races bears witness to the fact that the language question more than any other question was apt to arouse mutual misunderstanding and recrimination.

To have such an issue raised at a moment when mutual tolerance and co-operation were essential to a successful prosecution of the war was unfortunate in the highest degree. It made each nationality suspicious of the other, and on the one hand the old arguments of the Anglo-Canadians that a French Catholic Quebec which was none too loyal and wished to dominate the whole country and on the other hand the argument of the French Canadians that an inferior status instead of an equal partnership was being forced on them cropped up once more. The Nationalists, who felt deeply and on the whole sincerely about the rights of the French language, were not sorry to use the consequent confusion as a means of embarrassing the government and its war policy, which had never had more than their qualified approval. The fact that Regulation Seventeen applied to only the first form of the elementary schools was sometimes overlooked in the heat of the controversy. It was also forgotten that the Ontario majority, although favoring an adequate training in English for every school child, was by no means opposed to the teaching of French when it was desired by the parents and consistent with training in English. Moreover, it was sometimes practically difficult to teach both languages properly in one-room rural schoolhouses. The French Canadian minority was actuated as much by emotion as by reason and was possessed by the fear that the provision in Regulation Seventeen, which limited the teaching of French to those schools in which it had hitherto been taught, was a deep-dyed plot to prevent the opening of any further separate schools in Ontario. It should be recalled that the French Canadian population of Ontario had been steadily increased by the invasion of the eastern counties by Quebec farmers, who had in many cases pushed English-speaking people out and formed compact French and Catholic communities of their own. By the beginning of the war there were more than 200,000 French Canadians in Ontario out of a total population of some two and one-half million.

When the excitement rose to fever pitch, in the course of 1915 and 1916, the Separate School System of the province was practically in suspense. French-English schools were closed in protest against the regulation, children's strikes were organized, the Department of Education was defied by the English-French Separate School Board, with the result that the provincial authorities stopped the grant to the bilingual schools while French Canadian school commissioners were fined and imprisoned. Passive disobedience was largely resorted to, and even in 1917, after the Privy Council had decided that Regulation Seventeen did not infringe upon the French Canadians' constitutional rights and the Pope himself had appealed to them for tolerance, there were more than one hundred and fifty out of a total of three hundred schools that were still disobeying the provincial Department of Education.[2]

The polemics of Bourassa in the press, in speech, and pamphlets reached and no doubt disturbed great numbers of French Canadians who were by no means out and out Nationalists. The rumors of dissensions within the Church, which were fed by the attacks of an ardent Nationalist, Olivar Asselin, on the hierarchy for ultra-loyalty in approving the government war policy, helped to disturb people. The whole matter was a vicious circle in which Nationalists worked on war-minded French Canadians, and they in turn disturbed loyal Anglo-Canadians, and the only result was doubt and hesitation and a general slowing up of French Canada's war effort. The danger to Canada's war effort involved in the school dispute lay in the fact that it turned the minds of French Canadians away from the issue of war overseas, which essentially was foreign to them, and focused them on their usual preoccu-

[2] For Ontario School Dispute, see O. D. Skelton, "The Language Issue in Canada," in Queens University, *Bulletin*, No. 23, 1917.

The Revival of National Conflict 95

pation—the defense of their own particular French Canadian nationality.

The Ontario school dispute shook all French Canada to its foundations. Not only in Quebec but in Manitoba and New Brunswick French Canadians were stirred by the plight of their compatriots in Ontario. Wherever in Canada the French tongue was spoken, wherever there was a French newspaper or magazine, there the wrongs of the Ontario minority were aired. It had been proven in the past that the question of language and of religion, to which the language problem was so closely related, was apt to bind all French Canadians together in an indissoluble alliance in defense of what they considered their inalienable rights. Mgr. Bruchesi, Archbishop of Montreal, found an echo in the hearts of most of his compatriots when he said that "liberty of the mother-tongue, liberty of the national school and liberty of the confessional school, these are the conclusions logically and implacably recognized by the fundamental principle of our constitution." [3] It is not without significance that the opinions of so eminent and so conservative an ecclesiastic as the Archbishop of Montreal differed only in degree from the outpourings of the most fervid and fanatical partisan of the Ontario minority. The unity of all French Canadians on the Ontario school question should have been a warning to those in charge of Canada's war effort that it would be wise to do everything to foster French Canadian good feeling, especially by granting the privileges of the separate battalions and the French-speaking officers of which Quebec was so desirous.

All types of French Canadians, regardless of their political affiliations, were deeply disturbed by the bilingual agitation. Naturally the Nationalists were the most vociferous and used it as a means to attack the government. They were largely responsible, by

[3] Bruchesi, Mgr., *Le Problème des races*, in *Proceedings and Transactions of Royal Society of Canada*, IX, Series 3, 1915.

means of their intense publicity, for making a major political issue out of what had started as a provincial dispute. Bourassa, master of the pen and equally master of the spoken word, expert in the appeal to the emotions of his countrymen, himself a strange mixture of sincere patriotism and demagoguery, poured forth by means of pamphlets and speeches and especially in the columns of the *Devoir*, the full measure of his brilliant propaganda. Armand Lavergne was an able seconder of his efforts, and all the Nationalists and those who sympathized with them followed their lead. They demanded that the French Canadians of Quebec should help their brethren of the Ontario minority with every means at their command, by sending money to keep the schools going, by petitioning the federal government to disallow the obnoxious school laws as unconstitutional, and by constantly reiterating the right of French Canadians to speak their own language and have it taught to their children in all the provinces of Canada.[4]

As Bourassa became more convinced that real Canadian interests were being neglected in order to send men and money to help England, he began gradually to ridicule the Canadian war effort and to assert openly that Quebec had contributed a larger proportion of native soldiers than "loyal" Ontario.[5] In a series of speeches made by Bourassa and his lieutenants throughout the province of Quebec, these arguments were brought before a large public, and an eloquent pamphlet by Bourassa on the rights of the French language was given wide circulation. Bourassa told his readers that in the present crisis the Ontario government was following the same principle of oppression of the French Canadian minority as those in favor of English and undenominational education had pursued in Manitoba in the 1890's and in Alberta and Saskatchewan in 1905. Bourassa maintained that in the present Ontario attempt to pass anti-French laws there was a direct violation of the cardinal principle of confederation, that Canada

[4] *Devoir*, May 20, 1915.   [5] *Devoir*, February 15, 1915.

The Revival of National Conflict 97

was not an English but a British country composed of both English and French elements, both endowed with completely equal rights and privileges.[6] The Nationalist leader not only believed, as did most of his compatriots, that their language was the best means of preserving their own culture and faith but also constantly asserted that French was the language of the higher civilization, the medium of communication between the superior minds of humanity by reason of its clarity, its flexibility, and universality. A good deal may be said for Bourassa's thesis on the value of French, but it was hardly a popular theory in the English-speaking Canada of 1915, and it only helped to disturb racial feeling.

On the other side of the political scene the Liberal Prime Minister of Quebec, Sir Lomer Gouin, spoke with deep sincerity at the opening of the 1915 session of the provincial legislature of the necessity of helping the French Canadian minority in Ontario. In the federal Parliament French Canadian members of the House of Commons and of the Senate alike spoke frequently of their pride in their race and in its civilization, of their refusal to accept any inferior status for it, and of their insistence on an equal partnership for the French Canadians in the upbuilding of the Dominion.[7] The press of the cities and the rural centers alike united in their enthusiasms for the cause of the "oppressed" minority in Ontario. There were columns in every issue dealing with the happenings in the sister province and with the collection of funds to help those who were generally termed *nos blessés d'Ontario*. Most of the larger newspapers, especially the *Devoir*, devoted long articles to the history of the French language and its teaching since confederation. Old quarrels, such as that over the Manitoba schools in the 1890's, were rescued from oblivion, and old animosities were stirred up. The more extreme papers formed the habit of applying the adjective "Prussian" to the methods of the

---

[6] H. Bourassa, *La Langue française au Canada*.
[7] Hansard, *Senate*, 1915, pp. 62, 114.

Ontario authorities.[8] But it was by no means only the extremist press that became passionate over the bilingual issue.

The newspapers and periodicals with a religious orientation were especially noteworthy in their defense of their coreligionists of Ontario. The *Semaine religieuse* of Montreal and that of Quebec, two small broadsheets published by the diocesan authorities of those cities, and the *Petit canadien,* organ of the powerful St. Jean Baptiste Society, vied with each other in weekly articles on the wrongs suffered by the Ontario minority. The *Action catholique* added its more ponderous voice to the general chorus. The vehement attitude of the church press naturally acquired great authority because of the pronouncements not only of Archbishop Bruchesi but also of Cardinal Begin himself, who told his flock that it was the "noble duty of the French and Catholic province of Quebec to come to the aid of those who suffer and of those who fight ... until full justice is done."[9] The press of the cities was undoubtedly more moderate, but their intense preoccupation with the racial problem was very noticeable. In April, 1915, the *Presse* was featuring a series of editorials on the history of English maltreatment of French Canadians at the same time that it pleaded in other columns for better racial feeling. The *Patrie* was constantly reiterating its disappointment that the racial unanimity prevalent at the beginning of the war had been succeeded by such bitter animosity.[10]

The revival of partisan politics, which succeeded the party truce of 1914 to a considerable degree, had a part in destroying the unanimity of all Canadians which had marked the outbreak of the war. On the whole the Liberals supported the government war measures, but there was an outbreak of decided opposition to the proposal to give votes to soldiers. The term of the Parliament elected in 1911 was nearly over, and the government was faced

---

[8] *Devoir*, December 11, 1915.
[9] *Devoir*, January 11, 1915.
[10] *Patrie*, June 9, 1915 *et seq.*

with the necessity of either getting Parliament to prolong its own life or going to the country for a fresh mandate. The Liberals feared that the government would reap all the benefits of the patriotic appeal their conduct of the war would call forth. Laurier's 1914 appeal for a party truce during hostilities would have greatly handicapped them in an election, and the Conservatives might easily have taken the opportunity to increase their majority. It was this fear that substantially increased the Liberal opposition to a government bill giving the vote to all soldiers aged twenty-one who were British subjects and who had lived thirty days in their districts. The Liberals saw in this measure a threat by the government, which was using its prestige and the control of the election machinery to roll up a solid soldier vote for themselves. Also, some of the financial proposals were criticized as being unsound, and the ugly scandals attached to the supply of munitions and boots to the army were considerably exploited by the Liberals.

There can be little doubt that the war-supplies scandals helped to influence many Canadians against the national war effort. The period of economic depression that had preceded the war had been rapidly succeeded by one of extraordinary prosperity. Factories for making munitions of war, boots, uniforms, and war equipment in general sprang up in Canada. It was inevitable that the haste with which they were organized and the opportunity offered to make huge profits should lead to abuses. The Liberals, especially Sir Wilfrid Laurier, while maintaining their attitude of support for the government's war effort, did not hesitate on the other hand to reserve their right to criticize mistakes in war administration or negligence and corruption with regard to the military supplies. Sir Wilfrid Laurier made it very clear that the war was the only thing that he and his supporters thought worth concentrating on and that to win that war they wanted an army which should be well equipped. To that end the Liberals again and again pledged their support for any government measure that would help win the war. It is interesting to note that the scandals over military supplies divided the rural press of Quebec on strictly partisan lines. The Conservative *Courrier de St. Hyacinthe* accused the Liberals of having invented the military-boot scandal for their own partisan ends,[11] while the Liberal *Avenir du nord* insisted that, while the Dominion war policy should be supported, the government must on no account be allowed to escape its responsibilities.[12] This instantaneous and almost instinctive reaction of the rural press of Quebec is not entirely without significance. While the press of the large cities tried in the course of 1915 to maintain the party truce decided on at the outbreak of the war and emulated Laurier's dignified attempts at an unpartisan criticism of the maladministration of war supplies, the rural newspapers, so strongly impregnated with political bias, reverted to partisan strife at the first opportunity. The position of the Liberals was a difficult one, for they had pledged themselves to loyal support of all the government war measures, while they had absolutely no control over its policy and at the same time remained in opposition. This invidious situation tended to cause partisan resentment which was none-the-less real because it was often repressed in the interests of the country as a whole. In the case of French Canadian Liberals, their growing antagonism was increased by the Ontario schools agitation, and the ensuing division of opinion came to be exploited by the Nationalists for their own ends.

There can be no doubt that these disputes helped to tarnish the fine enthusiasm of all Canadians, which in 1914 had seemed to presage at last a united national policy for Canada. Nevertheless, in 1915 discontent still remained a minor issue, and on the whole all seemed to be going well with Canada's war effort. Canadians

---

[11] *Courrier de St. Hyacinthe*, April 17, 1915.
[12] *Avenir du nord*, February 26, 1915.

of both races were proud of the way in which the youth of the country had rallied to the support of Britain, of the rapid organization of the Canadian Expeditionary Force and its dispatch to the battlefields, where it was winning laurels for the Dominion. Canada remained safe and remote from the strife. It was this very safety and remoteness that enabled such disputes as the Ontario school controversy to attain wide proportions and permitted Bourassa to develop an anti-war propaganda that was to become a serious embarrassment to the military efforts of Canada.

In spite of the remoteness of Canada there were signs that the exigencies of war were seriously changing her relations with the mother country. The initial, and perhaps the most important, step had been taken even before the war, when Sir Robert Borden had been admitted to that holy of holies of imperial war policy, the Committee of Imperial Defense. From that admission to consultations for shaping the military efforts of the Empire and a share in its foreign policy were perfectly natural steps. A significant evidence of this evolution was the invitation issued by the British government to the Canadian Prime Minister to sit with the British cabinet. When Sir Robert Borden visited England in July, 1915, he accepted that invitation, and though he took no part in the discussions the presence of the Prime Minister of Canada was considered by many a precedent for the further representation of the self-governing Dominions in the councils of the Empire. It was symptomatic of the fact that the exigencies of war had made the Imperial Government fully realize that the Dominions, which were contributing so largely to the war effort of the Empire, could no longer be denied a voice in the control of its policy. Sir Robert Borden himself believed that the seating of Canada's Prime Minister at the cabinet board constituted a recognition of Canada's right to be considered a fully equal partner of Great Britain.

The extraordinary transformation of a peaceful people into a nation in arms continued to make enormous strides in the course of 1915. The second contingent of the Canadian Expeditionary Force, which included the Royal 22d French Canadians, sailed for further training in England in April. On April 10 the Prime Minister announced that there were already 36,500 Canadian soldiers overseas, 53,000 in Canada, and a total of 101,500 men of all branches of the service actually under arms.[13] An order-in-council of July 8 authorized the recruitment of 150,000 men, but by October it was recognized that even more men would be needed, and a limit of 250,000 was set.[14] Meanwhile, a Third Division was being organized, and by December 31, 1915, there were 213,000 men under arms, of whom more than 180,000 had been raised in 1915. Even that was not enough, and very shortly after the end of the year an appeal was made to bring the Canadian forces up to 500,000.[15]

Meanwhile, in March, 1915, the First Canadian Division had taken its place in the front line. At Ypres and at St. Julien the Canadians had sustained the continual onslaught of the Germans and the first gas attack of the war with magnificent courage, but their losses had been very heavy, in many cases as high as fifty percent of their strength. Throughout the summer, the First Division was under the heaviest strain of battle, at a period when the British Army lacked shells and when liaison between the troops was still feeble. In September the Second Division, which had been training in England throughout the summer landed in France. Thus it came about that within a year after the first Canadian soldiers had sailed from the Dominion there were two whole divisions, or approximately 40,000 Canadians, in the field. As a result it became possible to form a separate Canadian Army Corps under the command of a British general in France.[16] It must be

---

[13] Sir Charles Lucas, *The Empire at War*, II, 16-17.
[14] J. G. Hopkins, *Canada at War*, p. 6.
[15] *Canadian Annual Review*, 1915, p. 219.
[16] Lucas, *op. cit.*, pp. 108 *et seq.*

recalled that while Canada was responsible for the equipment, training, and immediate command of the Canadian troops both at home and in the theater of war, the troops were subject to the strategic plans of the British military authorities once they left their native shore. There was a considerable amount of disquiet in Canada over the control of Canadian soldiers by the British authorities. English, as well as French, Canadians, asked questions in Parliament, but the Minister of Militia made it quite clear that the military control of the Canadian Expeditionary Force and the choice of battalions destined for the front line lay entirely with the British military authorities.

It is difficult to assess the part played by French Canada in this speeding up of the Dominion's war efforts. The fact that it was not required that recruits must state on enlistment whether they were French- or English-speaking, but simply whether or not they were Canadian born, made any accurate estimate exceedingly difficult. It was well known that many French Canadians had gone overseas with the first contingent. The 14th Battalion Royal Montreal Regiment alone had a whole company, and there were many others scattered throughout the force. Recruiting for the 22d Battalion French Canadians which was part of the 2d Division had been exceedingly brisk, and the ranks had been filled in a very short time. Subsequently, other strictly French Canadian battalions such as the 41st, the 57th, and the 69th, had been raised in Quebec with great ease and enthusiasm, and by midsummer these battalions, totaling more than 4,000 men, were at full strength. As a result the French Canadians claimed with considerable justice that their compatriots were playing a large part in the country's war effort. Of one fact there could be no doubt, and that was that the proportion of British-born soldiers in the Canadian army still far exceeded that of the Canadian-born. It was authoritatively estimated that up to the end of 1915 the percentage of native-born soldiers was only 30, while the British-born

The Revival of National Conflict

constituted 62 percent, with the other 8 percent consisting of other nationalities.[17] It should be recalled that the number of British-born in Canada was proportionately large at the outbreak of the war. A great wave of immigrants from the British Isles had poured into the Dominion between 1896 and 1913. The 1911 census figures showed that the British-born constituted 285,858, or roughly 16 percent, of a total male population of 1,653,646 between the ages of eighteen and forty-five. At the same period there were 973,621 Canadian-born males in this age-group, so that the proportion of British-born to Canadian males between eighteen and forty-five was about one to three.[18]

Unfortunately, however, there were evidences by the middle of the summer of 1915 that things were not going smoothly. The year 1915 saw the beginning of the bad management of the Quebec recruiting situation. The military authorities committed blunders, such as appointing an Anglo-Canadian Protestant clergyman as chief recruiting officer in the French Catholic Province of Quebec, by assigning French Canadians to exclusively English-speaking battalions and by refusing to allow them to transfer to French-speaking battalions. Resentment was felt in Quebec over the apparent desire of the military authorities to exclude French Canadian staff officers from commands commensurate with their rank. Many French Canadians felt rightly or wrongly that Sir Sam Hughes would go to any lengths to keep the higher positions for his own Anglo-Canadian and anti-French friends. The relegation to minor posts of well-known French Canadians, such as General Lessard, highest ranking officer of the pre-War militia, Colonel Pelletier, South African War veteran, and General Landry was directly attributed by French Canadians to the anti-French and anti-Catholic prejudices of the Minister of Militia. These blunders caused bad feeling among the French Canadians which the Nationalists were not slow to turn to their own advantage by

---

[17] Lucas, *op. cit.*, p. 17.   [18] *Fifth Census of Canada*, II, 340.

an insistent propaganda on supposed wrongs suffered by the French Canadian minority in the Ontario schools. The Nationalists were emboldened to commence a real opposition to the government war policy, and they even went so far as to attack the attitude of the Catholic hierarchy toward Canadian participation as ultra-loyalist and contrary to Canadian tradition. In reply the Church newspapers called the Nationalists revolutionaries, but on the whole they did not think it necessary to defend their own support of Canada's war policy with any amount of force. In consequence of this rather fainthearted attack on the Nationalist attitude toward the war and its own open sympathy with the cause of the Ontario minority, the Church laid itself open, and with it, all of French Canada, to the whispered charge of veiled disloyalty to the cause of active Canadian participation. French Canadian officers were complaining that their battalions were being kept too long in Canada and that it was difficult to maintain discipline when the men were sent home on harvest leave and consequently tempted to desert and stay at home.

Little was done to allay the dissatisfaction in the French Canadian units with their continued inaction. In some cases officers of inferior capacity were kept in their commands simply because they had had long militia experience, and some officers whose standing in the community and general capacity were far greater were consistently ignored. It is a well-known fact that the French Canadian, especially if he comes from the country, is much more likely to follow an officer from those families that have been the leaders of the French Canadian communities for generations or even in some cases for centuries. Men of this caliber had no difficulty in the recruiting campaigns which they organized in the countryside in 1915, but they found that recruits grew restive when they were kept long months in Valcartier Camp or in winter barracks in Quebec city. The military authorities were not always wise in dealing with these cases of unrest among the

French Canadian units, and unfortunately the impression got abroad that the Quebec battalions were undisciplined and inclined to desertion. Such rumors were seized upon by people who always had been unfriendly to the French Canadians, and they gave a powerful momentum to the whispering campaign which alleged that Quebec was not doing its full duty.

It continued to be particularly unfortunate that the statistical methods employed by the military authorities did not permit a clean-cut estimate of the number of French Canadians who had enlisted. The lack of suitable records permitted a good deal of arbitrary guesswork on both sides, with racial bitterness as the only result. Apparently the government did not appreciate the danger to racial peace and consequently to a successful prosecution of the war involved in this question. It failed to take advantage of the early war enthusiasm of Quebec when many influential and patriotic French Canadians were by no means content with the formation of the 22d Battalion but wanted to raise a larger unit such as a brigade of four battalions to be exclusively composed of their countrymen. Early in the 1915 session of Parliament, when a French Canadian member asked whether the government actually desired to form such a French Canadian brigade the Minister of Militia replied in the vaguest manner that the formation of three new French Canadian battalions was still under consideration. Seemingly the government failed to realize that evasion about the number of French Canadian soldiers embittered their own compatriots who were proud of Quebec's effort and supplied ammunition to the detractors of everything French Canadian. In the course of the Parliamentary session, Sir Sam Hughes, in reply to a direct question from a Quebec member as to the number of French Canadians in the first contingent, said evasively that there had probably been between three and six thousand but that in his opinion whatever the number Quebec had done its duty.[19] Such

---

[19] Hansard, *Commons*, 1915, p. 1549.

vagueness on the part of the military authorities made exaggeration of every sort only too possible. The essence of the matter was that those who were prone to disparage the war efforts of Quebec made the number of French Canadians who had enlisted as small as possible, while the French Canadians were naturally disposed to overrate it. The rural press was especially prone to make large assertions. On April 29 the *Bien Public,* of Three Rivers, claimed that there were 10,000 French Canadian soldiers, while the Joliette *Avenir du nord* estimated on August 6 that the number was as high as 13,800. The very fact that there was so much assertion and counter-assertion proved that there was much uneasiness about Quebec's war efforts. While many English-speaking Canadians became critical of the war attitude of French Canada, the French Canadians for their part deeply resented what seemed to them a libel on the war efforts already so well initiated by their countrymen. There was indeed a strong body of opinion in Quebec which believed that the fanatical Orangemen of Ontario, whose war cry had always been "Down with Popery and Quebec domination," were deliberately trying to discredit French Canada's war efforts for political purposes. The apparent difficulties with regard to getting the government to authorize more French Canadian units and to securing higher commands for French Canadian officers, coupled with the fact that the Minister of Militia, Sir Sam Hughes, had always been known to be a member of the Orange Order, lent color to these suspicions.

In October a muddle-headed attempt was made to enlist the support of the more extreme nationalists by the offer of the command of a French Canadian battalion to Armand Lavergne. The Lavergne affair had a good deal of repercussion, as it provided the Nationalists an opportunity to give their standpoint on enlistment and Canadian participation the greatest publicity through the medium of one of their most prominent leaders. Armand Lavergne had come to be known as the most able and trusted of

Bourassa's lieutenants, and his opinions were considered to represent the Nationalist viewpoint as a whole. In an open letter to Sir Sam Hughes, the Minister of Militia, Lavergne refused the government's offer of a command. He reiterated the well-known pre-war principles of the Nationalists against the involvement of Canada in imperial wars, or in any war which was not for the actual defense of the Dominion, especially as long as Canada had no control over imperial foreign policy. The real importance of Lavergne's refusal and the publicity given it lay in his bold insistence that his compatriots, like himself, would not consider enlisting for any overseas adventure, no matter how interesting, until the wrongs and abuses inflicted on their brothers in Ontario had been righted; and until a reign of liberty and justice was well established in Canada, they would not attempt to impose one on other nations. Lavergne realized that the essential *Canadienisme* of the French Canadians was beginning to make its appeal to many of his compatriots and was helping materially to turn their thoughts away from the active and enthusiastic war effort that had seemed so possible in 1914.

The newspapers of French Canada, especially in Quebec and Montreal, did their part in the first months of 1915 to maintain an interest in recruiting among their compatriots. But the undercurrent of resentment at what was considered calumny of the French Canadian war effort was becoming evident. The Montreal *Presse*, which was assiduous in its publication of news of the French Canadian battalions and in stimulating recruiting, urged its readers to remember that "solidarity of sacrifice should extinguish the quarrels due to prejudice ... and should render indissoluble the harmonious union which unites the two great races." [20] The *Presse*, however, felt constrained to reiterate that the French Canadians were doing their share and that the satisfaction they felt in doing their duty was enough to prevent them from feeling disturbed at the per-

[20] *Presse*, April 16, 1915.

The Revival of National Conflict 109

fidious suspicions with which jingoes attempted to destroy their loyalty.[21] In similar vein the *Patrie* proclaimed its satisfaction with the progress of recruiting and told the Nationalists that their policy of preaching to the French Canadians that they should not enlist was "to ask them to close the glorious period of their history and to begin another of shame and ignominy." [22] The conflicting emotions of the French Canadians may be illustrated by the fact that at the very moment that newspapers like the *Presse* and the *Patrie* were trying to maintain harmony between the races the *Devoir* was publishing a series of articles violently attacking Britain's treatment of minorities in general and Ontario's treatment of the French Canadians in particular. While the press of the metropolitan centers was doing its best to maintain an attitude of loyalty and patriotism, it is noticeable that the rural press reflected the growing indifference of the province to war issues. After the first flurry of interest in the war it was evident that local happenings had resumed their rightful places on the front page of the rural newspapers. Long columns were devoted to conventions of Papal Zouaves or to anniversary celebrations of favorite priests, while the bare announcement that three new French Canadian battalions were to be raised did not even bring forth editorial comment.[23] Even the parliamentary debates in Ottawa were not commented upon at any length, while there were frequent references to the struggle in Ontario over bilingual schools.[24]

In spite of this growing indifference the rural press kept within the limits of loyalty and opposed the more extreme views of Bourassa and the Nationalists, especially if the paper in question was a Liberal organ. The *Avenir du nord* asserted that Bourassa would not succeed in finding a justification in the Canadian Constitution for the regrettable rôle he was playing in attempting to turn people's minds not against Germany but against Britain.[25]

[21] *Ibid.*
[22] *Patrie*, July 22, 1915.
[23] *Etoile du nord*, July 18, 1915.
[24] *Ibid.*, November 25, 1915.
[25] *Avenir du nord*, December 24, 1915.

The Montmagny *Peuple,* for example, did not hesitate to attack Bourassa openly and to tell him that Canada had very good reason to defend England, for it was in London that French Canada could always claim her legitimate national rights with the greatest possibility of success.[26]

In the confused situation there arose a rumor in the midsummer of 1915 that the government was considering the possibility of introducing compulsory military service. There seems to have been no reason for this report, but it was distinctly embarrassing to the government and to all who were urging men to join the colors. The Nationalists, for their part, neither denied nor affirmed the truth of the conscription rumor, but it was of some advantage to them in their growing anti-British campaign. Those who appreciated the danger of this equivocal situation undertook an active recruiting campaign in Quebec in the course of the summer. French Canadian leaders of every political complexion went up and down the province urging their compatriots to enlist. Even the ex-Nationalist Minister Blondin urged his compatriots to sink their local grievances and to show by enlisting that their hearts were with the Allies.[27] Conservatives of the old school like Postmaster-General Casgrain expressed the hope that active Canadian participation would bring about a better racial feeling.[28] Rodolphe Lemieux, a leading Liberal, addressed many recruiting meetings and even went to Toronto to denounce the doctrines of the Nationalists as unrepresentative of his countrymen's feelings toward the war. Laurier himself did not hesitate to say that "it is the duty of Canada to give to Great Britain in this hour all the assistance that is in her power." [29] The French Canadian press, in general, ridiculed the conscription bogey, and the *Patrie* and *Evénement* did not hesitate to accuse the Nationalists of having

---
[26] *Peuple,* October 29, 1915.
[27] *Canadian Annual Review,* 1915, p. 25.
[28] *Canadian Annual Review,* 1915, p. 276.
[29] *Patrie,* July 12, 1915.

The Revival of National Conflict 111

invented it.³⁰ The *Presse* urged the initiation of a great recruiting campaign to show that conscription was unnecessary.³¹ The Nationalist *Devoir* pointed out that the government had already done so many unexpected things in the course of the war that it would not be surprising to see it resort to compulsory military service. The *Devoir* asserted that in the first instance the conscription scare was due to the leaders of industry who were coercing their employees into enlisting—a theory to which even the Conservative *Evénement* subscribed.³²

It was not surprising that in this sultry atmosphere of mistrust on the one side and hesitancy on the other, there was an actual riotous outbreak. At the Parc Lafontaine, in Montreal on July 23, a recruiting meeting of the 41st French Canadians attended by many thousands was broken up with cries of "We don't want conscription," and recruiting posters at the offices of the *Presse* and *Patrie* were torn down by columns of rioters singing "O Canada," the national hymn of the French Canadians.³³ The *Devoir* in its account of the disturbance condoned the action of the rioters whom it estimated as having amounted to more than 12,000, while the *Gazette* stated there were no more than 1,500. The French press in general was swift in its condemnation. The *Patrie* warned French Canadians to "beware of compromising the good name of Quebec forever and of losing for the French Canadian race its prestige and its honor," ³⁴ while the *Action catholique* pointed out that in its opinion the best way to stop conscription was to enlist in large numbers.³⁵ In fact, every organ of French Canadian opinion, whether Liberal, Conservative, or Nationalist, came out against conscription during this period. It is noticeable that after the flare-up of the Parc Lafontaine riot the

---

[30] *Evénement*, July 8, 1915.
[31] *Presse*, July 20, 1915.
[32] *Devoir*, July 26, 1915. *Evénement*, July 8, 1915.
[33] *Devoir*, July 24, 1915. *Gazette*, July 24, 1915.
[34] *Patrie*, July 26, 1915.
[35] *Action catholique*, July 26, 1915.

province quieted down. Quebec does not easily take to violence, and its use generally prejudices the cause with which it is associated. Throughout the autumn of 1915 large recruiting meetings were held in the cities throughout the province with considerable success. Even the rural press did its share in telling the French Canadians that they must appreciate that Canada was sending soldiers to fight in Europe to safeguard her own liberty and her own interests.[36] It spite of this effort, Henri Bourassa and his Nationalist followers kept the bilingual school question and thus the racial issue constantly before the French Canadian public.

Bourassa's evolution from a qualified supporter to a bitter opponent of Canadian war participation was of great significance. The Nationalist espousal of the cause of the Ontario minority had aroused racial hatred, but their anti-war policy seriously divided French Canadian opinion. It was not that Quebec turned from an essential deep loyalty to the British crown nor even that the great majority of French Canadians approved of all that Bourassa said, but it made them hesitate to give full unstinted support to the war policy of the government of Canada. People and press were made uneasy by Bourassa's anti-war propaganda. Great newspapers, such as the *Presse* and *Patrie,* commented sadly on the fatal divisions between the two Canadian nationalities and blamed the Nationalists for the accusations made against French Canadian loyalty.[37] At the end of 1914 Bourassa was still able to give qualified approval to an active participation, but even then he was already saying that Canada should be careful to contribute only within the limits of her capacity and that she should consider how to help the Allies with industrial and agricultural products as well as with men. Although the Nationalist leader was careful to reiterate that Canada as an Anglo-French community bound to Great Britain and France by a thousand ties had a vital interest

[36] *Courrier de St. Hyacinthe,* October 2, 1915.
[37] *Presse,* June 9, 1915. *Patrie,* August 7, 1915.

The Revival of National Conflict 113

in their preservation, his conclusion that other means than the mere sending of soldiers should be seriously considered seemed to indicate that Bourassa's influence was to be thrown against recruiting, and so it was interpreted in anti-French-Canadian circles.[38]

Bourassa's changing attitude was well indicated by the title of a very long and quasi-legal pamphlet called *Que devons-nous à l'Angleterre*, published in 1915. In analyzing the duties and obligations of Canada toward the mother country he made no direct suggestion that the Dominion should default in the war participation that she had voluntarily assumed in August, 1914. But the Nationalist leader pointed out clearly to his compatriots that by the various fundamental agreements between Canada and Great Britain, such as the Constitutional Act of 1791, the British North America Act of 1867, and the various Militia Acts, Canada's military obligations were confined to the defense of her own territory, while Britain as sole mistress of the Empire's foreign policy was bound to assume the full burden of imperial defense. It is easy to see that this somewhat sophistical argument was very likely to impress simple people with the idea that Canada had no obligations whatever in the present crisis. The impression of Canada's lack of responsibility could only be increased by Bourassa's many examples which purported to prove that ever since the days of Joseph Chamberlain imperialists in Britain had been attempting to secure the automatic co-operation of the self-governing Dominions in all the wars of the Empire.[39]

As Bourassa's viewpoint against the government war policy became clearer, he used every possible opportunity of showing that the English-speaking Canadian leaders were sacrificing Canada for the Empire. Arthur Meighen's famous statement that if necessary he would bankrupt Canada to save the Empire was held up

[38] H. Bourassa, *The Duty of Canada at the Present Hour*.
[39] H. Bourassa, *Que devons-nous à l'Angleterre*.

as evidence time and again, as was the Prime Minister's remark, shortly after his sitting with the London cabinet, that an Empire like the British was worth living and dying for.[40] The conscription scare of midsummer, 1915, afforded Bourassa the opportunity of saying that such a measure was by no means impossible for the simple reason that it was quite in line with the Canadian government's policy of truckling to the imperialists in London. As Bourassa developed his hymn of hate against imperialism, he urged his compatriots with all the eloquence at his command to adopt the new "nationalism" which should place the interests of their native land above all other interests and to insist on the essential principle of Dominion autonomy which would oblige her to defend only Canadian soil. Such an appeal could not but attract people like the French Canadians who naturally were more concerned with their own narrow interests than with a war three thousand miles away. In that alone lay the strength of Bourassa's propaganda and the danger to a successful Canadian war effort.[41]

If Bourassa appealed to many who were inclined to be "agin the government," the controversy between the *Action catholique* and Olivar Asselin distressed an even wider circle of earnestly devout and conservatively minded French Canadians. It was an indication of the disturbed state of public opinion in Quebec. In the course of 1915 Asselin, who in spite of his Nationalist affiliations had joined the army, boldly attacked the war policy of the Canadian hierarchy as contrary to tradition. The *Action catholique* as the recognized organ of the hierarchy had been criticized before by many as having gone too far in its approval of the policy of active Canadian participation. The Nationalists and Asselin were perhaps the most frank in their criticism, but the existence of any criticism at all on the matter indicated that the great body of the faithful

---

[40] R. B. Borden, *Canada at War, Speeches*, July-December, 1915, privately printed.
[41] Bourassa, *Le Devoir, son origine, son passé, son avenir*.

The Revival of National Conflict 115

was wavering from the enthusiastic loyalty which had been the general rule in 1914. Olivar Asselin boldly asserted that in the Pastoral letter of September, 1914, the Canadian hierarchy had gone contrary to tradition by interpreting the military obligations of Canada in an imperialistic and antinational sense for the first time in Dominion history by approving the dispatch overseas of Canadian troops.[42]

Asselin did not hesitate to accuse the hierarchy of having desired, above all things, to stand well with the imperial authorities and with the federal government by taking this point of view. The authority of the bishops in matters ecclesiastical was questioned in no way, but the fact that the obligation of the Canadian state rather than that of the individual Canadian citizen to come to the military aid of England had been recognized, was proof to Asselin that the Church had exceeded its powers. For this break in the traditional policy of the hierarchy, Asselin openly, and with passionate and sometimes even scurrilous invective, blamed the editors and those who controlled the policy of the *Action catholique*. Asselin even ventured to assert that Cardinal Begin of Quebec was too old to appreciate what was going on, and in consequence the real instigators of what he termed the "antinational and imperialist" attitude of the Quebec hierarchy were the auxiliary Bishop Mgr. Paul Eugène Roy and the Abbé D'Amours, editor of the *Action catholique*. These dignitaries were accused of having twisted the statement of the bishops' Pastoral, which called for obedience to legitimate authority, to mean obedience to Great Britain's legitimate authority rather than to that of the Parliament of Canada. Asselin, who felt deeply the call of France in her present hour of peril and who entered the army to come to her aid, insisted not only that the bishops in their impatience to attach Canada forever to the British crown had shown more zeal than dignity, but by generally abusing France in order to detach

[42] O. Asselin, "*L'Action catholique*," *les évêques et la guerre*.

French Canadians from that country had destroyed their pride of race and in so doing had compromised the survival of French speech and thought.

Asselin's criticism of the bishops' attitude toward Canadian participation was much more contradictory than that of the more orthodox Nationalist who was beginning to oppose participation in any form. It was because Asselin was trying to reconcile his belief in the obligation for participation of the individual with the necessity of maintaining the traditional attitude of strict Canadian autonomy, blended with loyalty to the British crown, that his argument was significant, for it represented the perplexity in which thousands of his compatriots were beginning to find themselves. Asselin evidently felt that he was speaking not only for the puzzled laymen among his compatriots but for some of the priests, for he called his pamphlet a "plea for the freedom of thought of laymen and the lower clergy in political matters,"[43] and asserted that the *Action catholique* had warned the country clergy against compromising the loyalty of French Canadians to Britain by any criticism of the government's war policies. Asselin believed the priests owed obedience only in matters of religion and morals, and as a result a priest who disagreed on the necessity for active war participation with the bishop did not necessarily fail in church discipline. That this opinion was shared by many good churchmen is shown by the statement of so devout a man as Bourassa himself, who in discussing the policy of the *Devoir* insisted that while clerical opinion on matters political was always to be respected, it was not necessarily to be obeyed.[44] In the last analysis, the opinion of Asselin was that while the individual Canadian had an obligation to fight for the cause of Britain and France the Canadian state would be more faithful to its own interests if it limited its military effort to the defense of its own territory.

[43] Asselin, *op. cit., passim.*   [44] Bourassa, *op. cit.*

The Revival of National Conflict 117

It is obvious that the *Action catholique* could not have subscribed to Asselin's doctrine, having once adopted the validity of the bishops' Pastoral and its approval of Canadian participation. In addition, the hierarchy for whom it undoubtedly spoke had a healthy fear of the dangers in which the Nationalist movement might involve the French Canadians. They had long feared that the Nationalists were in the process of developing a form of philosophy which perilously resembled the ideas of the French revolutionaries and which therefore should be abhorrent to any good churchman. As early as September, 1914, the *Action catholique* had pointed out that the loyalty owed to Britain by Canadians was based on the rigorous obligation of obeying that authority which God had placed over them, and that it would be a grave error to think that sovereignty belonged to the people who therefore owed no obligations save those they had assumed for themselves.[45] The duty of loyalty was in no way affected by the good treatment that French Canadians had received at the hand of Britain nor even by the occasional injustices meted out to them. The measure of help was to be entirely dependent on what was needed to attain victory, and in the last resort its extent depended on Britain alone.[46]

The Nationalists insisted that by this statement the *Action catholique* meant that Canada should contribute men and money, but the editors asserted in return that they had never wished to dictate the means of Canadian participation and that their only desire was to maintain the colonial tie in the form in which it then existed and to carry out their bounden duty of helping Britain in the present war, which in no way implied that they were imperialistic.[47] The *Action catholique* was firm in pointing out that it was an historic and generally recognized truth that the great majority of French Canadians were happy to live under

[45] *Action catholique*, September 11, 1914.
[46] *Ibid.*, September 14, 1914.
[47] *Action catholique*, September 23, 1914, February 1, 1915.

the protection of the British flag and that it would be a great pity to change their present political status in relation to the Empire.[48]

The *Action catholique* considered the Church the great bulwark of French Canadian rights and privileges. While inspiring the French Canadians with her spirit and with her teachings, the Church had never fallen into the errors of a pagan imperialism nor into that of a revolutionary and excessive nationalism. As a result the Church taught the faithful that there were duties and obligations toward the sovereign power ruling Canada which should of necessity be discharged. These duties could be accomplished without adopting the exaggerations of an over-insistent imperialism, and similarly the rights of French Canadians could be defended by the precepts of Christian law without adopting the exaggeration of a nationalism which was becoming more and more inspired by the false principle of nationality, of which the revolutionary origin was only too well known. With this refusal to accept the appellation of being either imperialists or Nationalists and standing on the old tradition of unquestioning loyalty to Britain, the hierarchy joined issue with anyone who opposed the official participation of Canada in the war.[49]

The year 1915 closed in doubt and mutual distrust between the two Canadian peoples as these controversies attracted more and more attention. Large masses of English-speaking Canadians were beginning to believe that French Canada was not fully loyal to the Empire, in this, its hour of need, and that Quebec was not taking its full share in the defense of Canada. For this feeling the propaganda of Bourassa and the Nationalists must be held largely responsible. On the other side, thousands of French Canadians were convinced that a great injustice was being done their brethren in Ontario and were beginning to weary of the war effort, which they no longer felt it essential to support. Besides, they felt deeply hurt that their enthusiastic response to the call

[48] *Ibid.*, September 2, 1915.   [49] *Ibid.*, March 9, 1915.

for men, money, and supplies at the outbreak of the war had apparently had no further result than the injustice of the Ontario school dispute and the calumnies against their race's war effort. There was misunderstanding and a growing antipathy on both sides. The unanimity of feeling which to a certain extent had prevailed even as late as the beginning of the year had definitely disappeared. Instead, there was disillusionment and mutual suspicion, and the transition stage marked by 1915 was soon to develop into open dissension between the two Canadian races.

VI

French Canada on the Defensive, 1916

WHILE 1915 had been for the French Canadians a hesitant year, in which they had been torn between the call of their racial brethren in Ontario and that of the larger Canadian patriotism which the appeal for active war participation involved, 1916 was to see French Canada definitely on the defensive, her hesitation hardening slowly but surely into resistance to the pressure being brought to bear on her. The great majority of French Canadians were convinced that their war effort had been worthy of their race and that the criticisms and attacks made against it were a mass of invidious calumnies. As a result, they began to feel "nationally," and their reactions to any question involving war issues or the language controversy were conditioned less by their normal political orientation than by their racial prejudices and emotions.

The difficulties of the war were producing a definite French Canadian "nationalism" which the coming of conscription in 1917 was to crystallize into an almost unanimous passive resistance to the war policies of the Canadian government. In 1916, however, there were still many French Canadians who were honestly trying to adjust the difficulties between the two races and to do all in their power to bring Quebec's war effort up to the highest possible level.

The last days of 1915 witnessed the appeal of the Prime Minister for a total number of 500,000 men for the army. Up to the end of 1915, 213,000 men had already enlisted, so that the new call involved the raising of more than a quarter of a million more.[1]

[1] Sir Charles Lucas, *The Empire at War*, II, 31.

In the course of the preceding six months the authorized number of soldiers had been doubled. Of this new force it was estimated that Ontario could raise about nine divisions, while the quota of Quebec was to be between three and four divisions. The response to the government's appeals was excellent at first, and in the first six months of 1916 approximately 120,000 men joined up. After that the men were much slower in coming in, so that the second half of the year saw only about 40,000 recruits.[2] Obviously, the need of munitions factories was great, and by 1916 there were more than six hundred of these plants, employing some 300,000 men who might otherwise have gravitated to the army.[3] These munitions factories had a great economic appeal to young workers, for they paid much higher wages than other industries—wages which far exceeded those of the army. The appeal for increased agricultural production was another factor which helped to keep many able-bodied young farmers at home and away from the ranks of the army. Obviously few of those patriotic young men born in the British Isles who had rushed to the colors in 1914 and 1915 remained.

All these factors helped to slow up recruiting as a whole, and to them was added the growing indifference and hostility of Quebec toward doing more than she had already done. The slowing up of recruiting seriously alarmed those who were most concerned with speeding up Canada's war effort, and there were many attempts made not only to analyze the difficulties but to solve them. The recruiting figures up to the beginning of 1916 were subjected to a searching analysis by a prominent Conservative senator, General Mason, in March, 1916.[4] General Mason based his deductions on figures supplied him by the census authorities and the Ministry of Militia. According to the census of 1911 the total Canadian-born males between the ages of eighteen to forty-

[2] *Ibid.*, II, 31 *et seq.*
[3] *Canadian Annual Review*, 1916, p. 253.
[4] Hansard, *Senate*, 1916, p. 406.

five had been 1,112,000, of whom 667,000 were English-speaking and 445,000 French-speaking. General Mason estimated that only 30 percent of the total number of recruits to date were Canadian-born, while the British-born constituted 63 percent and the foreign-born the remaining 7 percent. Of the Canadian-born, General Mason estimated that 85,000, or 28.5 percent of the total enlistments, were English-speaking, while 12,000, or 4.5 percent of the total, were men who had enlisted in battalions which were exclusively French Canadian or who bore French names in English-speaking battalions. Thus, the French Canadian males of the ages between eighteen and forty-five, who constituted two-fifths or 40 percent of the total population of that age, had supplied only 4.5 percent of the recruits.

General Mason was doubtless conscious that his figures would not be popular among French Canadians, and indeed they caused much acrimonious debate. As a result he was careful to point out his strong belief that the native-born of both races were not doing their full duty and that means must be found to get this class of the population to enlist. His suggestion was the adoption of the Derby Scheme, in force in England, which called for a registration of all available males as a means of ascertaining how best they could serve the country either in the army or in war industries, coupled with an urgent appeal to volunteer for active service. A few weeks before General Mason published his figures Lord Shaughnessy, the President of the Canadian Pacific Railway, made the statement that in his opinion the raising of 500,000 men seemed an almost unbearable burden for the country when it was taken into consideration that more than 300,000 were already engaged in war industries.[5] Among French Canadians, especially among the Nationalists, there was a good deal of feeling that Lord Shaughnessy's statement proved the point that Canada had done enough and that it would henceforth be wiser to concentrate on

[5] *Gazette*, March 10, 1916.

sending supplies rather than soldiers overseas. In fact, so widely was this opinion held that Lord Shaughnessy was obliged to explain that he had meant not to discourage recruiting but to organize it by allocating some recruits to the army and others to vitally important war industries and thus to prevent the recruiting of men who should be in factories or the employment of men who should be in the army.[6] When these suggestions for some scheme of registration for war service were made, the time for them was not yet ripe. But when the tide of recruits definitely slackened in the second half of 1916, a scheme was set on foot under the auspices of the federal government for the supervision of recruiting and the allocation of men to war industries.

It had been planned at first to set up a board which should supervise and co-ordinate recruiting throughout the Dominion, and as a result this body was actually established in August. But it was soon apparent that the war industries, as well as the army, needed men and that it would be wise to establish some means of ascertaining which of the men eligible were best suited to industry and which should be called upon to enlist. A National Service Commission was appointed in September under an order-in-council, and an appeal was issued to the manhood of Canada to enlist for overseas military service, and all Canadian citizens not able to enlist were called to serve their country in such capacity as might be useful to the nation as a whole.[7] It was stated that the National Service Commission would take an inventory of Canadian man power. This came to be interpreted by many as the prelude to an eventual conscription scheme and thus called for unconditional condemnation by the Nationalists and all those opposed to further active participation. In organizing the National Service Board the government attempted to secure the support of all Canadians regardless of party lines. Nevertheless, the compo-

[6] *Ibid.*, March 10, 1916.
[7] *Canadian Annual Review*, 1916, pp. 327 *et seq.*

sition of the Board was considerably criticized as being too predominantly Conservative. The Prime Minister had indeed asked Sir Wilfrid Laurier to co-operate with it, but the Liberal leader had refused the invitation. He apparently felt that the National Service Board, under the chairmanship of the Conservative R. B. Bennett, was to be conducted on partisan lines and believed that a fundamental mistake had been made in urging enlistment as the primary need rather than to ascertain first the essential needs of war industries. Laurier's reservation somewhat invalidated his sincerely patriotic support of the National Service scheme and gave an opening to the enemies of French Canada to say that the plan was being sabotaged in Quebec. In spite of these difficulties, those in charge went ahead and urged all men to sign National Service cards.

Some newspapers tried to point out that it was necessary to abide loyally by the National Service scheme because the interests of all citizens must be subordinated to the good of the State if the Empire and Confederation were to be preserved.[8] In other quarters mistrust of the scheme was evident, and Laurier was praised for having refused to serve on the National Service Board.[9] One paper asserted that the Prime Minister had originally proposed raising 500,000 men and that it was his responsibility alone to see that they were secured, while a rural weekly hinted broadly that the National Service scheme was undoubtedly designed rather for raising soldiers than for securing men for the war industries.[10] The government was careful to point out that the National Service scheme involved no threat of conscription, but realizing that the future might make such a measure necessary for the preservation of the State it no longer pledged that conscription would never be introduced.

There can be little doubt that this somewhat equivocal attitude

---

[8] *Courrier de St. Hyacinthe*, December 23, 1916.
[9] *Soleil*, October 23, 1916.
[10] *Bien public*, November 30, 1916; *Soleil*, October 23, 1916.

French Canada on the Defensive, 1916

of the government influenced Quebec against the scheme, in spite of the fact that French Canadian leaders in Church and State had urged their compatriots to sign and fill in the National Service cards. The registration of the population for National Service did not take place until January, 1917, when more than one and one-half millions in all Canada responded to the questionnaire. There were disturbances at National Service meetings in Montreal and Quebec addressed by the Prime Minister, by R. B. Bennett, and by French Canadian leaders, such as E. L. Patenaude and Chase Casgrain, who spoke in support of the scheme. An attempt had been made in Quebec to make the meetings symbolic of nonpartisanship and national unity by having both Roman Catholic and Protestant clergy on the platform, but in spite of this the French Canadian speakers were howled down, and there were cries of "We want Bourassa and Lavergne." When R. B. Bennett, as director of National Service, rose to speak, the great majority of the audience left the hall in a body.

The ever-growing demand for men and more men for the armies of Canada was based on the imperative needs of war. It was for this reason that men of sincere patriotism sought every means to raise a further quota of Canadian manhood for active service and that any attempt to stem the tide of recruiting was often branded as treason. One hundred and sixty-five thousand men were sent overseas in 1916, and still came the demand for more.[11]

By the spring of 1916 there were three divisions in France, and in August a fourth was added.[12] In the spring the Canadian troops, under the command of Sir Julian Byng, distinguished themselves at the St. Eloi Craters and at Sanctuary Wood, and in July they took their valiant part in the bloody battles of the Somme which alone cost them more than 25,000 casualties.[13] At Courcelette, in

---
[11] Lucas, *op. cit.*, II, 31.
[12] *Ibid.*, II, 121.
[13] *Ibid.*, II, 147 *et seq.*

September, the Canadian Corps won a brilliant victory in which the 22d French Canadians bore a gallant part, but here, too, Canadian losses of 6,000 dead and wounded were a measure of their courage. The 5th Brigade alone, which included the 22d French Canadians, had 1,000 casualties. These losses were in themselves an earnest call for reinforcement in order that the valiant efforts of the Canadian troops might not be in vain. By the end of 1916 more than 280,000 men had been sent overseas to England and France since the beginning of the war, and another 100,000 were still in training in Canada.[14]

It had been decided that the need of reinforcements was so great that men would be sent over in drafts as quickly as possible instead of being attached to the home battalions, which still had a relation to the old territorially organized militia units. Six reserve brigades, with a total of twenty-six battalions, were formed in England, and each battalion became a reinforcing unit for a definite front-line battalion.[15] The territorial nature of these reserve battalions was at first rather lost sight of. As a result the battalions which had already been raised in Canada and the new drafts were broken up and sent wherever they were most needed. This system had its importance as far as the French Canadians were concerned, for they especially resented the breaking up of their battalions and the sending of men to units in which French was not spoken and where the customs of their people were unfamiliar. As time went on the army authorities did their best to send all French Canadian drafts first to the reserve battalion of the 22d in England and then to the 22d itself at the front. The confusion of policy and the fact that many men wrote home to protest against being sent to other units caused French Canadians at home to feel that their men were being treated in an unfair fashion and that their religion and customs might be interfered with as a result. The devout French Canadian especially feared the contamination that close association

[14] *Ibid.*, II, 31.   [15] *Ibid.*, II, 153-54.

with Protestants and English-speaking people might have on the simpler souls among their compatriots.

As a further measure to ensure the efficient control of the Canadian Expeditionary Forces, a Ministry of the Overseas Forces of Canada with headquarters in London and under the direction of a cabinet minister, was established, in October, 1916. For some time previously, there had been a good deal of friction between the Minister of Militia and the military authorities overseas. Sir Sam Hughes, though a most active and zealous officer, had a tendency to assign more powers to himself than was usual under a system of responsible government. During his frequent visits overseas, he did not hesitate to advise the Canadian officers in the field how to conduct operations and on one famous occasion even attempted to give Lord Kitchener some lessons in strategy. The Prime Minister, in the fall of 1916, came to the conclusion that the establishment of an overseas War Office was vitally necessary to the efficient running of the army, and by order-in-council of October 28 the Ministry of Overseas Military Forces of Canada was established.[16] Sir Sam Hughes, who was very angry at what seemed to him an usurpation of some of his powers, attempted to establish an Overseas Military Council under his own orders. Naturally, Sir Robert Borden could not tolerate this insubordination and asked the Minister of Militia to resign. By the establishment of the Overseas Ministry the complete control of all Canadian troops in the United Kingdom and in France was taken over by the Canadian government. The system under which the troops in training in England had been under the command of a British general was given up. A Canadian general staff was set up in London, and a section of it was established at General Headquarters in France to act as a liaison agent between the British High Command and the Canadian Corps. By these important changes Canada secured an army entirely controlled by her own govern-

[16] Lucas, *op. cit.*, II, 30.

ment, independent of, though co-operating with, the British Armies, and paid, officered, trained, and controlled by Canada alone.

By 1916 French Canada was no longer able to disguise from herself the fact that her recruiting effort was considered inadequate by the rest of the Dominion. In press and pulpit, on the lecture platform, and by means of pamphlets French Canadians of every political allegiance discussed this thorny problem. The newspapers defended the patriotism of their compatriots or pointed out that French Canadians must be excused for lacking a definite military spirit. Some few newspapers were ready to admit that the recruiting effort of Quebec had been a failure, while others hastened to refute such an idea with impassioned reasoning and many statistics. Those French Canadians who were definitely opposed to further active participation attacked recruiting in the boldest possible manner and generally helped to make the confusion of French Canadian opinion worse. French Canadian officers at the front, distressed at the apparent lack of co-operation at home, wrote open letters urging their compatriots to enlist and to appreciate the vital issues at stake. Over all the controversy there hung always the specter of conscription as something that might easily be introduced if recruiting did not pick up in the desired degree.

Meanwhile the number of French Canadians who had actually enlisted continued to be a matter of acrimonious dispute. The lack of accurate statistics served only to increase the bitterness. General Mason's estimate had been 12,000 French Canadians up to the early part of 1916,[17] while Rodolphe Lemieux insisted that there were 17,500;[18] and in July the *Canada* optimistically asserted that there were no less than 50,000 French Canadians[19] in the army, while in October the *Presse* asserted that there were no more than 16,000.[20] The estimate of 50,000 by the *Canada* included

[17] Hansard, *Senate*, 1916, p. 406.
[18] *Ibid.*, *Commons*, 1916, p. 3435.
[19] *Canada*, July 17, 1916.
[20] *Our Volunteer Army*.

French Canada on the Defensive, 1916 129

10,000 French and Belgian reservists besides more than 4,000 Acadians from the maritime provinces. On the other hand the detractors of the French Canadians claimed that these figures were all grossly exaggerated and that there had never been more than 5,000 in the army and, adding insult to injury, charged that in the French Canadian battalions "They enlist in retail and desert wholesale." [21]

A further source of confusion as to the number of enlisted French Canadians was the lack of accurate information as to the battalions that had gone overseas. The 22d was at the front in 1916, and three other battalions, the 41st, the 57th, and the 69th, had been broken up and poured as reinforcements into the ranks of the 22d. However, as each of these battalions had been recruited to full strength, an estimate of close to 4,500 French Canadians at the front would not be very far from accurate. Speaking in the House of Commons Rodolphe Lemieux mentioned thirteen distinctively French Canadian battalions that had been enlisted since the beginning of hostilities.[22] Allowing for the fact, which Lemieux admitted, that many of these battalions were at half strength, there must have been between eight and nine thousand French Canadians in the ranks of the infantry battalions in Canada and overseas by the middle of 1916. When French Canadians in other branches of the service or in English-speaking units are added, General Mason's estimate of 12,000 is seen to have been fairly near the truth.

It was generally acknowledged, even among French Canadians, that it grew harder to secure recruits in the course of 1916. Recruiting officers who at the beginning of the year had obtained half a battalion easily, by midsummer were able to raise only a few hundred. By some this was attributed to the seasonal factor that made harvest hands very much in demand in Quebec, when all were

[21] *Our Volunteer Army*, quoting *Orange Sentinel*, August 21, 1916.
[22] Hansard, *Commons*, 1916, p. 3281.

called upon to raise more food for the Allies, and by others to the ever-growing demand of the munitions factories for more workers.[23] The dispatch to Bermuda of the 163d Battalion, which Olivar Asselin at considerable personal sacrifice had raised for service in France, decidedly annoyed French Canadians and made them feel that they were not wanted at the front. There was further disappointment that the military authorities failed to send overseas a whole French Canadian brigade, which had been provisionally organized at Valcartier in the summer of 1916 and then broken up into separate units.

There was indeed within the ranks of the army itself evidence of active dissatisfaction with the methods by which French Canadians were treated. In July there were serious disturbances in the 206th Battalion of French Canadians. The officers of the Battalion were blamed and sent home. Before leaving the unit the commanding officer of the 206th went so far as to address his men and tell them that the main reason for the dismissal of the officers was the mere fact that they were French Canadians and in consequence not in favor with the authorities. The men were covertly advised to profit by this experience and to desert. The offending officer was subsequently tried by court martial, convicted, and sentenced to a term in prison. The unfortunate incident of the 206th Battalion was an isolated occurrence, but the fact that order-loving and generally obedient French Canadians could go so far as to rebel against constituted authority was a striking instance of the degree to which discontent and mistrust had developed.[24]

All of these factors militated against the success of the French Canadian recruiting effort, but it is none the less difficult to assess which of them was the most important. Perhaps the fact that French Canadians as a whole had too many reservations about enlisting was as important as any, though it did not appear openly. Some like

[23] Hansard, *Senate*, 1917, p. 414, letter of Col. Migneault to Senator Landry.
[24] *Canadian Annual Review*, 1916, p. 353.

Asselin believed voluntary participation of the individual was justifiable while that of the state was to be frowned upon. Others like the Quebec *Evénement,* while preaching full and loyal adherence to the Government's war program, nevertheless asserted that the duty of helping Canada's war effort was a relative one which every individual was entitled to judge on its merits.[25] Many felt—and especially the country press—that Canada was sending too many men and was draining herself dry for a cause that only concerned her indirectly. The day-by-day pronouncements of such adverse critics as Lavergne and Bourassa could not help but influence men who in their secret hearts had reservations as to the rightness or the necessity of rushing to the defense of England. When Lavergne told them early in 1916 that every French Canadian who enlisted was a traitor to his own country because he was subordinating the interests of his Ontario brethren to those of far-away England, the man who had always been taught that his main duties and interests lay in his native land could not help being affected. Finally, the ever-growing ferment over the bilingual schools in Ontario, the appeals for hundreds of thousands of signatures for a petition of disallowance of the hated law, the mass meetings of sympathy for the sufferers, and the impassioned speeches of the more prominent French Canadian leaders in Parliament on the wrongs endured by the Ontario minority, could not help exciting the French Canadians and turning them not only against their English-speaking fellow citizens but also against the policies of the mother country.

The more remote the community the more intense was the feeling, and, in May, the Quebec *Evénement,* whose support of the Government's war policy was beyond question, asserted that the great majority of French Canadians were opposed to the idea of any participation in the war and that recruiting was a fiasco which it was wiser to admit than to conceal. For this failure, the *Evéne-*

[25] *Evénement,* January 5, 1916.

ment blamed the lack of a sense of military vocation among the French Canadians and what had now become open antipathy to the cause of Britain. In the opinion of the *Evénement,* the hierarchy had done its best to resist this tendency by the mass of the lower clergy; the leading politicians and the bourgeoisie were either indifferent or openly hostile to Britain.[26] It was the appeal to the innate fear of overseas entanglement in the arguments of men like Lavergne, in the sermons of rural curés, and in the editorials of the rural press, always closer to the instinctive reaction of the people than the more cosmopolitan press of the cities, that showed how the wind was blowing in Quebec.

The *Evénement* in its frank admission that French Canadian recruiting was a failure went further than others, but all the French newspapers were admitting by 1916 that something was wrong with recruiting, though none except strictly Nationalist papers ever deviated from at least an attitude of loyalty. The *Presse* was always much preoccupied with proving that French Canada was doing her part, though it did not fail to admit that the proportion of English-speaking Canadians was far greater.[27] French Canadians were warned that they would be reduced to impotence politically if they insisted on skulking in a corner.[28] The large metropolitan newspapers never tired of telling their compatriots that it was their bounden duty to enlist, and even in some cases, that Quebec could and should do much more than she had done to date.[29] In fact the *Presse,* while frankly admitting that a large and convinced part of the French Canadian population was not favorably inclined toward a war which seemed to them to be waged primarily for the interests of Britain, urged them to appreciate that if Canada were to traverse the present crisis without the help of French Canadians their collaboration would never again be asked for. The rest of Canada would feel that they had mis-

[26] *Evénement,* May 26, 1916.
[27] *Presse,* March 21, 1916.
[28] *Ibid.,* June 5, 1916.
[29] *Soleil,* August 4, 1916.

French Canada on the Defensive, 1916   133

understood their duties as British subjects and that those who had refused to undergo the heat and pain of the struggle should not expect to partake of the advantages of victory.[30] The attitude of the *Evénement* was scored as defeatism and a calumny on French Canadians in some quarters, and it was pointed out by the stanchly Liberal *Canada* that the *Evénement* should rather blame the ex-Nationalist ministers, who since 1911 had been preaching that Canada should never involve herself in any imperial war and who now were beating the drums of enlistment at every opportunity. In some circles it was vehemently asserted that men of an essentially agricultural province like Quebec were much less likely to leave the land to which they were attached than were the footloose industrialized young men of Ontario.[31]

It is not without significance, however, that active opposition to the war began and was most notable not among the young farmers of remote Quebec but among the young industrial population of Montreal. The fanatical attacks on French Canadian culture and civilization which the Ontario school controversy had produced were advanced as another potent reason for the falling off of Quebec recruiting.[32] The total inability of some people in the province of Quebec to realize the magnitude of the task to which Canada had set her hand was marked by the proud statement of *Le Bien public*, of Three Rivers, on July 6 that "ten or twelve 'brave sons' of the town" had already enlisted for active service in 1916. In spite of this ignorance all the rural press, as well as that of the large cities of Quebec, reported the recruiting meetings that were held in the course of the year and published the recruiting advertisements; but it was obvious, none the less, that fewer men were responding to the appeal of the recruiting officers, for fewer figures were given on the number of men that were raised.

In this growing perplexity of French Canada over the recruiting

[30] *Presse*, January 14, 1916.
[31] *Canada*, July 21, 1916.
[32] *Ibid*.

situation, it was noticeable that the hierarchy maintained its attitude of strict loyalty and approval for Canada's war effort. The words of Mgr. Bruchesi, the Archbishop of Montreal, "we owe to Great Britain a loyalty which should go as far as shedding our blood for her,"[33] were typical of the sentiment in the higher ranks of the clergy; but it is noticeable that there were murmurs among the lower ranks, and a certain Abbé Guibeault openly denounced Canadian participation, adding that to fight Germany was ridiculous.[34]

A strong note of defense of Quebec's war effort was struck by Rodolphe Lemieux who asserted that his province and the Roman Catholic Church were wholeheartedly pro-war, and only Bourassa, who in no way represented Quebec public sentiment, was opposed. But even so ardent a defender of French Canada's part in the war had to admit the slowness of French Canadian recruiting, for he added that when Quebec became better informed as to the issues at stake the world would see a vast improvement in the number of her enlistments.

The marked silence of the *Action catholique* on the issues of the war showed how deeply the clergy were disturbed by the rising tide of bitter controversy. When Lavergne made fiery anti-British speeches, they were not commented upon in the *Action catholique*, and when the *Evénement* branded recruiting in Quebec a failure, the organ of the hierarchy termed it an unfortunate article.[35] But the editors who avoided the more obvious issues of the war did not appear to realize that in their own policy of constantly fighting the Ontario school battle in their editorial columns, they were adding enormously to the bad feeling between the two Canadian nationalities.

In the confusion and perplexity that marked the reaction of French Canada to the recruiting situation there were some earnest

[33] *Evénement*, January 10, 1916.
[34] *Patrie*, April 25, 1916.
[35] *Action catholique*, May 27, 1916.

French Canada on the Defensive, 1916   135

and patriotic citizens who tried to make their countrymen appreciate that a failure in recruiting would not only endanger the cause of the Allies at the front but would seriously affect the status of the French Canadians at home. The excellent work of the Montreal Recruiting Association under the chairmanship of Sir Alexander Lacoste was an example of the attempt to swing French Canada over to more active participation. Another instance was the attempt of Olivar Asselin to persuade his compatriots that in enlisting as individual Canadians rather than as part of an official state war effort they would find a way out of their perplexity, but it fell on stony ground. Asselin succeeded in fact in raising his 163d Battalion to war strength as a result of an intensive recruiting campaign, but his efforts on the lecture platform and by means of pamphlets to explain the justice of his cause met with little success. Perhaps his feeling in the matter was too complex and subtle for the man in the street to understand. Asselin again and again stressed his utter detestation of the wrongs done to the Ontario minority while urging his compatriots to forget the quarrel by going to fight overseas.[36] An attempt to explain his contradictory, though undoubtedly sincere, attitude at a large meeting in Montreal in January, 1916, was a signal failure. Not only was the audience increasingly cool to the speaker, but the mention of Bourassa and Lavergne was met with thunderous applause, and the meeting finally ended in disorder.[37]

Unfortunately, the efforts made to persuade French Canada to improve her recruiting effort only served to cause further acrimonious controversy. In each case the Nationalists seized the opportunity to denounce patriots who made such efforts as foolish and misguided men who were endangering the cause of French Canadian culture at home in fighting other peoples' battles overseas. The pamphlet issued in the autumn of 1916 by the *Presse,* of

[36] Asselin, *Pourquoi je m'enrôle,* Montreal, 1916.
[37] *Presse,* January 22, 1916; *Devoir,* January 22, 1916.

French Canada on the Defensive, 1916

Montreal, as an analysis of the recruiting problem was less critical, on the whole, of what Quebec had done; but nevertheless it was undoubtedly intended as a means of stirring up French Canadians to a greater effort.[38] The *Presse* admitted from the first that the province of Quebec had been lacking in the proper amount of zeal, but it claimed that when the number of native-born soldiers was taken into consideration Quebec did not lag so very far behind Ontario. In the opinion of the *Presse,* recruiting had been almost as slow in Ontario as it had been in Quebec once the reservoir of British-born was exhausted. The claim was made that Quebec had enlisted a total of 16,000, or 1 percent of her eligible male population, while Ontario's total was admitted to be 42,000, or 2½ percent. Of the 16,000 it was claimed more than 9,000 were French Canadians. Granting the disparity of Quebec's and Ontario's war showing the *Presse* tried to assess the reasons which were responsible for it. The French Canadian's deep feeling of insult and resentment resulting from the treatment meted out to his compatriots in Ontario was held to be the main cause. The control of the recruiting system by English-speaking officers, the fact that there was less chance for French Canadians to be promoted and decorated than there was for their fellow soldiers of English blood, and the policy of breaking up French Canadian units at the front or even of sending them to stations such as Bermuda rather than to the front, as had been done with Asselin's 163d Battalion, all these factors were considered potent causes of French Canadian resentment. The *Presse* felt that the fact that Ontario had many more unmarried men and more of a city population should be taken into consideration in justly assessing the respective war effort of the two provinces. Another argument in defense of the proportionately small number of Quebec soldiers was that while Ontario men enlisted in all branches of the service those of Quebec were apt to join only the combatant battalions. It was evident from

[38] *Our Volunteer Army.*

some of the arguments that the *Presse,* like many a French Canadian, was ready to seize upon arguments that held little weight in order to defend its native province. But the really significant thing about the *Presse* recruiting pamphlet lay in the fact that in spite of its defensive argumentation it clearly admitted that Quebec had not done its part and in its earnest appeal to French Canadians to make their war effort equal that of Ontario.

An open letter, by Captain Talbot Papineau of the Princess Patricia's to his cousin Bourassa, published in the autumn of 1916, was an attempt to turn the minds of French Canadians from the bitter internal controversies then agitating them to what every soldier at the front thought far more important, the victory of Britain and the Allies.[39] Like Bourassa, Captain Papineau was a descendant of the great tribune of the people, Louis Papineau, and perhaps for this reason he was hopeful that they would listen to him with respect. He appealed to Bourassa and through him to his compatriots to realize that the one essential fact to govern their conduct should be that Canada was at war and that Canadian liberty had to be protected. In Papineau's opinion, the French Canadian, because of his loyalty to both England and France, had a double reason to participate; and in so doing he had an unexampled opportunity of proving to his English fellow citizens that he, as well as they, was actuated by a love of their common country and the wish that the talents and energies of both races should be united in the future to create a happy nation. Those who like Bourassa opposed Canada's war effort were warned lest the men at the front should return after the war with revengeful feelings in their hearts against those who had stayed at home and had given them no support. In a final eloquent appeal Papineau said that while he wrote, French and English Canadians were fighting and dying side by side. Would their common sacrifice go for nothing or would it cement the foundation of a true Canadian

[39] *Gazette,* July 28, 1916.

138 French Canada on the Defensive, 1916

nation, independent but spiritually attuned to the two mother lands of England and France?

In his reply to Captain Papineau, Bourassa expressed the very core of the French Canadian position on active war participation.[40] It summed up in brilliant fashion that instinctive recoil from foreign involvement that lay at the heart of the French Canadian opposition to imperial obligations. Others among his countrymen had tried to express this feeling, but it had remained for Bourassa to focus the attention of all Canada upon Quebec's dislike for the war. The Papineau controversy afforded Bourassa an excellent opportunity for making his attitude against war participation clear. The Nationalist leader explained that he had changed his opinion as to Canadian participation since 1914 because he realized that he had been mistaken in thinking that Canada's intervention had been freely made by a united nation. Instead, it had been the result of the age-old policy of sacrificing Canada to the needs of the Empire. To an old anti-imperialist like Bourassa the German form of imperialism or that of Russia or England or even of France was equally abhorrent, and as a result he believed that Canada had a different mission to fulfill on the American continent than to bind her fate to that of the imperialist and acquisitive nations of Europe. In reply to Papineau and those who agreed with him about the necessity for increasing Quebec's war effort Bourassa asserted that it was the essentially anti-imperialistic spirit of French Canadians that made them averse to enlisting in great numbers. The French Canadians were more Canadian in their tastes and in their interests than any other group in the Dominion. The perturbations of Europe, even of France and England, were no more than far-away events to them, with which they had little connection even though their sympathies were naturally on the side of France against Germany. In spite of their pro-French sympathies, the French Canadians felt no more obligated to fight for

[40] *Devoir*, August 5, 1916, for Bourassa's reply to Papineau's letter.

French Canada on the Defensive, 1916

France than the French themselves would feel obliged to defend Canada if she were attacked by the United States or Japan or even by Germany. Given these essential feelings it was only natural that recruiting should be in inverse ratio to the "Canadianism" of the individual. The British-born naturally was more eager to fight for his native land than the English-speaking Canadian, and he, in his turn, enlisted more readily than French Canadians, all of whose interests lay at home. The abstention of French Canadians from a wholehearted participation in the Dominion war effort Bourassa laid to their instinct to fight only for the defense of Canadian soil and their faith in the old tradition that Britain in her turn was obliged to defend them. As for the bilingual question, Bourassa asserted that it was only a secondary reason for French Canadian dislike of active participation. The fact that Quebec's population was so largely agricultural was advanced by Bourassa as another and important explanation for the French Canadian attitude, for he asserted that men whose lives were attached to the soil were much less apt to desire foreign adventure than the inhabitants of cities. Bourassa left no argument against active participation untouched, but if he had mentioned none but the essential one that French Canada was opposed to foreign entanglements because she wanted to conserve all her energies for her own development, it would have been enough. There was probably not one among his compatriots, be he ever so favorable to Canadian participation, that could remain unmoved by the appeal to conserve French Canadian manhood for the service of Canada alone. Bourassa had appealed to the deep, unspoken instincts of the French Canadian race.

The bitterness of those French Canadians who had given unstinted support to the cause of Canada's war effort from the beginning of hostilities was reflected in the open letter of Papineau. His viewpoint was echoed by another French Canadian officer, Captain Gustave Lanctot, who had originally been in Asselin's 163d Battalion but who on being sent on a special mission to England had had himself transferred to an English-speaking battalion which went to France.[41] Writing to a friend in Canada Lanctot asserted that while Europe was full of praises for the 22d Battalion of French Canadians it was astonished at the indifference of Quebec to the war and even more so at the fact that certain newspapers were actually carrying on anti-Ally propaganda in war time. Lanctot asked whether there was any awakening of public opinion in Quebec or if French Canadians were people who refused to live the life of idealism and duty. The anguish of those French Canadians who were at the front was made plain in this appeal of Lanctot to his compatriots for a realization that they were fighting for Canadian liberty and against the possibility of seeing Germany extend her dominion to the shores of the St. Lawrence.

The letters of Papineau and Lanctot created a certain stir, and there was even some comment that the moment had come for French Canadians to realize that as British subjects of French descent they had a duty to help the Allies; but unfortunately for the cause of an active French Canadian participation they came too late.[42] The tide had set against enlistment in Quebec, and the unceasingly clever propaganda of Bourassa and the Nationalists in the press and even in Parliament continued to keep it flowing.

Armand Lavergne had given the watchword at the very beginning of 1916 when he said that henceforth French Canada should not give a man or a cent or a gun[43] and that the man who enlisted was lacking in respect toward his country. If it were a question of being unfaithful to either the Empire or Canada, Lavergne asserted that he for one would choose to betray the Empire rather than his own native land. In the *Devoir* Bourassa was constantly

---

[41] For Lanctot's letter, *Gazette*, October 25, 1916.
[42] For commentaries on Papineau-Bourassa letters see: *Gazette*, July 28, August 7, 1916; *Evénement*, August 12, 1916; *Patrie*, August 7, 1916; and *Canada*, August 8, 1916.
[43] *Devoir*, January 13, 1916.

French Canada on the Defensive, 1916 141

urging that Canada turn from continuation of her present military policy to a limited participation which should be more in proportion to her own resources.[44] To a request to aid the national recruiting campaigns Bourassa replied that it would be better to form a society to protect individual liberty.[45] Bourassa constantly whipped up the fears of the French Canadians that if voluntary enlistment was definitely pronounced a failure, conscription would be resorted to by telling them that the government would have no other alternative, for they had promised to raise 500,000, and to do so by the voluntary system was becoming impossible.[46] Day by day, week by week, the *Devoir* never ceased to reiterate its opposition to recruiting, its insistence that Canada had done enough, and that it was her duty to look to her own interests at home. Sometimes Bourassa attacked imperialism. Sometimes he ridiculed the efforts of Ontario patriots to discredit French Canadians. Occasionally, he openly hinted that England was in dire straits and needed the aid of Canada's manhood. Every means of attacking and discrediting the Canadian war effort was employed. Can there be any doubt that this able and unceasing propaganda, this appeal to instinct, played a very important part in the slowing up of French Canada's war effort which became so marked in the course of 1916?

There was disturbance of recruiting meetings in Montreal in August, and there were some who blamed the ever-growing virulence of the Nationalist propaganda.[47] In any case, these events were recurring at frequent intervals and were symptomatic of the heated atmosphere of Quebec, which was disturbing all classes of the population. The triumphant return of the Liberal government of the province at the April elections was a further indication that Quebec was more than ever attached to principles and policies

[44] *Devoir*, January 19, 1916.
[45] *Ibid.*, April 15, 1916.
[46] *Ibid.*, August 18, 1916, September 7, 1916.
[47] *Devoir*, August 25, 1916; *Peuple*, September 1, 1916.

142   *French Canada on the Defensive, 1916*

which were opposed to those held by the party in power at Ottawa. The growing disquiet of the Liberals with their own equivocal position became noticeable in 1916. In spite of the fact that Laurier had agreed to allow the government to extend the life of Parliament, which was to have expired in 1916, the Conservative majority was slightly uneasy about the support to be expected from the Liberals.

The year 1916 was marked by the enactment of a large number of war measures by order-in-council.[48] It was naturally much easier to impress Parliament with the urgency of measures so enacted than to submit them for long and possibly acrimonious debates. The Liberal feelings were manifest when Sir Wilfrid Laurier, as leader of the Opposition, moved for a parliamentary inquiry into the purchase of war material and asserted that the Shell Committee of 1915, which the government itself had appointed, had not been above suspicion of partisanship.[49] Throughout the year Laurier never ceased to reiterate his unalterable opposition to any project for compulsory enlistment, and it was obvious that the Liberals were beginning to be preoccupied with the fear of such a project, especially after the Prime Minister, in advocating the National Service scheme, had admitted that it might be necessary in the future.[50]

In the course of 1916 the Nationalist anti-war propaganda attained a very high degree of effectiveness. Bourassa and his followers had become very bold, and in any other belligerent country they would doubtless have been sent to concentration camps as fomenters of sedition and treason. It was naturally through the columns of the *Devoir* that the daily wave of Bourassa's anti-war propaganda, combined with his constant appeal for the bilingual

---

[48] As in England, orders-in-council were ordinances passed by the Governor-General-in-Council, i.e., the cabinet, and later given retroactive legislative sanction by Parliament.
[49] Hansard, *Commons*, 1916, p. 1571.
[50] Lucas, *op. cit.*, II, 34.

schools, swept over the reading populace of Montreal and far into the remote back country where the *Devoir* and its weekly edition, the *Nationaliste,* had many readers. It was, however, in his pamphlets that Bourassa had scope for fuller argument and a wider application of his great powers of persuasion. In order that these pamphlets could reach a wider public they were frequently reprinted in the columns of the *Devoir* and even in rural newspapers that had a Nationalistic bent. Besides the pamphlets Bourassa and his lieutenants used the lecture platform as a means of spreading their doctrines. By the intelligent use of all these means of propaganda the Nationalist ideas were constantly kept before the public, and no opportunity was lost to give them the utmost publicity and to put their opponents on the defensive.

The greatest strength of Bourassa lay in the fact that he was in himself an appealing figure. His quick wit and matchless command of the French language and the truly Gallic grace with which he used it struck even the casual observer. It is very obvious that Bourassa was a man with the widest interests, for even at a time when he was devoting daily columns to such controversies as the bilingual schools or conscription in 1917 he had time to analyze the wider implications of the war, such as the future of Poland or the results of the Russian Revolution. He was by no means a narrow bigot or a fanatical partisan, though at times he seemed to be. He was a man to whom fighting seemed to be the breath of life. His sincerity was evident, even to many of his opponents, and in it lay much of his strength. More than anything else, what appealed to his own countrymen about Bourassa was that he was a real Frenchman in the cultural rather than the political sense of the word, one who combined grace with courage, logic with wit, and deep learning with eloquence.

It is noticeable that even in the midst of a passionate polemical argument Bourassa could retain a wider view than was common to the Canadian controversialist. In his analysis of the rôle of the

Devoir in the war he pointed out that to him the Canadian race conflict was merely an incident in a five-hundred-year struggle between the English and French races, between the Gallo-Roman and the Anglo-Saxon civilizations, between Roman Catholic order and Protestant disorder.[51] The feeling of Bourassa that this war was but another imperialist venture caused him to assert his opposition in ever greater degree as he felt the imperialist nature of Canadian intervention becoming accentuated. To his mind Canadian intervention had been the result of a definite plan on the part of the "imperialists" who had gained the support of Canadian social leaders, of the newspapers and even of certain Catholic theologians. In mentioning the Catholic theologians Bourassa undoubtedly meant to attack the hierarchy, for he analyzed their attitude as being a renewal of the old seventeenth-century Gallican *Régalisme,* of subservience to the king, representing the sovereign power of the State, rather than to Rome. The bishops' Pastoral, Bourassa held, was outside the episcopal tradition of the Canadian hierarchy, and in consequence it should not be considered necessary to obey it as dogmatic teaching or as discipline. The Nationalist leader hinted strongly that some of the bishops who had signed the Pastoral Letter believed that it went too far in adherence to a wide Canadian participation. Bourassa insisted that, in spite of the admonitions of the bishops' Pastoral, Canadians remained free to adhere to the old tradition of Canadian autonomy and free to resist excessively large enlistments or even the giving of too great amounts to war charities. French Canadians were urged to remember that in the first century of their existence under British rule they had maintained their status by a constant stubborn struggle for their rights, while the period since 1867 had been a succession of lamentable defeats as a result of a false principle of race conciliation and compromise. Let them now stand up for their rights, not only in Ontario, but also in every other prov-

[51] H. Bourassa, *Le Devoir et la guerre.*

ince of Canada, not only with regard to the school question but with regard to the recruiting situation, and as a result they would be much more likely to be respected by their fellow countrymen of English speech. Such advice in 1916 could not but stir up mutual distrust and animosity.

In a series of lectures given by Bourassa in the winter of 1916 the Nationalist leader not only revealed his own views on the national problems that were dividing Canadian opinion but also proposed bold solutions for them.[52] Imperialism was still the principal enemy that Bourassa saw, and his efforts went to an assessment of the factors which had caused it to triumph over the older principle of Canadian military autonomy by which Canada had been considered responsible for her own defense while Britain assumed the external defense of all parts of the Empire. In Bourassa's opinion this principle of Canadian military autonomy should have been altered only with the consent of the Canadian Parliament, for Britain had no right to involve the self-governing Dominions automatically in any and every war in which she was engaged unless their own territory was in danger. If the Canadian Parliament had wished a national intervention, it should have so stated in 1914 and proceeded to a declaration of war. In the opinion of Bourassa the acceptance of the principle that when Britain was at war Canada as a part of the Empire was automatically at war also constituted a revolutionary act in Canadian constitutional history. For this reason Bourassa felt that the French Canadian hierarchy had much to answer for in having approved automatic Canadian intervention. In the early days of the British régime the leaders of the Canadian Church had been content to stay within the limits of a strict loyalism and had never recommended that Canada should contribute men and money to the wars of Britain. In the wars of the American Revolution and of Napoleon the Canadian hierarchy had blessed the cause of Britain,

[52] H. Bourassa, *Hier, aujourd'hui et demain*.

ordered *Te Deums* sung for her victories, and urged Canadians to enlist for the defense of their own homes. This tradition had been continued when prayers were offered for the Allies in the Crimean War and when Canada was urged to see to her own defense in the course of the American Civil War; but no men had ever been sent abroad during those conflicts. The break had come with the dispatch of volunteers to the South African War in 1899, and now the Church was actually supporting a cause which was based on the imperialist need of England to get Canadian soldiers to fight her battles. Bourassa felt that the imperialists had used every means to exploit Canada economically by the invasion of British capital and the seduction of Canadians by titles and social honors. The attempt to get Canada automatically to fight England's battles overseas was only another step in the game.

It is interesting and significant that at a time when the mother country was at war and the great majority of Canadians were deeply concerned for her ultimate safety and survival, Bourassa dared to say that England's enemies were a result of her own wars of conquest and spoliation, her monstrous ambition to paint all the map of the world "red," and her arrogant domination of the seas. It was strong language to use about Britain in a British dominion; but there was more to come, and French Canadians were asked whether they owed gratitude to Britain for her attempts to denationalize them, for her attempts to interfere with their language and religion, for her "theft" of the Jesuit estates, for Lord Durham's report, and the iniquitously unjust Act of Union of 1841. The answer was vehemently negative, and Bourassa told his compatriots that if they wished to show real gratitude to Britain they would maintain intact Canada's autonomy, her traditions and her liberty, and finally her right to remain at peace within her borders. In his eagerness to demolish the case which had been built up for Canadian intervention Bourassa ridiculed all the reasons that were usually brought forward. The claim that the Allies were fighting to protect small peoples was held up against the record of Britain in South Africa and Egypt or of Russia in Poland. Were the Allies fighting for liberty and democracy, when they were all oppressing minorities within their own territories? French Canadians had been told that they were fighting for the salvation of France; but they owed no love and gratitude to France, and the claim that they should be obliged to fight for their former mother country was as absurd as to say that the Brazilians should fight for Portugal or the United States for England. Bourassa asserted that the only possible results of Canadian intervention would be a greatly increased debt and taxes and the militarization of Canadian life. Canada would lose her status as an autonomous Dominion and would become completely dependent on the mother country, who, as a result, would once more revert to her ancient policy of anglicizing Canada.

What was the solution? First of all, Bourassa told Canadians, they should stay at home and eradicate evils that they found there, such as the interference with the rights of a minority in Ontario. The French Canadians were the sole possessors of the essentials of French civilization in North America who for three hundred years had been rooted in the soil. It was for them to protect their hard-won rights as British subjects and to seek an honorable solution for their problems. The independence of Canada was by all odds the most desirable solution in the opinion of Bourassa, but he acknowledged that it was a highly improbable one. Independence, Bourassa considered the simplest solution and the one most consonant with British tradition; for when the Canadian Dominion had been created, it had been John A. Macdonald's ideal to see Canada absolutely independent under the crown. Under independence there would be economic advantages in a trade open to the whole world rather than in one largely restricted to Britain and the United States. There would be racial advantages when the Anglo-Canadians discovered that Canada was their only country and when they were no longer torn by their sentimental feeling for England. As a result they would cease trying to anglicize the French Canadians, who were as essentially Canadians as they themselves. But the greatest advantage of independence would be that in contrast to conditions in the present war, when all of Britain's enemies were enemies of Canada, an independent Dominion would have to deal only with her own enemies, which are nonexistent. Annexation to the United States would be more likely, especially since American economic interests were intent on exploiting the Dominion. Bourassa opposed such annexation, even though he asserted that the United States would allow Quebec to rule herself, because he feared that for the French Canadians it would mean gradual racial and national absorption. Some system of imperial association or partnership was the most probable solution in Bourassa's opinion, and he believed it would be better than the anarchy obtaining at the moment. A system of imperial representation would correct some of the evils of military imperialism, the colonial horizon would be enlarged as the Dominions were forced to consider problems outside their own countries, and this very enlargement would serve as a useful schooling for eventual independence. As for Canada, Bourassa felt that she must gradually develop a foreign policy which should recognize the imperative necessity of defensive alliance with the United States and close association with England, who was her best friend in Europe. Disarmament would be sought, and above all Canada would be granted the right of neutrality in wars which did not directly menace her.

The power of Bourassa's ideas lay in the fact that he knew superlatively well how to express them and, most important of all, that they were ideas which were of the French Canadian soil from which he and all his countrymen sprang and which had the strongest possible appeal to them all. It was the spirit of *Canadienisme* that Bourassa preached, the philosophy that made the men of Quebec believe that there was no country like their own, that there was no reason to fight for anything except their own immemorial rights and privileges and to be interested essentially only in those very things that touched the preservation of their own particular forms of civilization. Acting under the stress of sentiment and emotion an Asselin or a Papineau might feel impelled to fight for France, the cradle of their race, but to the great mass of the French Canadian people Canada was their home, their country, the only land worth living in or dying for. They could not see that she was in any danger because the Allied battle line three thousand miles away bent before the German onslaught. They had tried to help the English, but their efforts had been belittled and ridiculed. Why should they try to do any more for them? Better far to stay at home in the Quebec they loved, and if *les Anglas* should try to force them, English-speaking Canada would feel the whole weight of a determined though naturally pacific resistance. It was this spirit that Bourassa understood and to which he appealed; and because he did so, the resistance of thousands of his compatriots to Canada's war effort was enormously increased.

It should not be thought that there was no opposition to Bourassa's ideas among French Canadians. As far back as September, 1914, when Bourassa had sounded the first notes of criticism of Canadian participation and of discouragement of Quebec's enthusiasm there had been protests from the cultured young élite among French Canadians which was then offering itself for enlistment. In an article in the *Patrie* of October 3, 1914, Gustave Lanctot sharply attacked Bourassa as being unrepresentative of Quebec, whose sons had died for liberty in 1837, and as insulting the proudest traditions, the courage, and the very loyalty of French Canada. In a pamphlet which was given the widest circulation in 1916 the Abbé D'Amours, editor of the *Action catholique,* attempted to refute the more violent of Bourassa's anti-war theories as being themselves opposed to the best French Canadian traditions.[53] D'Amours and the higher clergy, for whom he doubtless spoke, had grown alarmed lest the Nationalists should seriously compromise the religious and national rights which the French Canadians had so painfully acquired, and they were distressed besides at the race hatred and anti-Catholic feeling, which D'Amours himself asserted was greater than it had been for fifty years. D'Amours insisted that Bourassa's principles—his idea of a free and sovereign people able to dispose of its destinies, his denial of the right of conquest unless accepted by the conquered, and his approval of national egoism—were all equally false. To D'Amours and his school Nationalism in the widest sense was un-Christian and revolutionary; for true Christian patriotism taught that a nation like an individual had a right to protect its position, but the egoism and utilitarianism of the Bourassa school of Nationalism was contrary to morality and the true interests of the people. D'Amours asserted that the Bourassa Nationalists had tried to group French Canadians outside the jurisdiction of the authorized heads of the Church and had taught that its opinions on matters political need not necessarily be obeyed, and, as a result, the forces of French Canadianism and Catholicism had been divided.

In an examination of Bourassa's solutions of the Canadian problem D'Amours dismissed independence as being contrary to the will of the majority of Canadians and as leading to the total subservience of French Canadian rights to the will of the Anglo-Canadian majority. D'Amours felt not only that annexation would be the end of Canada politically and ethnically but also that as a result the Canadian soul would entirely disappear and lose its peculiar characteristics as surely as Louisiana had been submerged and assimilated by the United States. Bourassa's fears of an imperialist yoke and the automatic participation of the self-governing dominions in imperial wars D'Amours considered grossly exag-

[53] *Ou allons-nous? Lettres d'un "Patriote."*

gerated. The Abbé's solution of the problems vexing French Canadian opinion was the maintenance of the *status quo* if the rights of all French Canadians in Quebec or in the western provinces were to be maintained at all. D'Amours called for a Canadian patriotism which not only should seek to maintain the present confederation with all its advantages and obligations but should also, while giving its primary loyalty to Canada, remain wisely attached to the British connection. The Canadian patriot should seek to make friends and allies for his country rather than to isolate her by a policy of national egoism. God had preserved the French Canadians, and it was, therefore, their obligation to see that their patriotism had a truly Christian basis. D'Amours advised his compatriots to beware of forming a Catholic party or a Nationalist school of thought which since it was not truly Roman Catholic would expose French Canadians to all the dangers peculiar to a Catholic group in a predominantly Protestant country.

The definition of de Maître, that a man's country or *Patrie* was the whole land which submitted to the rule of the sovereign, whoever he might be, was employed by D'Amours in a final eloquent appeal to the French Canadians to realize that as long as Canada was British territory it was of the very essence of Canadian patriotism to be British and to be attached and devoted to the sovereign and the civil society to which they belonged. They were urged to realize that the Canadian Parliament had been within its indisputable rights in deciding on Canadian war participation and that the Nationalist attempt to dispute this Canadian authority and the right of Britain to be supported was neither legitimate nor prudent. French Canadians were advised to be careful lest they dissipate the strength needed for defense of their legitimate rights at home in a useless fight against irrevocable decisions. D'Amours's pamphlet was an able presentation of the conservative point of view regarding Canada's status in the Empire and her duty in the existing conflict. It was in the direct tradition of the Canadian Church, which had always maintained that French Canadians should be loyal to Britain. To D'Amours and the more conservatively minded churchmen Britain had been not only the bulwark against racial assimilation and against any interference with the ideas on faith and morals inculcated by the Church but also a sure defense against the dangers of Americanization or contamination by doctrines of revolutionary France. It seemed essential to them to preserve the British connection at all costs. The D'Amours's pamphlet marked a decided division of opinion among the French Canadians as to their duty in the war. Time was to prove whether the traditional loyalism of D'Amours and the hierarchy or the isolationism, or *Canadienisme,* of Bourassa and the Nationalists was to be the stronger.

The *Bonne Entente* movement was another attempt on the part of well-meaning citizens of both races who had become alarmed at the bitterness of racial feeling to bring about an improvement in the relations between French- and English-speaking Canadians. In the course of 1916 and 1917 the sponsors of the movement arranged good-will visits of prominent French Canadians to English-speaking towns in Ontario and the return of English-speaking citizens to Quebec. There were many speeches made on both sides urging racial conciliation, and civic receptions were held in some instances. The newspapers did their best in the course of 1916 to give the *Bonne Entente* movement favorable publicity. But though there was some decrease in racial bitterness as a result of the attempt to make the two provinces of Quebec and Ontario better acquainted with each other, the net result was not very great. The bitterness of the bilingual-school dispute went too deep, and even though there was some assuagement of racial hatred the smoldering quarrel sprang into full flame again at the proposal for conscription in 1917.

The year 1916 saw the full flowering of hatred and bitterness over the bilingual schools of Ontario, and not only did this controversy increase bad feeling between the races but also it was one of the most important factors in turning the minds of French Canadians away from the war issues. The incredible fact that in the press of French Canada in 1916 almost as much space was devoted to the unhappy agitation over the bilingual schools as to the news of the war was literally true. Large newspapers like the *Presse* and *Patrie* tried to be conciliatory on the subject. Partisan papers like the *Devoir* were shrill and almost hysterical. But all united in a passionate interest in the subject and in keeping it before the public. The *Devoir* devoted a special column to news of the bilingual controversy every day for months and even published frequently a sample petition to the Governor General praying for federal disallowance, which it urged its readers to sign.

In 1916 the bilingual question had definitely become a federal one. Those who opposed the now-famous Regulation Seventeen felt impelled to take the matter to Ottawa and hoped to find there more sympathy than they could find in the provincial Parliament of Ontario. From the beginning, the Dominion government took its stand on the fact that education, by virtue of the British North America Act, belonged exclusively to the provinces, and Sir Robert Borden made this very clear to a delegation of French Canadians who waited on him in February. In this stand the federal government was supported by all the Conservatives, with the natural exception of Nationalist members from Quebec. The Liberals as a whole followed the lead of Laurier, who while he admitted the government to be justified in refusing disallowance for a school law of the province of Ontario nevertheless urged conciliation and compromise in an issue which to him seemed unfair to the French Canadian minority in Ontario. That the division of opinion was largely on racial rather than on party lines was clearly shown in the debate over the resolution brought in by a Quebec member, Ernest Lapointe, which suggested that the Legislative Assembly of Ontario should be called upon to make it clear that the "privi-

154 French Canada on the Defensive, 1916

lege of the children of French parentage of being taught in their mother tongue be not interfered with." [54] The Ontario Liberals did support the Lapointe resolution as the means of conciliation which Laurier himself believed it was, but eleven western Liberals voted with the government, a clear indication that the West, embittered by the war issues and essentially English-speaking and Protestant, was no longer ready to follow the lead of the old French Canadian and Catholic leader.[55] Laurier was so saddened by this defection of some of his Liberal followers that he seriously considered resigning, but he was persuaded not to do so. After considerable discussion the Lapointe resolution was defeated by a vote of one hundred and seven to sixty.

It was clear from the discussion of the resolution that while the West was definitely opposed to any concession to the demands of the French Catholic minority in Ontario and while the Liberals were still willing, though against their better judgment, to follow Laurier's lead, the province of Quebec stood behind him to a man. The division on purely racial lines which the conscription issue of 1917 was to bring about was already visible a year before. The solidarity of Quebec was further shown by the triumphant return of the provincial Liberal government under the leadership of Sir Lomer Gouin in April, 1916, when the Conservatives managed to obtain only seven seats as against thirteen in 1911.

The press of the large cities attempted to tone down the passions aroused by the Lapointe resolution. On May 11 the *Patrie* asserted that even the most fervent champions of the French language admitted that politics was largely responsible for the complications surrounding the bilingual issue. The *Devoir*, on the other hand, maintained a violence of tone and a passion of argument that could not help attracting a great deal of attention. Its

[54] Skelton, *Life and Letters of Sir Wilfrid Laurier*, II, 478.
[55] *Ibid.*, II, 478 *et seq.*

comments were so often reprinted in other newspapers that they attained a wide publicity even outside the province, and there can be small wonder that they were often quoted in Ontario as representing the opinion of a united Quebec. When the *Devoir* spoke of 4,000 children being deprived of instruction at Ottawa, of one hundred and twenty professors unpaid, and of parents obliged to guard the schools from the invasion of the Ontario school authorities, and when it concluded that the only reason for all this disturbance was the refusal of the entire French Canadian population of Ontario to consent to the moral assassination of their race it was only natural that readers should be startled.[56] When this sort of argument was repeated with eloquent variations day after day and week after week the general effect of such a cumulative attack on the English-speaking Canadians was one of intense resentment throughout Ontario.

The resignation of Senator Landry from the speakership of the Senate in order to devote himself entirely to the cause of the Ontario minority was symptomatic of the ever-growing preoccupation of French Canadians with the bilingual-school question. The petition signed by Cardinal Begin and twenty-one French Canadian bishops for federal disallowance of the Ontario school law was further evidence, if any were needed, that French Canadians to a man felt the call of their brethren of the Ontario minority. The hierarchy might disagree with the Nationalists on the issue of Canadian participation in the war, but when it came to the rights of language and religion for French Canadians they were as Nationalistic as any Bourassa or Lavergne. The appeal of the bishops was in reality a legal brief which asserted that the province of Quebec as a contracting party to the British North America Act had caused a clause guaranteeing certain rights and privileges to Roman Catholics to be inserted in that act. These rights had included the election of school inspectors, the engaging

[56] *Devoir*, March 10, 1916.

of teachers, the choice of the kind of school acceptable to themselves, and in addition the guarantee of a proportional part of the provincial educational revenues. All these rights which had been declared inviolable by Section Ninety-three of the British North America Act of 1867, in the opinion of the hierarchy, were being invalidated by the Ontario School Law of 1915. The only possible result of such an attack on the Constitution would be a revival of bitter racial conflict and the breakdown of the pact of confederation.[57]

The claim that the Ontario school laws violated the confederation pact was the center of the legal argument for disallowance, but the underlying cause of the whole matter was the French Canadians' fear that because the 1915 law gave the Ontario Minister of Education the right to declare what was and what was not a bilingual school, all possibility for the minority to obtain any more new schools was at an end if the law were to be upheld.[58] The federal Minister of Justice had replied to the signers of a petition for federal disallowance that in his opinion the school law was *intra vires* and that it was therefore within the rights of the provincial legislature to have passed it and that it had in fact been so held by the Ontario courts. In the minister's opinion the terms of Regulation Seventeen which formed the basis of the statute were acceptable and fully protected the rights of Roman Catholics in Ontario.[59] In spite of the uncompromising attitude of the government of the Dominion that the Ontario school law was not liable to federal disallowance the wave of petitions piled up more than 600,000 signatures. Meanwhile the Ontario school law had been questioned in the prescribed way in the courts. An appeal from the decision of the Canadian courts which had upheld it had been taken to the Judicial Committee of the Privy Council

[57] P. Landry, *Le Désaveu*, Quebec, 1916. Contains the bishops' appeal.
[58] *Ibid.*, reply to report of Minister of Justice, May, 1916.
[59] *House of Commons, Sessional Paper, 271/A, 1916*, in Library of Parliament, Ottawa.

in London, and in October, 1916, this body handed down its decision. It was to the effect that as Section 93 of the British North America Act applied not to the rights of language but to those of the religion of the king's subjects the Ontario law of 1915 was in fact *intra vires*. At the same time it declared unconstitutional the legislation creating a government commission to control the Ottawa schools which was to succeed the former Separate School Board largely composed of French Canadian Catholics.[60]

It is noticeable that although the Privy Council decision upheld the constitutionality of the Ontario school law, it did not arouse the storm of abuse from Quebec which might have been expected. The main reason for this lay in the undoubted respect of the French Canadians for the force of law. They would go to any length as long as their rights were in question and they had the power to seek legal and constitutional redress. But when the supreme court of appeal of the Empire had given its verdict, there was on the whole an acceptance of the inevitability of that verdict by the great majority of French Canadians. It is particularly striking in this regard that the very newspapers that had for months been devoting many columns to the rights and wrongs of the school dispute commented with moderation on the Privy Council decision and then abandoned the question to a large extent. Perhaps one of the most important reasons for this assuagement of controversy and the ensuing appeasement of an inflamed public opinion was the Encyclical Letter of Pope Benedict XV on the bilingual-school issue, published in September, 1916.[61] With dignity the faithful were reproved by the Pope for not having discussed the matter with calmness and moderation and for having allowed so much bitterness to enter into the controversy. Conciliation was to be sought; and if that should prove impossible, there were recognized authorities within the Church to whom

[60] *Canadian Annual Review*, 1916, pp. 530-31.
[61] *Action catholique*, October 28, 1916.

Catholics might appeal for judgment and whom they must obey.[62] Newspapers and periodicals were ordered to refrain from fomenting discord, and priests were urged to give their flocks an example of moderation and of toleration by understanding both the English and French languages. The Pope held that the Ontario government was entirely within its rights in requiring the adequate teaching of the English language, which was that of the majority of the inhabitants of that province, while the French Canadians for their part were justified in demanding adequate protection for their own language. Moderation and toleration were urged as the prime duties of all good Catholics, and the bishops were enjoined to lead the faithful into the path of conciliation.

The reaction of French Canada to the Encyclical Letter of the Pope was on the whole one of profound respect, though there were some dissenting voices. Newspapers like the *Action catholique* quite naturally advised a sincere adherence to the principles propounded by the head of Catholic Christendom. The *Devoir* considered it the part of wisdom to make no comment at all. In the cities and in the rural districts the press of Quebec united in a wholehearted submission to the wishes of the head of the Church. Once more, as in the past in Canadian history, Rome had played the historic rôle of a moderator of passions as she had done in the course of the bitter controversy over the Manitoba schools in the 1890's. The Papal Encyclical was naturally a bitter disappointment to the more extreme partisans, but the great majority of French Canadians, with the clergy at their head, bowed to the

---

[62] The command of the Pope that there should be mutual toleration among Catholics was a reference to the old quarrel between English-speaking and French-speaking Catholics in Ontario. Those who had founded the Catholic churches of the province had been largely Irishmen and they had come to resent the invasion of thousands of French Canadians into their dioceses who in time practically absorbed the churches for themselves. As a result of this bad feeling between Irish and French Canadian Catholics the former had been very little interested in the latter's campaign for the rights of the minority in the Ontario schools. So bitter had the feeling become that early in 1916 the Vatican had already made an appeal for peace and conciliation among Catholics to the English-speaking Bishop of London, Ontario, Mgr. Fallon.

inevitable and recognized, as Rome meant them to do, that after all they were living in a state that was predominantly English-speaking and Protestant and where they were not the only ones to possess rights and privileges. There can be no doubt that the Papal Encyclical was of great value in calming the bitter interracial feeling. If the religious issue in all its fury of unchained passion had been added to the racial differences which in 1917-18 divided Canada into two hostile camps, the dispute might indeed have been a far more serious matter and might even conceivably have led to civil war.

With the declaration of a truce in the dispute over the Ontario schools at the close of 1916 the Dominion was enabled once more to turn its entire attention to the war. But it was no longer a united Canada that contemplated the demand that came from the front for men and ever more men to help defend the Allied battle line in France and Flanders. The bitterness of the bilingual dispute had alienated the interest and support of many thousands of French Canadians. The anti-war propaganda of Bourassa and the Nationalists had done its part to make many other thousands feel that it was more patriotic to seek to maintain the rights and privileges of their race at home than to seek adventure overseas merely for the greater glory of Britain. The appeal had been made to the French Canadian's essential desire to remain at home and enjoy his patrimony rather than to seek foreign adventure, and it was to be heeded in far wider circles than English-speaking Canada had dreamed of. Even in the ranks of the Church, there was division of opinion as to whether Canada should do more or whether it would not be better to conserve her energies for the future. French Canada was not only increasingly indifferent to the war issues, but she was alarmed lest in spite of them she might be forced to contribute more men and money. English-speaking Canadians had grown thoroughly distrustful of French Canadian loyalty, a distrust which the fulminations of the more violent anti-imperialist Nationalists had done much to increase. Everyone admitted that French Canadian recruiting was lagging far behind, and it seemed inevitable that if the war continued something must be done to obtain reinforcements for the hardpressed Canadian troops at the front. The bogey of conscription loomed very large at the close of 1916 and nowhere larger or more fearsome than in the province of Quebec.

VII

The Conscription Conflict of 1917

THE YEAR 1917 saw Canada involved in the greatest crisis in her history. It was the year of conscription, the year when Canada's war effort seemed on the point of going for nothing because the nation was split in twain, and it appeared likely that the Confederation would be divided into the two component parts of which it had been composed, wrecked on the jagged rocks of Nationalism. Passion and partisan spirit and racial and religious hatred walked the streets unchecked. Appeals to reason went unheard. Men distrusted their neighbors' patriotism and their personal honor simply because they did not belong to the same race or religion. Old party loyalties went by the board. Old political allies called each other "traitors" and "criminals" simply because they happened to differ as to the part Canada should play in the war. English-speaking Canada rallied behind the government for a vigorous prosecution of the war by every means at the disposal of the Canadian people. French Canada united behind the aging Laurier in a solid block of Liberals, Conservatives, and Nationalists, alike in a determined opposition to any measure which should force Canadians to fight overseas. It seemed indeed as if the end had come of the great experiment whereby two ancient rivals had agreed to live together in peace.

At the beginning of the year it was evident that voluntary recruiting had failed. This failure led to a National Service scheme which was in reality an inventory of the man power of the country, taken in January, 1917. The response of the population was on the whole satisfactory, and the Director of National Service, R. B. Bennett, was able to announce that 80 percent of the men between seventeen and forty-five, to whom registration cards had been sent, had replied. The classification of the male population was an elaborate one. The main divisions were two age groups of which the first consisted of the men between seventeen and thirty and the second of those between thirty-one and forty-five.[1] These groups were in turn divided into married men with no dependents who were not engaged in essential war occupations and men who though married and without dependents were engaged in war industry. There were further subdivisions for men with dependents and for married men of the two age groups. A total of 1,549,360 men returned cards to the National Service Board, and of this number 475,363 were considered eligible military prospects. Of the latter number only 4,660 men were skilled shipbuilders, munition or mine workers, while 183,727 were farmers, and 286,976 were engaged in nonessential occupations.[2]

While French Canada as a whole loyally adhered to the National Service registration, there were misgivings in certain quarters. Some newspapers, while urging their readers to fill in the National Service cards and to attend the meetings being held to explain the scheme, added the reservation that every citizen—his card once signed—was free from all obligation and could resume his entire liberty of judgment.[3] It was suggested that the National Service scheme was not only impractical and incomplete but also very possibly a mere prelude to conscription. The fear that National Service was but a mask for eventual adoption of conscription was very widespread throughout French Canada. The Nationalist press was eagerly suggesting this very thing, while

---

[1] Statement of R. B. Bennett, Director of National Service in House of Commons, September 20, 1917, in Hansard, *Commons*, 1917, pp. 6086 *et seq.*

[2] In considering the respective recruiting effort of Ontario and Quebec, it is interesting to note that while the former province had 186,252 military prospects under the National Service registration, the latter had only 79,700. It is possible that the registration was more efficient in Ontario than in Quebec, but it must be remembered that the French Canadian marries earlier than the Anglo-Canadian and rarely has a small family.

[3] *Soleil*, January 24, 25, 1917.

The Conscription Conflict of 1917   163

the vagueness of the National Service scheme itself seemed to lend color to the idea. But if there were misgivings about National Service in some quarters, especially in those affected by Nationalist propaganda, the Church, for its part, gave the project the full weight of its approval. Archbishop Bruchesi, of Montreal, announced that he would not only sign the National Service card himself but also urge all his priests and the citizens generally to follow his example.[4] Cardinal Begin, of Quebec, instructed the clergy to tell their flocks that the National Service questions should be answered in full and that the demands made were not only just and reasonable but also motivated by reasons of public interest which precluded any attempt to escape from the duty incumbent on every good citizen.[5]

There was undoubtedly a certain justice in the feeling that there was too much vagueness in the idea of a registration for National Service. The government, while it realized that recruiting had definitely slowed up by the end of 1916, was itself not altogether sure what had better be done. Doubtless it was being urged by some military experts both in Canada and overseas to introduce compulsory military service. But the government hesitated to bring up such a proposal, knowing full well what a storm of protest it would undoubtedly raise in Quebec, especially as most of the cabinet, from the Prime Minister down, had so often promised that conscription would never be introduced. The National Service scheme was a compromise and an attempt to get a clear picture of the man power available to the government for war purposes. Nevertheless, once the inventory had been taken little was done with it. Men continued to enlist at a slow rate and laborers went to the war factories, but no organized effort was made for some time to allocate them to either of these branches of the Canadian war effort. In February, 1917, Sir Robert Borden went to England,

[4] *Canadian Annual Review*, 1917, p. 303.
[5] *Circulaire au clergé*, issued by Archbishopric of Quebec, January 4, 1917. Copy in possession of writer.

and Parliament was adjourned to await his return with the latest information as to how Canada could best reorganize her war effort. It was apparent that the needs of the Allies, conditioned by the ever-growing submarine menace and the great losses at the front, had enormously increased. The cry for help was going out from Britain to the Dominions, and Canada, as the nearest and oldest of the self-governing possessions, was thought most likely to heed the call.

The results of Sir Robert Borden's visit to Britain were not publicly known until his return in May, 1917, but his assumption of a seat in the Imperial War Conference and later in the small war cabinet which had recently been organized called for a good deal of comment in Canada. Before the Parliament recessed Sir Wilfrid Laurier had remarked that it was incomprehensible to him how Sir Robert Borden, who was not a member of the Parliament at Westminster, could take part in the sittings of the cabinet of Great Britain.[6] The Canadian Prime Minister had no such misgivings about the course he was pursuing.[7] In his opinion recent events had made it essential that the Dominions should have a voice in the control of the war, and in consequence it was not only natural but also necessary that their representatives should sit in the Imperial War Cabinet. The Imperial War Cabinet itself was in fact a subcommittee of the larger British cabinet to which had been added the representatives of the self-governing Dominions by the invitation of the Prime Minister, Mr. Lloyd George. Sir Robert Borden was convinced that this innovation constituted a constitutional procedure which might well be followed even after the close of hostilities for the further governance of the Empire. He believed that actually there were two cabinets within the body of the Imperial War Cabinet: one, the Imperial War Cabinet as a whole, advised the crown in matters of general

[6] Hansard, *Commons*, 1917, p. 2392.
[7] From *Canada at War, Speech of Sir Robert Borden*, in *House of Commons*, May 18, 1917, privately printed.

imperial concern; while the other, the British War Cabinet of five men, were advisors on matters which concerned the United Kingdom alone. In the opinion of Sir Robert Borden the proposals for such an imperial cabinet, which he attributed to Lloyd George, would in no way affect the self-government of the Dominions, for the ministers who represented them would be responsible to their several parliaments just as the Prime Minister of Great Britain was responsible to the Parliament of the United Kingdom. It was obvious at the time that while the war made such a meeting of the representatives of the Dominions with the imperial cabinet not only useful but imperative, any permanent arrangement would require further and lengthy deliberation after the war.

It is doubtful whether the full significance of the proposals for the inclusion of the self-governing Dominions in a future imperial cabinet was appreciated in Canada, preoccupied with the National Service scheme, with echoes of the bilingual dispute, and with last frantic efforts to stave off conscription. The Nationalist press, it is true, asked whether the Canadian Prime Minister would make imperial co-operation conditional on further mortgaging of Canadian blood, and the Liberal organs remarked that it would be both regrettable and dangerous to resolve problems of imperial relationships under the influence of the exaltation of the moment.[8] But while such objections to Sir Robert Borden's solution of constitutional imperial relations were published from time to time, surprisingly little attention was paid to the project.

In the spring of 1917 the government attempted to raise a Home Defense Force in order to release for service overseas regulars who guarded vital points within Canada. From the very outset this force proved unpopular, and very few recruits were secured for its ranks. After a three-month trial the scheme was given up in June, 1917. It seemed to be no easier to raise soldiers for the de-

[8] *Devoir*, February 13, 1917; *Soleil*, February 23, 1917.

166   *The Conscription Conflict of 1917*

fense of Canada at home than to reinforce the line of battle in France.

Coincident with the attempt to raise men for home defense, there was a last attempt, by two prominent French Canadians, Major General Lessard and Hon. P. Blondin, to stir their countrymen to an appreciation of what was at stake for Canada by stumping the province of Quebec for recruits. General Lessard was perhaps the best known French Canadian officer in the prewar militia, one who had done much for French Canada's war effort and who had been considered for the command of the proposed French Canadian brigade in 1916. The Hon. Mr. Blondin had resigned his cabinet office as Postmaster General to accept a commission. The Lessard-Blondin recruiting mission went throughout the length and breadth of the province, holding recruiting meetings. In most cases they were politely if not enthusiastically received, though there were isolated cases of riotous resistance and Colonel Blondin was assaulted by rowdies near Three Rivers.[9] When this last attempt to raise French Canadian recruits by the voluntary system came to an end only ninety-two men had been obtained in the whole province of Quebec;[10] there could not have been any more striking illustration of the indifference and hostility of French Canada to the Dominion's war effort. The wholehearted enthusiasm of 1914 had turned to bitter mistrust and open opposition by the summer of 1917.

The resignation of Blondin made necessary the appointment of a successor to his cabinet position and a subsequent bye-election. The government made one last despairing attempt to gain Quebec sympathy by the appointment of Alfred Sevigny, who had begun his political career as a supporter of Laurier but had later gravitated to the Nationalist camp. It was not a very astute move on the part of the government, for although Sevigny had renounced

[9] *Presse,* July 16, 1917.
[10] Hansard, *Commons,* 1917, p. 2627, Statement of Sir E. Kemp, Minister of Militia.

his extreme Nationalist views and had been an ardent supporter of Canada's war effort, the Liberals considered him little better than a renegade, and when he was actually returned for Dorchester by some 250 votes he was even accused in some quarters of having bought the election.[11] In spite of the feeling aroused against Sevigny his election proved nevertheless that Quebec was still not altogether devoid of approval for the government's war policy, and the solidarity which the conscription proposal was to bring had not yet taken final form.

However, there could be little doubt that feeling against further active participation was rising in Quebec. In April and May, before the attack on Colonel Blondin, troops passing through the province of Quebec had been pelted with rotten vegetables, with ice, and in some cases even with stones. To the flood of criticism that this sort of incident evoked in English-speaking Canada the French Canadians replied that the troops had brought it on themselves by openly taunting the youth of the towns through which they passed for not being in khaki.[12]

In spite of the rising tide of opposition to further war participation there were some in French Canada who still hoped and believed that their countrymen could be made to see the seriousness of their own position at a time when Canada was calling for all her sons to help her and when only French Canadians seemed reluctant to heed the call. The press of the cities did all in its power to give publicity and encouragement to such efforts as the Lessard-Blondin recruiting mission and constantly insisted that those who violently opposed a further war effort were but an irresponsible minority. Even before the introduction of the bill for compulsory service the *Presse,* of Montreal, was asserting that if such a measure became necessary it would be religiously observed in Quebec by an order-loving and peaceful people, who, while

---

[11] *Soleil*, January 29, 1917.
[12] Hansard, *Commons,* 1917, p. 2754, speech of Mr. Boulay.

they might fight against an idea as long as it was tenable, would obey any law once it had been enacted.[13]

Following the failure of the scheme for raising the Home Defense Force and the fiasco of the Lessard-Blondin recruiting mission, coupled with the disquieting news of the war, all of Canada, especially Quebec, had become uneasy. It was obvious that the war was at a crisis and that something would have to be done to revivify Canada's lagging war effort. Naturally there were some beside the Nationalists who believed that the time had come for an open acknowledgment that Canada had done enough.[14]

Other earnest men, appalled at the racial division and racial bitterness that were sweeping Canada, still hoped that something could be done to bring French Canadians back to a wholehearted participation in the Dominion's war effort. Among these was Ferdinand Roy, a distinguished lawyer of Quebec, who was actively associated with the law faculty of Laval University and who enjoyed considerable prestige in the community.[15] On the eve of the final enactment of the much-debated Military Service Bill, Roy published a pamphlet containing an eloquent appeal to French Canadians to reverse their anti-war attitude before it was too late, to enroll for active service, and to submit gracefully to the Military Service Bill when it had become the law of the land. Distressed at the clear-cut division on strictly racial lines, which the Military Service bill debates in the federal Parliament had shown, and the campaign of violent and riotous protest against conscription then raging in the cities of Quebec and Montreal, Roy appealed to his compatriots for reason, tolerance, and a new vision of French Canada's duty lest their national identity should be swept away altogether by the current of racial hatred. In Roy's opinion the war and the conscription bill, coupled with the fact that French Canadians had enlisted in smaller proportion than

[13] *Presse*, May 15, 1917.
[14] *Avenir du nord*, April 20, 1917.
[15] F. Roy, *L'Appel aux armes et la réponse canadienne française*.

had their fellow citizens of English speech, had put them in the deplorable position of being alone in opposition to the war policy of the Dominion. The causes of French Canada's abstention from a more active participation and of the united opposition of Quebec's members in Parliament to the conscription project Roy attributed to the racial war over the bilingual question, the unfortunate policy of the Borden government, the unskillful maneuvers of the Liberal opposition, the errors of the Nationalist propaganda, and the anticlerical tendencies of the French government, which had caused a weakening of the traditional ties between Quebec and France. The result of French Canadian opposition to participation was that all of English-speaking Canada was saying that Quebec was refusing to obey the patriotic duty it had itself assumed, while in the French province itself agitators were openly preaching resistance to conscription and were even preparing for civil war. This situation urgently demanded an inquiry by French Canadians as to their real duty, for their national honor was menaced and appearances tended to show that they were deserters from a cause to which they with all other Canadians had subscribed in 1914. Roy insisted that the cause of France and her Allies was the cause of civilization, in whose preservation the French Canadians should have a vital interest. Firmly opposed to conscription as he was, Roy nevertheless believed that as it was to be the law of the land and was furthermore the measure which the government considered the most efficacious means of aiding the cause of the Allies, French Canadians would be most ill-advised to protest further against a *fait accompli,* especially since the result of such an attitude on their part would be civil war. The only possible position for French Canadians to take in the existing crisis, Roy asserted, was a complete change of attitude and a proud unservile act of sacrifice, that is, the acceptance of military service. The time for discussion was past, and it was the duty of French Canadians to abandon further resistance, which not only was sterile but also might even be criminal and which could only increase their troubles. The sacrifice of their opinions, their pacific tastes, and of their very blood for the sake of the superior well-being of their race would be well worth while.

Roy's pamphlet was a very clear and dispassionate statement of the French Canadians' perplexity concerning the false position in which they felt themselves to be. Among the many causes for the failure of recruiting in Quebec Roy mentioned the breakup of French Canadian battalions, the slowness of promotion for French Canadian officers, and dislike for English-speaking recruiting officers who were constantly urging French Canadians to enlist and fight for England. He felt that the Liberals had been too subservient to the government and had not exercised an intelligent opposition. As for Bourassa, in Roy's opinion the Nationalist leader made a fundamental error in preaching "sacred egoism" in a country like Canada, where compromise between the races was utterly essential, and he had been equally mistaken in asserting that French Canada had no reason to fight for France, which was the mother of her civilization. Roy felt that the majority of the clergy were secretly on the side of Bourassa because of their dislike for modern anticlerical France.

Roy reflected the perplexity of many of his compatriots who deplored the more extreme manifestations of opposition to conscription and who felt that it put the whole French Canadian race in rather a false and not over-admirable position. To be the only ones in the federal Parliament to say "no" when a question so vitally affecting the safety of Canada was raised was to be in the wrong, even if the English-speaking majority was not wholly in the right. Roy was ready to admit that in the excited state of public opinion in Quebec it would be impossible to bring about any great amount of voluntary enlistments, and in consequence he stressed the necessity of his compatriots' bowing to the inevitability of the Military Service Act and by so doing bringing

The Conscription Conflict of 1917

about a modicum of racial peace. French Canadians should remember that they had a definite mission, in being not French but French Canadians. They owed to England all the obligation due to an ally, to France life itself, and to their own native province a realization of her ancient motto *je me souviens,* which alone should cause those with French names to be the first to respond to the call to arms.

That the sincerity of so modest a man as Ferdinand Roy attracted attention was evident in the letters he received from many well-known French Canadians, hesitant and perplexed like himself. The letters to Roy summarize very well the varying shades of opinion current in Quebec in the summer of 1917 on the all-important problem of French Canada's reaction to conscription. A prominent French Canadian senator, while approving of Roy's ideas, put the entire blame for the failure of French Canadian recruiting on the attitude of the English-speaking provinces on the bilingual school question. Senator Dandurand, Liberal leader in the upper house, and Sir George Garneau, former Mayor of Quebec, wrote Roy to tell him of their hearty approbation. On the other side was a long letter from Armand Lavergne, who repeated all the stock Nationalist arguments, demanded a popular referendum on the question of conscription, and added significantly that if such a consultation were refused by the government, it would be necessary to call the people to arms for the defense of democracy in Canada.[16] The curé of one of the prominent churches of Quebec city wrote as his opinion that Bourassa had

---

[16] That even some of the hierarchy were being swept into the current of what at the beginning of the war they would have termed disloyal opposition to the government's war policy was made evident by an editorial of the *Action catholique* on July 31, 1917. The organ of the Quebec hierarchy asserted that Roy was mistaken in asking for French Canadian participation merely because of sentiment for France and the cause of the Allies. In their opinion French Canadians should not be concerned by what others said of them, and their only duty was to safeguard the existence of their own country which was being asked now to support an effort which was beyond its strength, even though it might be suitable to a European country where militarism had been built up for centuries.

succeeded in paralyzing the good intentions of French Canadians and in securing the support of a large part of the clergy, who instead of urging their flock on to make the necessary sacrifices were keeping silent when they were not in active opposition. A very highly placed ecclesiastical educator wrote stating that in his opinion the attitude taken by Quebec on conscription was regrettable but that the manner in which her opposition was being exploited was equally so.[17] In this attitude of suspicion that Quebec's opposition was being used as a means of discrediting the French Canadians as a whole the writer of this letter was not alone. Even today there are many French Canadians who sincerely believe that there was a distinct plot on the part of fanatical enemies of the French Canadians not only to discredit Quebec's war effort but also actually to weaken it in every possible way in order that they might undermine the position of the French-speaking provinces. The pamphlet of Ferdinand Roy was a reasonable plea for an eleventh-hour reversal of the policy of opposition to active war participation by French Canada. Unfortunately, at a time when passions were aroused it was too much to expect that it would be heeded by the great mass of the people, though in the quiet and peace of his own home many an intelligent man might agree. Passion and prejudice were the order of the day, and it was only natural that Bourassa should more readily be listened to than Ferdinand Roy.

When the Prime Minister returned to Canada from England and a visit to the front in May, 1917, it was widely known that he brought with him a plan for the reorganization of Canada's war effort. It was an open secret that Sir Robert Borden would propose some form of compulsory military service. Since the beginning of the year recruits had been coming in more and more slowly.[18] All the world knew that the Allies were in difficulties.

[17] The name of this ecclesiastic must remain anonymous, by request of F. Roy.
[18] There had been 9,194 in January, 1917, but the number had shrunk to 6,407 by May. See J. G. Hopkins, *op. cit.*, p. 84.

The Conscription Conflict of 1917

The submarine warfare was making greater inroads on British shipping than had been expected. Russia had thrown off the age-long yoke of the Tsars and stood hesitating, more intent on internal reorganization than on her flagging war effort. The United States, it is true, had just entered the war on the side of the Allies, but it was appreciated that it would be a long time before she could make her potential military strength felt on the western front. It was a grave situation for the Allies; and the Prime Minister, who had been admitted to the innermost councils of the Empire, was deeply impregnated with its seriousness when he rose to state the government's intention of introducing a measure of conscription in the House of Commons on May 18, 1917.[19]

Reviewing the war situation the Canadian Prime Minister pointed out that if the war were to be won a great military effort lay before the Allies, especially in view of the fact that Germany had been able to put one million more soldiers in the field at the beginning of the 1917 campaign. It was necessary for the Allied armies, of which the Canadian corps formed a vital part, to hold the line; and for this reinforcements were an absolute necessity. Four Canadian divisions were at the front, and more than 326,000 Canadians had gone overseas to swell the ranks of the Expeditionary Force.[20] It was a magnificent effort, but more was needed. The Prime Minister stated that he had reluctantly become convinced that the voluntary system of enlistments was no longer able to yield substantial results. It was his belief, sincerely held, that the battle for Canadian liberty was being fought on the plains of France and Flanders and that the time had come to invoke the authority of the State to provide reinforcements for those gallant men who were defending that liberty. There was only one course possible if the sacrifices of Canadian soldiers were not to go in vain, and as a result the government was proposing to provide re-

[19] Hansard, *Commons*, 1917, pp. 1515 *et seq.*, Sir Robert Borden.
[20] *Ibid.*

inforcements on a basis of compulsory selective conscription. The number of men required would not be less than 50,000 and probably would be nearer 100,000.

With the announcement by the Prime Minister of a bill for compulsory military service Canada was plunged into the midst of one of the most serious crises in all her history. In spite of this fact the casual observer visiting Montreal, a hotbed of opposition and disturbance in those June days of 1917, would not have noticed that there was much amiss. The streets were full of citizens going quietly about their business. The hotels were full of American tourists whose cars carried intertwined British and American flags, which were heartily cheered by the populace. The campus of McGill was filled with soldiers ready to depart for overseas, and occasionally a body of troops would march to the docks for embarkation amid throngs of applauding spectators. Nevertheless, the metropolitan city of French Canada was seething underneath this seeming peace and quiet. In the French Canadian quarters of the city, far from the hotels of the American tourists, were held each night anti-conscription meetings attended by people in thousands and addressed by passionate men urging their compatriots to resist conscription to the limit. These scenes were duplicated in the city of Quebec and throughout the length and breadth of the province. The French Canadian press, stunned to find that the conscription measure was actually imminent, bore witness to the resentment and the perplexity of the entire French Canadian people. It was a moment when French Canada stood at the crossroads. Would her habit of loyalty and her age-long obedience to authority be maintained? Or would her passionate dislike for any compulsion and her deep feeling of resentment at the insults which fanatics were hurling at her burst into the flame of open revolt? These were the questions that anxious patriots were asking themselves in the critical days after the introduction of the Military Service Bill at Ottawa. It was indicative of the tense atmosphere at the time that the meeting of the National Unity Congress, in Montreal, at the end of May, 1917, passed comparatively unnoticed. The National Unity Congress was the outgrowth of the *Bonne Entente* movement of the previous year organized by a Toronto publicist, Arthur Hawks, who had sought to enlist Canadians of both races in a campaign for mutual toleration and unity. It was particularly significant that one of the prominent French Canadian delegates, Mgr. Gauthier, Auxiliary Bishop of Montreal, took the opportunity of pleading not for racial unity but in passionate defense of his compatriots' war efforts.[21]

The Prime Minister had always realized the gravity of the situation which conscription would bring about as long as there was so much opposition to Canada's war effort in Quebec, and for that reason he had made an earnest attempt at securing the co-operation of the Liberals in a coalition government before introducing his Military Service Bill in Parliament. On May 29 Sir Wilfrid Laurier received the Prime Minister's invitation to join the government and to assist in the creation of a cabinet of both Liberals and Conservatives under the leadership of Sir Robert Borden. It was proposed that the new coalition government should proceed to get the Military Service Bill passed through Parliament at once. Sir Robert Borden at first suggested that the entry of the Liberals into the government obviated the necessity of an election; but as this proved to be unsatisfactory to the Liberals, it was proposed that as soon as the Military Service Act was passed the new government should seek the verdict of the country. Pending this popular endorsement conscription was not to be enforced.

Sir Wilfrid Laurier asked for time to think the matter over, but he at once expressed his regret that the government had not seen fit to consult him before bringing in the Military Service Bill. After a week of consultation the Liberal leader declined the proposal to join a coalition government. His refusal was based on the

[21] *Semaine religieuse de Montréal*, June 1917; see, also, *Presse*, May 21, 1917.

feeling that he should have been previously consulted regarding the proposed measure if he were to form part of the responsible government of Canada and that for him to accept office now would be not only a denial of his own principles but also an assumption of responsibility for a policy which he had had no part in making and for which he would be bitterly attacked. The Prime Minister and the Conservatives would be the only ones to derive political benefit from such a scheme for coalition. Laurier was in a very difficult position. He knew that many of his Liberal supporters in Ontario and in the West were anxious that he should join a coalition, while on the other hand Quebec Liberalism was solidly opposed to any such project if conscription were to be its price. There were many Liberals who even believed that the Conservatives had lost their grip on the country and that if Laurier would only hold out the party would have a very good chance at victory in a general election. The Liberal leader himself not only was opposed to conscription on principle but also was convinced that the reason a voluntary system of enlistment had failed was chiefly because Canada as a whole had reached its limit of man power. To him there seemed no possibility that the number of men asked for could be obtained, and time was to prove that he was right.

It was a bitter moment for Laurier, who had spent his life in the service of the ideal of the racial pacification of Canada; for he now feared that if he fought what he considered the subservience of Ontario to the ideas of English imperialists, he would be howled down simply because he was a French Canadian. On the other hand, if he accepted conscription in the interests of racial peace, his own province would turn against him and go over to the control of the Nationalist extremists. He believed that conscription meant racial cleavage, and for that he could not be responsible. He himself said that he had lived too long, but that what strength remained in him would still be devoted to the cause of racial peace. It seemed to him that the only wise thing was an appeal to the people on the question of conscription. Given the strong feeling in the English-speaking provinces, which had the majority of votes, conscription would probably be upheld; but Quebec would have a chance to speak her mind, and he could devote his energies to convincing her that the verdict of the majority must be upheld.[22]

If the opinion of French Canada was almost unanimously opposed to the proposal for conscription, that of English-speaking Canada was no less clear cut. Immediately after the announcement of Sir Robert Borden the Montreal *Gazette,* the most influential English paper in the Dominion, said on May 19 that since there was no other way the government had done its duty in proposing the measure and that the people should accept it and make it effective. The very patriotic Tory organ, the *Mail and Empire,* of Toronto, asserted on June 11 that in refusing to enter a coalition government Laurier had missed the chance of performing the greatest possible service for Quebec by making her one with the rest of Canada in the present crisis and of destroying for all time the efforts of agitators to sow discord between the two races. The attitude of the French Canadian press, though in general vehemently opposed to conscription, had not as yet crystallized. On May 28 the Montreal *Presse,* while reserving its judgment pending the parliamentary debates on the bill, urgently recommended a popular referendum. The *Patrie* argued on May 18 that the grave decision taken by the government should be given serious consideration and that after all the real object was the defeat of Germany at any cost. The loyally Conservative *Evénement,* of Quebec, was of the opinion on May 21 that conscription was a necessity which Canada was called upon to share with the other Allied nations. The Liberal *Canada* asserted on May 21 that the government

[22] For the account of Laurier's position on the coalition project, see Skelton, *op. cit.,* II, 506-16.

should be required to state why it had gone back on its repeated promise never to introduce conscription and added on May 24 that neither the government nor the Parliament had a mandate to impose its will on the people unless there were a popular consultation.

That the feeling of resentment against conscription was no less strong in the country than in the cities of the province was clearly shown in the rural press.[23] Laurier had supplied the Liberals with the essential *mots d'ordre* for opposition to conscription by saying that there should be no compulsory service unless the measure were approved by a majority of the voters and that a Parliament elected in 1911 on entirely different issues was now moribund and had no right to involve the people in so serious a matter unless their mandate were renewed by a general election. These themes were constantly reiterated by the Liberal press of Quebec. The Conservative press of the province was in a more difficult position at the outset of the conscription debates, torn as it was between its political loyalty to its representatives in the cabinet who had approved the Military Service Bill and its instinctive dislike for the principle of compulsory service. The Nationalists were in no such predicament. They had always predicted that conscription would ensue as the logical outcome of the policy of an active war participation.

Nor did the population seem in any doubt as to what should be done now that conscription was imminent. Immediately following the announcement of conscription by the Prime Minister protest meetings began to be held throughout the province, especially in Montreal. On the evening of May 23 three thousand people met at the Champ de Mars, and proceeding to the business section broke the windows of the *Patrie* with cries of "Down with conscription." On the same evening 10,000 were said to have attended an enthusiastic protest meeting at the Parc LaFontaine, in Mont-

[23] *Bien public*, May 24, 31, 1917; *Avenir du nord*, May 25, 1917.

real. The following evening the mayor of Montreal urged a meeting of 15,000 to put their trust in Laurier, but nevertheless the crowd got out of hand and proceeding down one of the main thoroughfares of the city again broke the windows of the *Presse* and *Patrie* and attacked any soldiers that showed themselves.[24] On May 26 the Montreal *Gazette* reported Armand Lavergne as saying that he would go to jail or be shot before he would accept conscription, and on May 29 the paper reported a huge anti-conscription meeting at Hull, an important French Canadian center immediately across the river from Ottawa, in the province of Quebec. The fervor of anti-conscription demonstrations was not confined to the cities—even in so quiet a town as St. Jerome 5,000 people held a protest parade early in June.[25]

The Nationalist press, while asserting constantly that Canada had done enough and that the limit of enlistments had been reached if the country were not to be ruined, was startled, as was all of peace-loving French Canada, by the degree of violence attained at the anti-conscription demonstrations. As early as May 28-29 the *Devoir* urged its readers to remain calm and to beware of *agents provocateurs* who might incite French Canadians to violence in order to discredit them with English-speaking Canada by placing them in the invidious position of seeming to be disloyal to the crown and rebels to the laws of the land. If among ten thousand peaceable manifestants only a handful indulged in excessive language or even violent acts the violent ones would be represented by enemies of French Canada as typical of the entire population. French Canadians were urged to listen to the voices of their religious leaders, who were asking God that the leaders of the nation might see the light, and furthermore to oppose conscription in a disciplined Christian manner and to meet the unjustifiable demands of the government, not with sterile violence but by orderly calm opposition. That the fears of the *Devoir* were not

[24] *Devoir*, May 25, 1917.   [25] *Avenir du nord*, June 8, 1917.

entirely unjustified was proved by the *Mail and Empire* on June 15, when it asserted that evidently the Quebec agitators were determined to stop completely the raising of troops, not only in their own province but also throughout the Dominion; and as this was pushing Quebec domination too far, the real patriots should form in a solid English-speaking bloc in support of Canada's soldiers.

With one or two exceptions the French Canadian press in town and country was preaching moderation and calm to their compatriots. It was obvious that French Canadians shrank from violence. Nevertheless the Nationalists felt that even now there was a need for frank criticism.[26] They pointed out that those French Canadian leaders who in their desire to promote racial tolerance had attempted to make Anglo-Canadians believe in Quebec's war enthusiasm had been very unwise. The Nationalists were convinced that the great majority of French Canadians believed that Canada had done enough for the Dominion war effort and that their sole obligation was to fight for their own native country. To force them to fight against their innermost conviction was to make revolutionaries out of the population of Quebec. Bourassa himself continued to attempt to calm his compatriots, as was shown by the resolutions passed at large meetings at the Monument National, in Montreal, on June 7, for which he was largely responsible. These resolutions expressed the unalterable opposition of French Canadians to any measure of conscription, as contrary to the principles of the Canadian constitution, their refusal to consent to any such measure unless the majority of voters approved it, and their firm belief that any further national effort for the Allied cause should be in the economic rather than in the military field. However, their determination as loyal subjects of the king to defend Canadian territory whenever it should be threatened was clearly expressed. To mark this loyalty the meeting, at

[26] H. Bourassa, *La Conscription*, reprint of articles first appearing in *Devoir*, May-June, 1917.

Bourassa's suggestion, had concluded with the singing of "O Canada" and "God Save the King."[27]

Nothing could better illustrate the attitude of the Church than a speech made early in June by Archbishop Bruchesi, of Montreal.[28] It reflected the surprised resentment at the change in the government's policy which was so prevalent in Quebec. Mgr. Bruchesi pointed out that the Church had done everything in its power to prove its loyalty. He himself had asked the Prime Minister whether the National Service cards in any way implied that conscription might be introduced and, receiving a firmly negative reply, had urged full co-operation with the National Service Board on all his flock. Now the Prime Minister, who had always stressed his own opposition to conscription, was proposing such a measure himself, and it was only natural to ask what had happened in England and at the front to change his mind. The Archbishop concluded by telling the faithful that during the conscription debate they were free to express their opinions, but that they should beware of going too far and should remain within the bounds of reason in the discussion. It was obvious that French Canada was rapidly becoming a unit in opposition to the war policy of the Dominion government, when one of the acknowledged leaders of the Quebec hierarchy came so near to open disapproval. The wave of opposition to conscription was fast sweeping all of Quebec with it. Even some of the Conservative supporters of the government in the province could not stand against it any longer, as was shown by the resignation of E. G. Patenaude, Secretary of State, Mr. Rainville, deputy speaker, and Mr. Pacquet, government whip for Quebec. The municipal councils of Montreal and Quebec recorded their overwhelming opposition to conscription. In spite of the attempt of Bourassa and others to check the passion which was breaking out so frequently, anti-conscription meetings of unbridled violence continued to be held through-

[27] *Devoir*, June 8, 1917.   [28] *Presse*, June 7, 1917.

out the summer, and for the first time there was public discussion of the possibility of Quebec's secession from the Confederation in the columns of the ultra-Catholic *Croix,* on June 15.

The debates on the Military Service Bill in the Dominion Parliament, which lasted for more than two months, were followed with a passionate interest throughout the country, but nowhere with closer attention than in Quebec. Nearly a month elapsed between the Prime Minister's announcement of conscription and his introduction of the Military Service Bill into Parliament, on June 11, 1917. In the meantime the whole weight of partisan passion had been thrown into the scale so that when Sir Robert Borden rose to address the Commons the country already knew fairly clearly how much support the government could count upon. Parliament as well as the country was plainly divided on the racial lines which were cutting across the conventional party divisions. Behind the government was the great mass of English-speaking Conservatives, and to it was added a determined band of Liberals of English speech who had broken away from Laurier's leadership in order to support conscription. On the opposite side was the solid bloc of French Canadians, who were for the most part Liberals, but who had been joined by many French-speaking Conservatives and even Nationalists. A few members of the old guard of English-speaking Liberals still supported their old leader.

The Military Service Bill introduced by Sir Robert Borden provided that all male British subjects between the ages of twenty and forty-five should be liable for military service.[29] The total number of men was divided into classes based on age and civil status which might be called up for service by proclamation when they were needed. The terms of exemption were very liberal. Men engaged in essential war industry were to be excused from

[29] *Acts of the Parliament of Canada, Seventh Session, Twelfth Parliament,* Ottawa, 1917.

service as were all conscientious objectors, and those who had special qualifications for the work in which they were engaged and could not be spared without upsetting industrial conditions. Exemption tribunals were to be set up in every military district, and arrangements were made for an appeal court which was to decide those cases appealed from the local tribunals, and as a last resort there was to be a central appeal tribunal in Ottawa.

In introducing the Military Service Bill, on June 11, the Prime Minister explained that although the Militia Act of 1904 in his opinion fully permitted the conscription of Canadians for service in Canada and even beyond Canada "for the defense thereof," the government had thought it wise to bring in this new bill which would allow for the selective drafting of men either for the army or for the needs of war industry in a way that the old militia laws did not recognize.[30] When Sir Wilfrid Laurier rose on June 18 to reply to the government all Canada hung upon his words, for here they knew was the center of the opposition to the proposed conscription law.[31] He began by stating that the government was proposing a measure which until April, 1917, it had said would never be resorted to and which in Laurier's opinion would do more harm than good to the cause which all Canadians had at heart. Furthermore, the law of the land which antedated Confederation by many generations declared that there should be no compulsory military service except to repel invasion, and there was obviously no danger of German invasion of Canada. The attempt on the part of the government to enact such a new and radical principle as was embodied in the Military Service Bill by means of a Parliament elected in 1911 on far other issues was a distinct abuse of authority. Laurier asserted that there were many people not only in Quebec but also throughout the Dominion who were honestly opposed to conscription, and that the only way to avoid bitterness and a sense

[30] *Ibid.*, *Fourth Session, Ninth Parliament*, Ottawa, 1904.
[31] Hansard, *Commons*, 1917, pp. 2329 *et seq.*, Sir Wilfrid Laurier.

of injustice and intolerance was a popular referendum on the measure. As far as his native province was concerned Laurier freely admitted that the French Canadians had not enlisted in sufficient numbers, but that, in his opinion, did not mean that they had degenerated. There were many reasons for apparent recruiting failure. For one thing, their attachment to France was far less than that of English-speaking Canadians to their mother country, for few French Canadians had had any relations with France since 1760. Besides, disarmament at the conquest and the subsequent and continuing paucity of French Canadian military organizations had played an important part in making the habitant uninterested in military affairs. The 1911 elections which the Nationalists had fought on the basis that Quebec should not be involved in the wars of the Empire had helped to turn the sympathy of French Canada away from aid to Britain, and the blundering recruiting policy of the government in the present war had been the final blow to any real measure of co-operation.

Nevertheless, and in spite of all bitterness and misunderstanding, Laurier pledged his compatriots to a loyal observance of the Military Service Act once it should become the law of the land. No one regretted Quebec's slowness in recruiting more than Laurier, but he felt that there was only one way out, and that was to appeal to the whole country, not to one section only, but to all sections. He believed that when the country had spoken, the question would be settled and all must submit to the law. In consequence Sir Wilfrid Laurier proposed an amendment to the Military Service Bill providing that further consideration of it should be deferred until the principle contained therein should have been submitted to and approved by the electors of Canada.

After the speeches of the Prime Minister and the leader of the opposition the House plunged into the full fury of the debate on conscription. The government supporters who were regular Conservatives gave the measure the full weight of their approval, reit-

The Conscription Conflict of 1917   185

erating and strengthening the arguments already advanced by their leader. Occasionally the bitterness of English-speaking Canada at what it considered the almost criminal slackness of Quebec cropped out, and bitter words were hurled across the House. Laurier was even told by a member of the cabinet that the only reason that he believed that Canada was not in danger of invasion and that he could sit comfortably in his seat was because he knew that the troops of the Allies would succeed in holding the line.[32] One English-speaking member insisted that the only reason that Canada as a whole was faced with conscription was that French Canada had failed to do her duty.[33] Laurier was accused of being responsible, even before the war, for Quebec's anti-British bias, and the impulse for Canadian independence was attributed to him besides, while his younger Liberal followers were accused of interference with the recruiting campaign in Quebec.[34]

It was not easy for the ex-Nationalist supporters of the government to approve of the conscription bill. Nevertheless, the Postmaster General, Sevigny, and other such men did their best to convince their compatriots not only of their own sincerity but also of the necessity for a measure of compulsion. Sevigny asserted that he saw no reason to resign simply because most of his compatriots were opposed to conscription. He defended Quebec's war effort and insisted that its comparative failure must be attributed to faulty organization.[35] Not all the ex-Nationalists continued to support the government. E. G. Patenaude, who had been Secretary of State, declared that, although he had always believed that the best interests of Canada required that she should give the fullest support to the Allies, he could not approve of the conscription bill, which he feared would imperil the country's unity and give rise

---

[32] Hansard, *Commons*, 1917, p. 2529, Hon. A. Meighen, Solicitor General.
[33] Hansard, *Commons*, 1917, p. 2547, Mr. Armstrong.
[34] *Ibid.*, p. 2715, Mr. Edwards.
[35] *Ibid.*, p. 2337, Hon. A. Sevigny.

186   *The Conscription Conflict of 1917*

to lasting internal divisions which in themselves would interfere with the smooth working of the proposed bill.[36]

Symptomatic of the cleavage of the country on racial rather than on the old party lines was the support of the conscription bill by English-speaking Liberals. As yet the defection of these Liberals from the leadership of Laurier was not as marked as it was to become later in 1917, but it was noticeable nevertheless. Old and tried supporters of the Liberal leader began to oppose his stand for a referendum, adding that Laurier was underestimating the seriousness of the war situation.[37] Laurier was stricken to the heart by these defections among his Liberal following, though he realized that many of those who were deserting him did so for motives of the highest patriotism. He held the government chiefly responsible, for he was convinced that by introducing conscription they had hoped to destroy the Liberal party because of the inevitable divisions that would ensue.[38] But there were still many English-speaking Liberals who stood by Laurier and argued that the conscription bill would bring inevitable disunion to the country and who accused the party in power of subscribing to the slogan of "win the war and damn Quebec," which would only result in a very hollow victory at best.[39]

The solid bloc of French Canadians who supported Laurier were perhaps more voluble than any others during the long weeks of the conscription debates. It seemed at times as if every single member from Quebec was bent on having his turn at attacking the government proposal. Those French Canadians who were well known and accustomed to speak in the House had the first say, but as the long debate dragged to its end many members of less importance rose for long and passionate speeches. The same atmosphere prevailed in the Senate where the bill came up for discussion

[36] *Ibid.*, p. 2931, Mr. Devlin, quoting Hon. E. G. Patenaude.
[37] *Ibid.*, p. 2660, Mr. Clark.
[38] O. D. Skelton, *Life and Letters of Sir Wilfrid Laurier*, II, 518-19.
[39] Hansard, *Commons*, 1917, pp. 2895, 2931, Messrs. Devlin and Knowles.

The Conscription Conflict of 1917 187

after its passage by the Commons. In the upper House the Liberals still had a substantial majority, and thus it was but natural that the division in the Liberal ranks which resulted in the passage of the bill was more noticeable than in the Commons. Most of the French Canadian orators repeated the arguments that Laurier had already made the basis of the case for opposition to the conscription measure, but there were additions and variations which showed the currents of thought that were agitating French Canada as a whole. It was noticeable that those members who represented far-away and isolated communities were, if anything, more vehement in their opposition than those living in the cities in close proximity to their fellow citizens of English speech. But hardly a French Canadian spoke against the Military Service Bill who did not insist that his compatriots felt deeply that the only country to which they owed loyalty and service was Canada and that to ask them to rush to the aid of France and England was asking a great deal too much.[40] The French Canadians' passionate resentment against the criticism of their war effort so frequently made in English-speaking Canada was often stressed, and orators asked bitterly whether the descendants of the oldest Canadian settlers were to be publicly ostracized merely because they had fallen a few thousand men short in enlistments. The French Canadians' instinctive dislike of compulsion in any form was brought up, and the government was urged not to attempt coercion but to appeal to the big heart of Quebec.[41] If only the campaign of slander against Quebec were to stop and good will were re-established between the races, it would not be necessary to put a conscription bill on the statute books.[42] The blundering recruiting policies of the government came in for much criticism from the Quebec speakers. Senator Landry accused the authorities of having systematically ignored rural Quebec in the enlistment campaigns

[40] For typical examples see Hansard, *Commons*, 1917, pp. 108, 3059.
[41] *Ibid.*, pp. 2428, 2430, Mr. Marcil.
[42] Hansard, *Commons*, 1917, pp. 2682 *et seq.*, Mr. Bureau.

188   *The Conscription Conflict of 1917*

and added that the population naturally resented the break-up of French Canadian units and the failure to organize the promised French Canadian brigade.[43] The intense resentment of Quebec because of the question of the bilingual schools was often brought up as a cause of the slowness of French Canadian recruiting. Senator Dandurand asserted that in 1915-16 the Nationalists had exploited the schools question to the full and as a result had succeeded definitely in bringing recruiting to a standstill in Quebec. He insisted that Quebec was convinced of the necessity for organizing agriculture and industry for war purposes and urged the government to see that this was done at once.[44]

The sincerity of the ex-Nationalist ministers was frequently questioned in the course of the debate in both Houses. That many French Canadians who had been elected as Nationalists were finding it hard to vote against the passionate disapproval of their compatriots became increasingly apparent in the course of the debates. Some asserted that, while they remained friendly to the Conservative party and believed in its sincerity concerning the necessity for conscription, they themselves as French Canadians could not approve of any such measure, for Quebec to a man was opposed to it.[45] Others showed the gradual crystallization of French Canadian sentiment into an unanimous opposition to the government war policy by statements repeating their Conservative sympathies, even their appreciation of the urgent war needs underlying conscription, but insisting that the deep feeling in their native province against the Military Service Bill made it impossible for them to support it.[46] The unfortunate incidents in Quebec, where troops had actually been stoned, were attributed by some of the French Canadian speakers to resentment at "persecutions" about their language, their schools, and their religion to which their com-

[43] Hansard, *Senate*, 1917, p. 414, Senator Landry.
[44] *Ibid.*, p. 338, Senator Dandurand.
[45] Hansard, *Commons*, 1917, p. 2825, Mr. Girard.
[46] *Ibid., Senate*, 1917, p. 373, Senator Beaubien.

patriots had been subjected, and it was repeatedly argued that such "insults" were indeed a justification for a passive resistance to any form of military assistance.[47] Occasionally orators even told their constituents, as Lavergne had done on many a platform, that not one French Canadian would enlist if he fully realized how badly Quebec was being treated.[48] Going even one step farther a French Canadian member assured the government that if it passed this measure his people might feel impelled to go to the limit in resistance and that the direst consequences might ensue.[49] It is significant, nevertheless, that this threat of open revolt against the enforcement of conscription was an isolated instance in the debate. The whole force of French Canadian opposition was aroused, however, when the government in the course of the debates moved to strike out the term "divinity students" from the list of exemptions on the grounds that the term was too inclusive. It could not have hit upon a more dangerous way of arousing Catholic suspicion and resentment. The echoes were heard in Parliament and in the press, and the clergy itself did not hesitate to express its intense disapprobation.[50]

It was only natural that the conscription debate should bring forth a discussion of the actual number of French Canadians enlisted in the army up to that time. It is noteworthy that in June, 1917, the government for the first and last time put the whole weight of its authority behind a statement of enlistments of French Canadians.[51] In reply to questions from the floor of the House the government stated on the authority of the Minister of Militia that while there were 125,245 Canadian-born members of the Expeditionary Forces speaking the English language, there were only 14,100 Canadian-born soldiers speaking the French

[47] *Ibid., Commons*, p. 2754, Mr. Boulay.
[48] *Ibid.*, p. 2962, Mr. Roch-Lanctot.
[49] *Ibid.*, p. 2551, Mr. Gauthier.
[50] For parliamentary discussion, see Hansard, *Commons*, p. 3557.
[51] *Sessional Paper, 143b*, June 14, 1917, Canada, Department of Secretary of State, in Library of Parliament, Ottawa.

language who had proceeded overseas from the beginning of the war to April 30, 1917. Of these 14,100, a total of 5,443 were French Canadian soldiers commanded by officers speaking the French language and serving with units organized in the province of Quebec, while 1,536 of the soldiers in Quebec units were serving under officers speaking English. There were, besides, 5,904 soldiers speaking the French language and serving in units organized in other provinces than Quebec. Finally, the total number of soldiers speaking French in the first contingent was officially stated to be 1,217. In reply to a question from a French Canadian member as to the basis the government used to determine who was a "French Canadian," in view of the obvious difficulties of name, and so forth, the Minister of Militia who presented this statement asserted that the greatest possible care had been taken in compiling the figures and that they were as approximately accurate as they could be.[52] He later added that the total enlistments up to June 30, 1917, were 424,456, with 329,943 overseas.[53] There can be little doubt

---

[52] Hansard, *Commons*, 1917, p. 2627, Sir E. Kemp, Minister of Militia.

[53] Aside from the official statement of the Ministry of Militia, the enlistment figures published by General Mason in the Senate attracted considerable attention. They were compiled according to General Mason from the figures supplied by the Ministry of Militia and the Dominion Census Office (Hansard, *Senate*, 1917, p. 429, Brigadier General Mason). General Mason showed that, while Ontario had supplied a total of 184,545 recruits up to July 15, 1917, the total number it might have been expected to produce, taking into consideration its male population between the ages of eighteen and forty-five (1911 census), would have been only 144,412, an actual excess in enlistments of 40,135. Quebec, on the other hand, with a similar population of 390,897, had produced only 46,777 recruits, an actual shortage of 50,176 against the 96,953 enlistments that the province should have produced. The total enlistments up to July 15, 1917, were officially stated to be 424,456. Obviously, the recruits from Quebec included many of English race and speech, while those from the other provinces had many French Canadians among them. Basing his conclusions on place of birth, however, General Mason asserted that up to June 30, 1917, there had been 132,265 Canadian-born English-speaking soldiers. These men constituted 19.8 percent of the total male population of Ontario and 40.2 percent of the total of soldiers overseas. Canadian-born French-speaking soldiers, on the other hand, were estimated to be 14,684, comprising 3.3 percent of the total male population of Quebec between the ages of eighteen and forty-five and 4.5 percent of the total soldiers overseas. The British-born amounted to 162,092, which was 52.8 percent of the total males and 49.2 percent of the total of overseas soldiers. The significance of General Mason's figures lay primarily in the estimate that the British-born constituted in 1917 almost 50 percent of the

that the small number of French Canadians which the official statement showed was a distinct shock to many people in Quebec. Even Sir Wilfrid Laurier felt impelled to question the figures in a statement to the House that in his opinion 20,000 was nearer to the correct total,[54] while some of his French Canadian followers asserted that the total number of their enlisted compatriots was 25,000 or even 30,000.[55]

It should be borne in mind that the total of 14,100 soldiers speaking the French language included not only those enlisted in Quebec and the western provinces but also Acadians from the maritime provinces. From the beginning of the war the attitude of the French-speaking Acadians had been extremely loyal, and the various interracial crises had affected them far less than their brethren in Quebec and Ontario. The bilingual school dispute had not touched them, while the Acadian people and especially the clergy had been very little affected by the Nationalist campaign against British imperialism and Canadian war participation. Acadian leaders, both laymen and clerics, had always stood for a policy of active Canadian participation, and now their representatives in Parliament and in the press were willing even to accept conscription in order to help win the war.[56] A whole battalion, the 165th, had been enlisted among the Acadians of the maritimes, and it was even claimed that in some cases 30 to 40 percent of certain English-speaking New Brunswick battalions were Acadians.[57] The Acadian representatives in Parliament urged their brethren of

---

Canadian army and in their close approximation to the estimate of French Canadians made by the government in June, 1917. There can, in consequence, be little doubt that the number of French Canadians in the army before the enactment of the Military Service Bill was in the neighborhood of 14,000.

[54] Hansard, *Commons*, 1917, p. 2398, Sir Wilfrid Laurier. Unofficial estimates continued to be made throughout the year, and it was again noticeable that French Canadian sources were apt to place the estimate rather high, as the estimate of 37,000 French Canadians in the *Action catholique* of December 31 showed.

[55] Hansard, *Senate*, p. 175, Senator Choquette.

[56] *Ibid.*, p. 347, Senator Poirier.

[57] *L'Evangeline*, Moncton, N. B., September 26, 1917.

French speech in Quebec to emulate the example of New Brunswick, where people of different races and creeds dwelt together in harmony.[58] But, while urging their French-speaking compatriots to realize that Canadian liberty was at stake in the present struggle, the Acadians asked English Canadians to understand that the slowness of French Canadian enlistments was due rather to the fact that Quebec had been misled and that she would fight as well as any other province if she were appealed to in the right way.[59]

It was an interesting sidelight on the history of the Acadians, whose bad treatment by the English had been the subject of song and story for close on two hundred years, that in this crisis of Canadian history they should be more demonstratively loyal than the French Canadians of Quebec whose political status and actual survival as a race had been in far less danger. Nevertheless, the reason may be found in the fact that the Acadians had felt themselves to be British ever since the famous naval scare of 1793, when they had enlisted gladly in the militia to defend their province against the revolutionary French.

The conscription debates dragged on for many weeks, but finally it was apparent that the time for a definite vote was at hand. On behalf of the government, the Minister of Justice, whose department would be called upon to administer the act, made a final plea for its passage.[60] Mr. Doherty insisted on the imperative need of the Allies for more men and defended the principle of selection whereby under the act men could be sent either to the army or to agriculture and industry according to their ability and the relative need of each. He denied that the government had any idea of coercing Quebec and pleaded for mutual conciliation between the races, while denying the practicability of the referendum proposed by the opposition. Laurier, in a final appeal against the bill, said with deep emotion that he had fought coercion all his life and

[58] Hansard, *Senate*, 1917, p. 406, Senator Bourque.
[59] *Ibid.*, p. 347, Senator Poirier.
[60] Hansard, *Commons*, p. 3016, Hon. Mr. Doherty, Minister of Justice.

had struggled to promote the union of the two Canadian races and that the inspiration which had led him through life would be his guide as long as there was breath in his body.[61]

Opposition to the Military Service Bill was obviously vain, for it was apparent from the first that, because of the defection of many Liberals and the general feeling that something must be done about recruiting, the government would command a comfortable majority. The test came when Laurier's amendment for a referendum was voted down 111 to 62, a majority of 49 for the government.[62] On the second reading of the bill divisions were drawn essentially on racial rather than on political lines. With the exception of nine ex-Nationalists from Quebec the Conservatives voted solidly for the bill. The English-speaking Liberals from Ontario voted 10 to 2 for the bill, while the French Canadian Liberals from Quebec voted solidly against, 37 to 0. The bill passed the Commons at its second reading 119 to 55, and at the third and final reading the government had a majority of 58 votes (102 to 44). In the Senate the government margin was much smaller, owing to the fact that there was still a Liberal majority in the upper House. When the Senate passed the clause canceling the proposed exemption of divinity students by the narrow margin of nine votes there was some hope in Quebec that the passage of the bill might be stopped altogether. But at the second reading the bill passed, with a government majority of 29, and at the third reading the government had a similarly comfortable margin. As a result the Military Service Bill became the law of the land after it had received the assent of the Governor General on August 29, 1917.

The Canadian press reflected the attitude of the people on conscription in the course of the debates on the Military Service Bill. With its usual moderation the Montreal *Gazette* summed up the Anglo-Canadian viewpoint on June 28, by asserting that none of

[61] *Ibid.*, 1917, p. 3721, Sir Wilfrid Laurier.
[62] For figures on voting on Military Service Bill, see *Canadian Annual Review*, 1917, p. 303.

the arguments advanced by French Canadians against further active participation because of the economic dangers therein involved for Canada could stand up against the imperative necessity for all belligerent countries to maintain their war effort for their own salvation.

The French Canadian press was almost solidly opposed to conscription from the beginning. The Quebec *Evénement* and the Montreal *Patrie* stood alone among the French Canadian newspapers in backing the government throughout. *Le Canada,* the chief Liberal organ in Montreal, supported Laurier in his opposition to the bill and in his demand for a popular consultation, and in fact, the tone of its opposition was almost as vehement as that of the Nationalist press. The people were told that it was their duty to protest against the iniquitous law and that Sir Robert Borden was willing to maintain himself in power by sacrificing the lives of Canadians.[63] After the final passage of the bill the *Canada* went so far as to assert, on July 25, that the government, in spite of Laurier's solemn warning, had succeeded in passing the death verdict of 100,000 young Canadians.

The influential *Presse* demanded a popular referendum and pledged that all loyal citizens throughout the Dominion would respect the outcome.[64] After the passage of the second reading of the bill the *Presse,* on July 12, began to insist that the government should seek the renewal of their mandate at a general election before enforcing the conscription proposal, and on July 16 it argued that such an election would be the only means of calming the racial passions and safeguarding the principles of real democracy. On July 28 considerable interest was aroused by an interview which the *Action catholique* had secured with Cardinal Begin. The eminent prelate did not hesitate to assert that the proposal that clerks, lay brothers, and members of Catholic novitiates

[63] *Canada,* June 15, 26, July 13, 1917.
[64] *Presse,* July 6, 1917.

should be subject to military service constituted a grave interference with the rights of the Church and one which all good churchmen should oppose.

As for the rural press of Quebec, it was equally united in its opposition to conscription. Even the Conservative Montmagny *Peuple* asserted on June 29 that, while it still favored Canadian participation and believed that the cause of the Allies merited sacrifices, it did not think that Canada need go as far as conscription. The *Etoile du nord,* of Joliette, supported the proposed referendum, and the *Avenir du nord* reiterated week after week that the conscription bill was an attack on the Canadian constitution, as well as a grave economic error.[65]

The *Devoir* never ceased its passionate opposition to the Military Service Bill. It did not hesitate to accuse the Prime Minister of having broken his solemn pledges against conscription, and it ridiculed the possibility that the change in his policy might be due to the exigencies of war rather than to political expediency.[66] On June 9, at the beginning of the conscription debates, Bourassa demanded that all enemies of the bill should stand together in petitioning the government against the measure and in insisting that it should not be enforced without a plebiscite. The *Devoir* branded as absurd the idea put forth by government leaders that the Allies' paramount need was men, and it added that the government would have been more honest if it admitted that it was embarking on an unlimited and dangerous war effort.[67] On June 28 the *Devoir* was saying boldly that if Canada were to survive, enlistment should stop altogether. Replying to an article in the *Gazette,* which had pledged the last man and the last dollar to the cause of the Allies, the *Devoir,* on July 20, insisted that it was time that all who were genuinely interested in the welfare of Canada and also in practical aid to the Allies should oppose a policy of

[65] *Avenir du nord*, May 25, June 1, 15, 1917 *et seq.*
[66] *Devoir*, June 4, 5, 1917.
[67] *Ibid.*, June 25, 1917.

suicide and economic bankruptcy and substitute for it a policy of rational conservation of men and of resources. At the close of the parliamentary debates the *Devoir* not only criticized Laurier for his acceptance of even a limited obligation of active participation but also accused the entire House of Commons of a total lack of understanding of the national interests of Canada. In the *Devoir's* opinion Parliament had shown a criminal neglect of the economic aspects of conscription and had failed to appreciate that it would contribute to the country's depopulation.[68] As a result of the unwillingness of Canadian statesmen to protect their constituents and the rights of the nation Canadian soldiers were fighting for the Empire in the same irresponsible manner in which the Senegalese tribes were forced by their chiefs to fight for France.

While the press reflected the opposition of the great majority of French Canadians to the conscription measure, the course of the debates had shown that there was no possibility that the bill would not become the law of the land. When the population realized this fact and the more important fact that the Military Service Act would be enforced throughout the Dominion, there was a flare-up of violent opposition in Quebec that boded ill for the peace of the province. Night after night, in July and August, anti-conscription meetings were held in Montreal that outdid anything that had previously been seen in French Canada in the course of the war. Young hotheads addressed the meetings and did not shrink from counseling their hearers to seek redress from the hated conscription measure by armed resistance.[69] Crowds numbering two and three thousand marched through the Montreal streets, breaking windows, shouting "Down with Borden" and "Long live the Revolution," and occasionally even shooting off blank cartridges.[70] One of the leaders, a certain Elie Lalumière, boasted that he was actively drilling five hundred men for resistance to conscription.[71]

[68] *Devoir*, July 26, 1917.
[69] *Gazette*, August 28, 1917.
[70] *Gazette*, August 29, 1917.
[71] *Ibid.*, July 21, 1917.

The Conscription Conflict of 1917

The disturbances reached a climax on the nights of August 29 and 30. After a crowd of some seven thousand persons had been urged to clean up their old guns and a collection had been taken for the purchase of arms, private soldiers, allegedly from the 22d French Canadians, had told of the hardships at the front and urged the young men not to enlist. Then the police attempted to break up the meeting. As a result one man was shot and four policemen were hurt.[72] There can be little doubt that although these riots were immediately caused by the passionate tension of the period the more underlying cause was the campaign of violent opposition to conscription mingled with incitements to violence, which had been going on in the province of Quebec ever since the first official announcement of the Military Service Bill.

That the Nationalists did not feel wholly unresponsible for the outbreaks was shown by a much-publicized article on "Sterile Violence" signed by Bourassa himself in the *Devoir,* on August 11. He argued that from the beginning his newspaper had pointed out the danger of any provocation to violence. Nevertheless the demagogues had undertaken the criminal, but sterile, task of serving the people night after night with the heady wine of hatred, vengeance, and blind anger. Instead of removing the menace of conscription, the agitators were only hastening its coming and providing deadly weapons for the hands of the enemies of French Canada. Indeed, to advise violent resistance in the name of the French Canadian people was to strengthen those who desired conscription in order to punish "the damned Frenchmen." Bourassa, in searching for the way out for the honest opponents of conscription, believed that once the law was passed every effort should be made to secure the election of the greatest possible number of anti-conscription candidates pledged to work for the repeal of the law. Meanwhile he firmly deprecated any talk of passive resistance. At the first sign of violence martial law would

[72] *Ibid.,* August 30, 31, 1917.

be proclaimed, and a number of acts usually lightly punished might involve heavy sentence. Bourassa was emphatic that any act of violence was in itself illegitimate and inexcusable.

The riotous disturbances of August 29-30 coincided with the discovery of a plot to blow up the residence of a prominent Anglo-Canadian magnate, Lord Atholstane. That Bourassa's fears were not groundless the immediate arrest of the agitator, Lalumière, went far to prove. This unfortunate incident further discredited Quebec in the eyes of English-speaking Canada, for it was felt that the province was sympathetic with those who in the last weeks had been openly preaching rebellion and resistance.

As a matter of fact, the situation in French Canada was far otherwise. Bourassa had spoken for a large group of his compatriots when he counseled against violence; and his counsel was quickly echoed by his colleagues of the French Canadian press. Especially the rural press seemed appalled at the outbursts of violence in Montreal. The Montmagny *Peuple,* on September 6, pointed out that the streets were distinctly not the place to fight; and the *Etoile du nord* said on August 16 that resistance to what was now the law was not only useless but dangerous, adding a week later that passive resistance was bad enough but that any active resistance would lead French Canadians straight to the abyss. After the bill had become law the *Etoile du nord* said that French Canadians must submit bravely to the ordeal. They should never miss an opportunity to drive those who were responsible out of power, but they should attempt no resistance beyond what was strictly legal.[73]

[73] *Etoile du nord,* August 30, 1917.

VIII

The 1917 Election and the Isolation of Quebec

"*Soyons nous-mêmes*"

WHILE Canada was convulsed by the bitter debates on the Military Service Bill, which was designed to provide reinforcements for the hard-pressed troops at the front, the Canadian Expeditionary Force had gone quietly about its business of holding the line in France and Flanders. At the beginning of 1917 there were 240,000 men overseas under the direct control of the newly-created Ministry of Overseas Forces.[1] There were now four divisions at the front, besides many soldiers in special services, such as the Forestry Corps, Railway troops, and the Medical Corps. In April, 1917, the Canadian troops, by means of thorough organization and excellent artillery co-operation, had performed the brilliant exploit of taking Vimy Ridge. The capture of Vimy had marked a considerable advance for the Allied lines; and the Canadians had taken many prisoners and guns, though their own casualties had been heavy, due probably to the extraordinary dash with which Canadian troops were used to advance. In August Sir Arthur Currie, a distinguished native of the Dominion, took over the command of the Canadian Corps. Later in the year the Canadians won another victory in the Paaschendaele-Ypres salient, but the loss of more than 16,000 men in the winning of part of a ridge which had to be abandoned a few months later was appalling indeed.[2] In the Paaschendaele-Ypres action the Canadians completed, after the British and Australians had spent themselves, one of the most expensive sustained attacks

[1] Sir Charles Lucas, *The Empire at War*, II, 153-206.
[2] *Ibid.*, p. 193.

of the war. The whole battle was intended to offset the Russian defection, but its final result was only to render the troops extremely dispirited. The year 1917, in which the Canadian troops, not the least among them the 22d French Canadians, had covered themselves with glory, had been also a year of heavy casualties; and the losses incurred in the course of the bitter fighting called urgently for reinforcements from home.

The insistent demand of the opposition in Parliament and in the press for a popular consultation on the conscription issue made a general election well-nigh inevitable. The Prime Minister made one more attempt in the course of the conscription debates to stave off an election and to bring about a coalition, but Laurier and the Liberals remained adamant. In proposing that Parliament agree to the prolongation of its own life for another year Sir Robert Borden insisted that it was only a temporary suspension of one feature of the constitution which he was sponsoring in order to avoid party strife in war time.[3] In reply Laurier said that in spite of the disunity prevailing in the country the only wise thing to do was to appeal to the people for their judgment.[4] For the Liberals to agree not to have a popular consultation would be an abdication of responsible government, the denial of democracy, and of the rights of a free people. The motion for a prolongation of Parliament for another year was passed, but the Prime Minister announced that he would not carry it out, since it would be useless without unanimous approval. It was obvious that there was nothing left for both sides except an appeal to the country by means of a general election, which was set for December, 1917.

While the country was in the throes of the electoral struggle the Military Service Act was put into force. On October 13, 1917, the first conscripts were summoned by royal proclamation to report in January, 1918. From the beginning, it was obvious that the number of exemptions asked for was very large in proportion

[3] Hansard, *Commons*, 1917, p. 3434.   [4] *Ibid., Sir Wilfrid Laurier*, p. 3484.

The 1917 Election

to those who were willing to accept service without further question. It was striking that the number of exemptions demanded was almost as large in Ontario as in Quebec. From the beginning there was some dissatisfaction with the workings of the act and more especially with the administration of exemptions. As early as November the *Presse* was defending its compatriots against the charge made in Ontario that the local boards in Quebec were exempting men in a wholesale manner, and it added that exemption claims were numerous throughout the Dominion.[5] As a matter of fact, there could be no doubt that the great power given to local boards in the matter of exemptions constituted a weakness in the act. But that Quebec was not wholeheartedly supporting further active participation was made plain in a *Presse* article which pointed out that if a large number of exemptions were granted in Quebec it was because the sending of too many men to the front could only result in interference with Canada's economic war effort. It was only too clear from the very beginning that the enforcement of the Military Service Act in Quebec would encounter great difficulties if it could be carried out at all. It should be remembered that conscription came into force after voluntary enlistment had failed and after the demands on agriculture caused by war needs had increased. In terms of population the drain had already been immense. Of the few that were available practically all were disinclined to go, and in the circumstances the farmers especially had a good excuse.

After the passage of the Military Service Bill the main business of the parliamentary session was at an end, though it was September before the Houses were able to adjourn, and the country prepared for the coming electoral campaign. In the closing months of the session the government had succeeded, in spite of the bitterest Liberal opposition, in passing the War Time Election Bill, by which women relatives of members of the Canadian Ex-

[5] *Presse*, November 23, 27, 1917.

peditionary Forces and women engaged in war industry were enfranchised.[6] Furthermore, those naturalized Canadians who had been born in enemy countries or were born before 1902 in countries where their native tongue was German were disenfranchised. There can be little doubt that the War Time Election Act created a special class of electors who might naturally be expected to vote for the government which had enfranchised them. The Liberals were especially resentful of the disenfranchisement of the enemy-alien voters, who, living largely in the western provinces, had been accustomed to vote Liberal. The opposition was also stirred up to resentment by the Military Voters Bill which set up machinery for counting the votes of soldiers. Soldiers were to be given on their ballots the choice of simply voting for or against the government, not for individual candidates. The Liberals claimed with considerable reason that the soldiers who were being paid and maintained by the government were most likely to vote for it, especially in view of the impersonal nature of the ballot.

The cleavage shown in the Liberal ranks by the debate over the Military Service Bill and later passage of the War Time Election bill brought to a head the simmering dissatisfaction of many Liberals with Laurier's leadership.[7] There was a growing body of Liberals, especially in Ontario, who believed that conscription was necessary and that only Laurier and the French Canadians stood against its adoption and enforcement. The leadership of the dissident Liberals was in the hands of a former minister under Laurier, Sir Clifford Sifton, of Manitoba. Throughout July many meetings were held in an attempt to bring the Liberals into line with a project for the abandonment of Laurier and a swing toward a Union government to be composed of Conservatives and anti-Laurier Liberals. But the movement was slow in gaining momentum, and there were not as many well-known Liberals

[6] Lucas, *op. cit.*, II, 48.
[7] Skelton, *Life and Letters of Sir Wilfrid Laurier*, II, 522-30.

who were ready to desert Laurier as had been believed. Nevertheless, Sir Clifford Sifton called a meeting of western Liberals, in Winnipeg, in August. A thousand delegates attended the Winnipeg convention and listened to Sifton's plan for an endorsement of conscription, the renunciation of the Laurier leadership, and the support of a Union government under a Liberal or neutral prime minister. Although there was much support for Sifton's scheme, especially in Manitoba, and although the West strongly favored conscription, the majority of the convention was unwilling to abandon the Laurier leadership; and as a result the agitation petered out, and the convention adjourned after having voted confidence in Laurier. The passage of the War Time Election Bill made it obvious, however, that the Liberals, deprived of much of their western support, would be very hard pressed, and many who had hesitated to agree with Sifton now hastened to rally to the support of a Union government to be organized not on their own terms but on those of Sir Robert Borden. There were still some Liberals who were unwilling to go to the Conservative camp, and in October an attempt was made to get Laurier to resign the leadership in favor of a conscriptionist English-speaking leader. Sir Wilfrid Laurier was willing to accede to the request, but the indignation of many of his followers decided him finally to retain the leadership.

Meanwhile, on October 12, Sir Robert Borden announced the formation of a Union government, which, under his own leadership, contained thirteen Conservatives and ten Liberals, including several who had served in the Laurier cabinet in the past. An attempt was made to secure the entrance of prominent French Canadians into the cabinet, but feeling in Quebec was much too strong against the government, and as a result the only French Canadians who would serve in the cabinet were Blondin and Sevigny, whose influence in Quebec had never been less. Those English-speaking Canadians, whether they were Liberals or Conservatives, who believed in the successful prosecution of the war at any cost naturally ranged themselves on the side of the government. Quite as naturally the overwhelming majority of French Canadians who were opposed to any compulsion to serve in the armed forces rallied behind Laurier. What Lord Durham's scheme for dominating the French Canadians had not been able to achieve, the passions of the war years had brought about. For the first time since French Canadians had been politically conscious, Quebec stood entirely isolated. Many of the soberer spirits among the French Canadians were appalled at this state of affairs, while the more daring tried to feel that there was a certain grandeur and rightness to a situation in which Quebec stood firm and alone on the rock of her principles.

With the exception of the Quebec *Evénement* and to a limited degree the Montreal *Patrie* the Quebec press reflected French Canada's almost unanimous opposition to conscription. The *Presse* gave unstinted support to the Liberal cause throughout the campaign and constantly reiterated that Laurier's ideas faithfully reflected those of the great mass of Canadians.[8] The menace of Quebec's isolation alarmed the *Presse,* and it did not hesitate to disclaim the accusations of disloyalty made against the province.[9] In its opinion French Canadians merely happened to differ on conscription with their fellow citizens of English speech, but the idea that because of that difference they were not interested in the cause of the Allies was entirely false. The loyalty to the person of Laurier was intense among French Canadians, and the *Presse,* on November 17, voiced this feeling in referring to Laurier, abandoned by his lieutenants of English speech and by the majority of Anglo-Canadian newspapers, as still remaining for thousands of Canadians, the knight *au panache blanc.* On the eve of the elections, the *Presse* commented on the striking unity of all French Canadians, moved by the same ideas and under the stress of the

[8] *Presse,* November 7, 1917. [9] *Ibid.,* October 25, 1917.

same necessity and added that absolutely no difference in principle now divided the Quebec Conservative from the Liberal,[10] for a united Quebec faced the rest of Canada.

The Liberal *Canada* abounded in the most vehement appeals to partisanship throughout the election period and spoke often of its belief that there was a conspiracy on foot to isolate and descredit Quebec.[11] The *Action catholique* appealed for calm but did not hesitate to state its unmitigated opposition to conscription and its conviction that the government was stirring up all English-speaking Canada against Quebec as a means of winning the election.[12]

It was only natural that the *Devoir* should lend its strength to the anti-government electoral campaign, but for some time there were doubts whether the Nationalist organ would support Laurier and the Liberals, whom they had long been accusing of being almost as anxious to bankrupt Canada to save the Empire as were the Conservatives. Early in November Bourassa made his position clear.[13] He appealed to all good Nationalists to join Laurier and the Liberals in their effort to defeat the Union government which in Bourassa's opinion represented the worst elements of both parties. The Liberal program was to be accepted in so far as it approached Nationalist policies and rejected where it differed from them. The Liberal scheme of a popular referendum was approved, but Bourassa stated that Laurier was very vague about what was to be done if conscription were disapproved of by the electors and asserted that essentially the Liberals were as anxious to continue the war effort as their opponents. Nevertheless, the Nationalists were advised that it would be worse than useless in the existing circumstances to take a separate stand. Of the two possibilities presented by the policies of the Liberals and Conserva-

[10] *Presse*, December 15, 1917.
[11] *Canada*, December 20, 1917.
[12] *Action catholique*, December 1, 3, 1917.
[13] *Devoir*, November 8, 9, 10, 12, 1917.

tives, support of Laurier was much the lesser evil. Unity with the Liberals would enable the opponents of government to defeat a large number of ministerial candidates. Nationalists, however, should exact promises from their Liberal allies not only that conscription would be repealed but also that any further active war effort should cease immediately. The result of the election clearly showed that the Nationalist sympathizers followed Bourassa's advice and threw the whole weight of their vote to the Liberal side.

The rural press further demonstrated the practically unanimous feeling of the province on the election issue. The *Avenir du nord,* of St. Jerome, said plainly that a vote for Borden meant that the hated conscription law would be enforced to the utmost, while a vote for Laurier meant that the law would be immediately suspended and submitted to the people for its verdict.[14] The *Courrier de St. Hyacinthe,* hitherto a Conservative paper, had been purchased by a Liberal in the course of 1917, and as a result was vehement in its demand that Canada, while remaining a part of the Empire, should first of all consult its own interests. Laurier was hailed as the people's champion, and the dangers of isolation were minimized.[15] *Le Bien public,* of Three Rivers, insisted that Quebec was a solid unit for the referendum simply because it desired the conservation of Canada's resources in men and money for Canadian uses.[16] A striking evidence of the unanimity of feeling in French Canada was the change of the Montmagny *Peuple* from its Conservative allegiance to wholehearted disapproval of the government on the issue of conscription. The *Peuple* announced that it had always been a Conservative organ, but that the Borden government had deserted the sane political principles of Macdonald and Cartier and hence was no longer worthy of support. Canadian participation, the *Peuple* asserted, was still jus-

[14] *Avenir du nord,* November 16, 1917.
[15] *Courrier de St. Hyacinthe,* November 17, 24; December 29, 1917.
[16] *Bien public,* December 20, 1917.

The 1917 Election

tifiable, but the best interests of Canada must be taken into consideration first.[17]

If the feeling of deep resentment and insult that the province of Quebec felt during the 1917 election is to be understood, the sentiments so clearly expressed throughout English-speaking Canada must be taken into consideration. The more partisan newspapers, especially in Ontario, but also in the West, abounded in the most violent attacks on Quebec and all she stood for. The Toronto *Mail and Empire* asked, on December 3, whether Laurier was for a German peace, and a week later an article announced that Laurierism was undoubtedly pleasing to the Kaiser. On December 11 the *Mail and Empire* carried a full-page election advertisement stating that a united Quebec wished to rule all Canada. Quebec's purposes were said to be: withdrawal from the war; the establishment of bilingual schools in every province; the weakening of the ties of British connection; and the political control of the Dominion. On election day, December 17, the *Mail and Empire* told its readers that a vote for a Laurier candidate was a vote for Bourassa and against the Canadian army at the front; it was a vote against the British connection and the Empire and a vote for Germany, the Kaiser, Hindenburg, von Tirpitz, and the German officer who sank the *Lusitania*. The man who had a son overseas was told that a vote for Laurier meant that he was ready to betray that son, for Laurier was the hope of Quebec, a menace to Canada, and totally satisfactory to the Kaiser.

Surely racial hysteria had seldom reached a higher pitch. The usual moderation and studied dignity of the *Mail and Empire* made this extravagance most amazing by contrast. The Toronto *Daily News,* on December 14, printed a map of Canada with Quebec outlined in black under the caption "The Foul Blot on Canada." Election pamphlets, freely circulated, asserted that Laurier had entirely capitulated to the desires and policies of Bourassa.

[17] *Peuple*, October 19; November 16, 1917.

The 1917 Election

Even the Manitoba *Free Press,* whose editor, J. W. Dafoe, had been a life-long Liberal, abounded in venomous attacks on Laurier and his followers. On December 4 the *Free Press* stated that Quebec had failed Canada and that this truth was very bitter to a Canada which had never failed Quebec. On December 7 the voters were told by the *Free Press* that the choice before them was for union and the war or for Laurier and disunion. Four days later the *Free Press* asserted that Quebec would neither fight nor pay. Even after the election the *Free Press* asserted that the issue had been whether Quebec should rule the country and whether for the remainder of the war the Canadian contribution should be conditioned by the approval of Bourassa or made in keeping with the desires of those elements of the Canadian people who had made the necessary sacrifices for the Allied cause.[18]

Given the intensity of feeling in Quebec, it was small wonder that the election campaign was fought in that province amidst scenes of unprecedented violence. Speakers for the Union government were universally howled down, rotten eggs and even more dangerous missiles were freely hurled at Unionist speakers, and officers in the king's uniform were refused a hearing. It was obvious from the beginning that Quebec would vote solidly against the government.

When the results were counted it was seen that for the first time in the annals of the province Quebec had returned a practically solid delegation to the federal House of Commons. Sixty-two of the sixty-five seats were captured by the anti-government forces in Quebec, and the Liberal majority amounted to 167,353, as compared with 44,461 in 1911.[19] The result in the rest of the Dominion was a triumphant return of the Union government. Ontario returned only eight out-and-out Liberals, twelve Union-Liberals, and sixty-two Conservatives. In the West, which was strongly for

[18] Manitoba *Free Press,* December 26, 1917.
[19] *Canadian Annual Review,* 1917, p. 643.

conscription, only two straight Liberals of fifty-five candidates were returned. The government majority in the country was seventy-one.[20] The soldiers' vote went ten to one for the government, and it was publicly stated by French Canadian officers that their men voted to uphold the government. The government obtained a popular majority of more than 300,000 and with it an undoubted mandate for the enforcement of the Military Service Act and the active prosecution of the war.

French Canada woke on the morning after the election to a realization that the isolation of Quebec was no longer a bogey but an accomplished fact. A solid Quebec delegation had been returned to the federal Parliament, but it was easy to see that faced with the stern and triumphant English-speaking majority there was little that Quebec's representatives could do to stop the policy of active Canadian participation which had been vindicated at the polls. The English-speaking press, for its part, did not mince words in making Quebec's position clear. The Manitoba *Free Press*, on December 26, stated that Quebec now knew that she was isolated and that the only reason for racial cleavage lay in Quebec's refusal to walk beside the rest of Canada along the road of national duty and sacrifice. The only help for Quebec was to join heartily in the prosecution of the war.

The French Canadian press realized the seriousness of the situation of their native province. Immediately after the election results were known the *Presse*, on December 18, told its compatriots that the different Canadian provinces should no longer live in a state of discord but should resume the task of building up Canadian national union.

The announcement by Mr. Francoeur, a member of the provincial legislature, that he would propose a motion at the 1918 session that Quebec should secede from the confederation focused public attention on the subject of Quebec's isolation and the solutions to

[20] Skelton, *op. cit.*, II, 541.

be sought. That even those who were accustomed to consider French Canadian problems with a certain amount of moderation and tolerance were stirred was shown in the editorial in the *Presse* of December 24. Asserting its firm belief that Quebec did not wish to secede, it added that if the English-speaking provinces considered that Quebec was interfering with their liberty of action, it might be wiser to terminate an alliance which no longer was based on the principles upon which it had originally been founded. In spite of all that had happened the *Presse* reiterated Quebec's unalterable loyalty to Britain and her desire to remain under the British flag whatever happened. The *Patrie*, which had with some difficulty managed to support the government in the election campaign, expressed, immediately after the victory of the Unionists, a hope for racial conciliation and refused to take seriously the Francoeur secession resolution.[21] The organ of the Liberals, *Canada*, on December 24 urged its compatriots to remain calm at all costs and not to be carried away either by Anglo-Canadian jingoes or by French Canadian extremists. The *Action catholique* reflected the divided feelings of the French Canadians. At heart they were opposed to any such radical solution as the secession of Quebec, but they did feel it necessary to air what they considered their just grievances. On December 27 the *Action catholique* said that it was very clear that Quebec could not decently stay in the Confederation if the sister provinces no longer considered her presence desirable. Nevertheless, the journal was firm in its opinion that the idea of actual secession should not be seriously entertained and that it would have been wiser if it had not been suggested. The organ of the hierarchy was convinced that Quebec's isolation was nothing of which to be afraid. The elections had united French Canadians as never before,[22] and this very unity should now prove to the rest of Canada that French Canadians not only opposed the

---

[21] *Patrie*, December 18, 22, 1917.
[22] *Action catholique*, December 27, 29, 31, 1917.

The 1917 Election

Military Service Act but also believed that Canadian military effort should no longer continue on the same scale as heretofore. Summing up the French Canadian position, the *Action catholique* told its readers that the isolation of Quebec made her position impregnably strong, but that the secession motion was decidedly inopportune and would only provide further means for a persecution of Canada from the extremist Anglo-Canadians.

As far as the Nationalists were concerned the threatened isolation of Quebec in no way frightened them. Bourassa told his compatriots not to be alarmed by the fact that Quebec stood alone.[23] The election had shown that those who had voted against the government, not only in Quebec but throughout the country, had been those who had been longest in Canada rather than newcomers who were ready for any adventure. In the existing situation, Bourassa asserted, it would be very unwise to seek conciliation with English-speaking Canada. It would be impossible in any case for the Union government, with its ultra-imperialist policies, to conciliate Quebec, and no representative French Canadian could honorably enter the cabinet or co-operate with such a body of men. French Canadians should remain aloof and strive to be the champions of right and truth and of real Canadian interests.

The rural press took its part in the discussion of Quebec's new position in the Dominion. The *Courrier de St. Hyacinthe* warned its compatriots against losing their heads because the Liberals had lost the election, while the *Etoile du nord* asserted that Quebec desired to remain a part of the Confederation only if she were wanted. If she were not, there would be no harm in seceding, for in any case Quebec remained a homeland for all French Canadians.[24] The Montmagny *Peuple* was of the opinion that the union of all French Canadians was the result rather of their fear of military service than of any united anti-English principles; and,

---

[23] *Devoir*, December 20, 22, 26, 1917.
[24] *Courrier de St. Hyacinthe*, January 5, 1918; *Etoile du nord*, December 27, 1917.

while it approved of the dignity of the Francoeur secession motion, it felt that Quebec's withdrawal from the Confederation was not to be seriously considered.[25]

The crushing defeat of the Liberals at the polls had merely brought to a head the ferment that had been brewing throughout French Canada in the course of 1917. As early as June 1 Bourassa had analyzed the racial question at some length. In his opinion it was unreasonable to expect the same attitude of mind, the same thought, and the same effort from the two Canadian races. There were, indeed, two concepts of Canadian patriotism. The Anglo-Canadian's double loyalty to Canada and to the Empire was quite different from the French Canadian's exclusive attachment to his native land. Separated from France for more than one hundred and fifty years, he had preserved a sincere affection for the old mother country. He was proud of her greatness, rejoiced in her successes, regretted her trials and her occasional errors, but in no way did he feel himself obliged to fight for France. According to Bourassa the two essential mistakes made in the treatment of French Canadians during the war were the assumption that French Canadians "loved" France and would fight for her and the attempt to get them to subscribe to the ideas of imperial solidarity current in English-speaking Canada.

The difference among French Canadians themselves on the proper status of their nationality was marked by the publication of several pamphlets in the course of 1917, all written by churchmen of some standing. The very fact that the conscription issue was disturbing the French Canadian state within a state, the Roman Catholic Church, was evidenced by the controversies between churchmen on the proper course for Canada to pursue. As early as 1915 Asselin's attacks on the hierarchy for the Pastoral Letter of 1914 had shown that even within the ranks of faithful churchmen there was division of opinion on Canadian war policy.

[25] *Peuple*, January 18, 25, 1918.

The 1917 Election 213

The controversy which with some interruption had continued thereafter between Bourassa in the columns of the *Devoir* and the *Action catholique* had kept the issue before the public. It was only natural that the passions aroused by the crisis of 1917 should add more fuel to the fire.

During the winter of 1917-18 a well-known priest, the Abbé Groulx, lectured to large audiences at Laval University, in Montreal, on the origins of Canadian Confederation.[26] Though the Abbé Groulx dealt primarily with the period of the 1860's, which preceded confederation, his evident preoccupation with the contemporary status of French Canada in the Dominion was very plain. He pointed out that in the 1860's the French Canadian leaders had believed that no material advantage nor any menace or seduction should turn the French Canadians from their task of defending the survival of the French race on this continent. Unfortunately their presentiment that Confederation might spell danger to their faith and to their very national existence had been proved only too true by 1917. The solemn promises made by Britain that the French language should be safeguarded had been too often broken, and now there was justification for the French Canadians' hesitancy to believe in British fair play. As to the religious rights guaranteed to the French Canadians in 1867, the Abbé Groulx felt that his compatriots had been too credulous in their faith that the Protestant English-speaking majorities in the other provinces would see that justice was accorded the French and Catholic minorities. The only result had been that, while the Quebec Protestants were fully protected, the Ontario Catholics had been forced to accept the *status quo* of 1867. The "Fathers of Confederation," in the Abbé's opinion, had been too insistent on provincial autonomy and had thus weakened the province's ability to intervene for the protection of minorities. The French Canadians themselves, he added, had often been too conciliatory, too

[26] Abbé L. Groulx, *La Confédération canadienne*.

moderate in their demands, too silent in the face of wrongs done them, and their present state was that of an impotent minority. The only results of confederation had been the vast increase of parliamentary corruption and the loss of the original ideal of a state based on civil and religious liberty and race equality. The difficulties with the minority problem had been greater than were originally anticipated; and the Canadian national soul, torn by racial conflict and menaced by a cosmopolitan European immigration, was now nonexistent. In conclusion the Abbé Groulx called on French Canadians to awaken and to be conscious of their race in order that they might be strong enough to help all their scattered brothers throughout the Dominion. French Canadian leaders were exhorted not to sacrifice their people for the dream of an unattainable racial unity and above all not to compromise the future by too favorable an attitude toward imperialism. The Abbé, in guarded language, was evidently concerned with telling his French Canadian fellow countrymen that they should insist upon their rights and not submit to coercion in any form, of which obviously the Military Service Act was the best known to his audience.

In the summer of 1917 an article on the doctrinal aspects of Canadian participation in the war was published over the signature of "Louis Romain" in the ecclesiastical weekly *La Vérité*, of Quebec. The author's interpretation of the hierarchy's attitude on Canadian participation attracted considerable attention. He asserted that as no distinct "contract" existed between Canada and Britain, the mother country could not legally require Canadian aid in time of war, and that, although the subject owed obedience to the sovereign, the involvement of a self-governing Dominion in all imperial wars was contrary to natural law. As a result and because kindness and charity alone required Canada to come to Britain's help, the idea that the bishops' Pastoral of 1914 had made Canadian participation an absolute obligation was based on a false premise. "Louis Romain" asserted that, in saying that Britain counted on Canada as of right, the bishops had meant, not that active participation was a duty or obligation but that it should be based on charity and mutual understanding. For in freely lending aid to the mother country Canada would be serving the common cause of the Allies and her own national interests at the same time. It would be absurd to pretend that the bishops were more interested in the welfare of Britain than in that of Canada or that Canadian citizens' duty to Britain in any way equaled the duty they owed to their own country.[27]

It is possible that in permitting the publication of "Louis Romain's" article the hierarchy were making him their unofficial spokesman. There was no doubt of the real discontent in Quebec and even within the Church itself with the official pro-war attitude of the Church. By the summer of 1917 this discontent was being rather openly noised abroad. Some among those prelates who had signed the Pastoral may have agreed with the majority of their countrymen that Canadian participation had gone too far and that conscription was to be opposed at all costs. Certainly churchmen such as Mgr. Bruchesi deeply resented the government's *volte face* on the conscription issue, and they may have felt that they had been tricked into persuading their flock that National Service would never lead to compulsory military service. It is conceivable that the hierarchy, worried at the disunion within the Church, might have officially maintained their attitude of strict approbation for Canada's war effort, while using unofficial spokesmen such as "Louis Romain" to spread the idea among the faithful that they were not and never had been adherents to the idea of automatic and unlimited Canadian participation.

[27] "Louis Romain," *La Participation du Canada à la guerre*, published in *Les Cloches de St. Boniface*, Manitoba, August 15, 1917, as reprint from *La Vérité*, of Quebec, July 7, 1917. The identity of the writer was hidden under the pseudonym "Louis Romain." From internal evidence it has been thought in well-informed quarters that it represented the opinion of a prominent ecclesiastic, Mgr. Paquet, Rector of Laval University, known for his distinctly ultramontane, hence "Roman," views.

The long and somewhat dialectical pamphlet *Halte-là, "Patriote,"* published at Rimouski by a certain "Jean Vindex," was avowedly a reply to the arguments for active Canadian participation contained in the pamphlet attributed to the Abbé D'Amours which had attracted so much attention the year before.[28] "Jean Vindex's" pamphlet dealt boldly with the division of opinion between the upper clergy of the cities and the lower clergy of the back parishes of Quebec on Canadian participation.[29] "Jean Vindex" asserted from the beginning of his argument that the time had come to combat the new imperialist school of thought which would willingly bankrupt Canada for the sake of the Empire and to which he believed the hierarchy now belonged. The pamphlet, which used the form of Socratic dialogue at considerable length, was of the firm opinion that while obedience to the authority constituted by God was naturally right, statutory law could exceed the limits of sovereign power when it commanded the citizens to perform any acts that were in contravention of the principles of natural right or which did not conform to the fundamental law of the land. The subject had an obligation to obey his sovereign only in so far as the latter was not exceeding his own rights. As a result of this theory "Jean Vindex" argued that there existed no extra-constitutional rights which the subject must obey and that it was erroneous to adduce such rights in justification of the idea of automatic Canadian participation in all British wars. Furthermore, there was no natural right or moral duty which obliged Canada to take part in imperial wars, and in consequence, Canadians might not be called on for military service merely because they were British subjects. Theoretically Britain could im-

[28] *Halte-là, "Patriote," que penser de notre école politico-théologique, de l'impérialisme qu'elle professe, du nationalisme qu'elle censure,* Rimouski, 1917.

[29] It has been stated in well-informed quarters that "Jean Vindex" was a certain Jesuit, Père Hermas Lalande. As the Abbé D'Amours had been trained in the Jesuit schools, the quarrel took on an added piquancy.

pose a conscription act on Canada, but actually this was impossible because it was inconsistent with the Canadian constitution.

"Jean Vindex" asserted that the doctrines of what he termed the "New School of Imperialists" were full of contradictions and bad logic. In his opinion the statement that when England was at war Canada was automatically at war also was true only in a passive sense. The dominions could not remain passively neutral in time of war, for they might be attacked; but they could be actively neutral by not participating except to defend their own territory. While denying repeatedly that either natural rights, theology, or the Constitution itself made Canadian participation a matter of strict duty, "Jean Vindex" agreed with "Louis Romain" that it was merely a matter of charity and convenience for Canada to help the mother country, even though, he added, not everyone believed that the Empire and the supremacy of England were indispensable to the existence of civilization. Besides replying to the hierarchy's theory of the duty of Canadian participation "Jean Vindex" eloquently defended the Nationalists from the charge of having advocated such dangerous and revolutionary ideas as national egoism and the principle of nationality. He differentiated between the egoism of Bourassa, who insisted that the government should place Canadian interests above all other interests, and the egoism of the Abbé D'Amours, who in his eagerness to conciliate the British authorities had gone to Rome and been instrumental in persuading the Pope to issue his famous encyclical of 1916 calling for moderation and toleration on the bilingual question. The members of the "New School of Imperialists" were accused by "Jean Vindex" of desiring to put Canada entirely at the disposal of the mother country and at the same time to forbid her any voice in the conduct of the war. They had entirely forgotten the fundamental duty of all Canadians, which was to put Canada and Canadian interests first.

In conclusion "Jean Vindex" boldly accused the "New School," with D'Amours at their head, of having dared to misrepresent the attitude of the hierarchy and of having twisted the meaning of the Pastoral Letter to suit their own theories. He exonerated the bishops from the errors and exaggerations which had resulted from the Pastoral and added that certain bishops who signed the Pastoral had since intimated that they never intended that it should rank as doctrinal teaching or disciplinary direction. According to "Jean Vindex" it was D'Amours and his followers who made it seem as if there were an implicit direction to the faithful to aid the cause of Canadian participation. For years many Catholics had kept silent out of respect for their bishops, but in the opinion of "Jean Vindex," the time had come to unmask the "New School" which was covering itself shamelessly with the mantle of the hierarchy in order the better to pursue its object of changing Canadian policies into automatic and complete subjection to the will of the British imperialists. The people must be informed of what was going on lest they come to believe that any solidarity existed between men like D'Amours and the rest of the clergy of Quebec.

The "Jean Vindex" pamphlet was an indication of the strength of the anti-war feeling in the heart of the province of Quebec by the summer of 1917. By that time the lower clergy were ready to declare open warfare on any policy which called for more than lip service to the cause of Canadian war participation, even if their spiritual pastors and masters demanded it of them. There could be no doubt that Bourassa had the great mass of the lower clergy back of him in his anti-British campaign and that the conscription bill, coupled with the unfortunate refusal to exempt divinity students, had put the seal on their hatred of the government. No effort at race conciliation, let alone any attempt to secure enlistments, would receive the support of the French Canadian clergy. It should not be forgotten that the clergy, while constituting a sort of intellectual élite, is socially of one class with the habitant and understands his prejudices and his enthusiasms. It stands to reason, therefore, that in moments of racial conflict and strife the country curé is the true spokesman of the French Canadian people; while city priests and the city prelates, who have had opportunity to travel and mix with men of both races, are bound to be more conciliatory and hence less representative of the masses. The fact that the lower clergy, who were accustomed to the iron-clad discipline of the Church, dared to oppose the stated opinion of their spiritual superiors in a matter in which, after all, the bishops had only expressed the centuries-old tradition of loyalty to Britain, was a revelation of the depth of the French Canadian's aversion to any participation in foreign war or to any interference with his peculiar sense of "nationality."

As 1917 drew to a close the situation of Quebec looked dark indeed. Wearied by the long and bitter struggle against conscription, which in spite of all her efforts had been in vain, she stood isolated in thought and sympathy from her sister provinces. The feelings of bitter resentment at the treatment accorded her, which she held to be contrary to the most elementary justice, were deep within the souls of most of her sons. The Prime Minister of Quebec, Sir Lomer Gouin, summed up the feelings of his countrymen when he said that, while they realized that people were trying to isolate Quebec, this was their own country and they could not help resenting such an attitude. Here they intended to live as the equals of their fellow citizens of other origins. They did not menace others, but they demanded nothing more nor less than justice.[30]

Would the new year bring Quebec's secession from the Confederation, or would the rest of the Dominion allow her to remain entirely aloof from Canada's war effort at a time when the needs of Britain and of the Allies had never been greater? This was the anxious question that many patriotic French Canadians asked

[30] *Presse*, November 14, 1917.

themselves as 1917 closed and the new year opened to the promise of the debate on the Francoeur motion for secession.

The platonic nature of the debates in the provincial Parliament showed that there was no danger that a sulky smoldering Quebec might flame up into rebellion as some English-speaking Canadians feared. Even the Quebec riots of three months later were more in the nature of a demonstration against the hated Military Service Act than an attempt at armed resistance. When the debates in the Parliament of Quebec had been finished and the motion for secession had been withdrawn by the proposer himself, a great wave of relief swept over Quebec that in spite of all that had happened she need not withdraw from that union of all the provinces of Canada to which she was more attached than she had known. Once again faced with the possibility of active nationalist "direct action," order-loving, obedient French Canada had drawn back content with having asserted its passionate devotion to its sense of nationality.

The essence of the Francoeur debate was the attempt to ascertain where the idea of secession had originated, what would be its eventual results for Quebec, and a firm insistence that no one really believed that French Canada seriously wished to consider leaving the Confederation.[31] In introducing his motion Mr. Francoeur stated that it was the direct result of the campaign directed against Quebec and of the general election just concluded. The proposer admitted that the campaign against Quebec had been due to the slowness of recruiting among French Canadians, but he added that nothing could justify the depths of insult to which the enemies of Quebec had descended. The real crime of Quebec, he believed, lay rather in the fact that the French province had a

[31] *Quebec and Confederation; a record of the debates of the Legislative Assembly of Quebec on the resolution proposed by J. N. Francoeur, 1918.* The Francoeur resolution read as follows: "That this House is of the opinion that the province of Quebec would be disposed to accept the breaking of the Confederation Pact of 1867 if in the other provinces it is believed that she is an obstacle to the union, progress and development of Canada."

different interpretation of the constitution from that of the other provinces of Canada. Confederation had been a compromise, and the Fathers had hoped that the grant of provincial autonomy would make racial conflict and racial oppression an impossibility. Quebec had always gone to the limits of conciliation, but it was different with English-speaking Canada, which was not content with Quebec's ideal of "live and let live." As a result, the position of Quebec in the Confederation had become untenable, and it would be wise to consider withdrawing from a pact which was no longer of any value.[32]

The majority of the speakers in this momentous debate stressed the feeling then prevalent in Quebec that the insults, the calumnies, and the injustices heaped upon their native province were responsible for the birth of the idea of secession. Many spoke of the fact that the violations of the Canadian constitution contained in such measures as the Military Service Act and the War Time Election Act caused many serious-minded men to doubt that Quebec could with honor remain where her every interest was not only unconsidered but also actually flouted. Others blamed their fellow citizens of English blood for having substituted a blind devotion to the interests of the Empire for a genuine Canadian patriotism.[33] Some of the more nationalistically minded members stressed this growing subservience of the Canadian government to the interests of the Empire rather than to those of their own country and even occasionally hinted that independence should be the goal of Canada.[34] Those who were opposed to nationalism blamed the school of Bourassa for the isolation in which Quebec now found herself.[35] They argued that the Nationalists had perverted the spirit of a large part of the population until they no longer thought of Canada but only of their province. The great dream of Cartier and the Fathers of Confederation of

[32] *Quebec and Confederation*, Mr. Francoeur.
[33] *Ibid.*, Mr. A. David.
[34] *Ibid.*
[35] *Ibid.*, Mr. Cannon.

founding a united bilingual nation had degenerated so that the Byzantine discussions of Bourassa were more important to French Canadians than the fact that Germany, the enemy of civilization, threatened her very existence. When England and France, united at last, called on Canada for assistance, the Nationalists could do nothing better than poison French Canadian opinion with their agitation against the cause of the Allies.[36]

There was noticeable a certain dignity in the reaction of the provincial legislators toward the isolation of Quebec. There was a feeling among them that there was something rather admirable in this nationality of theirs, animated by a great idea and endowed with an ardent desire to preserve the traditions of the past.[37] They were all united in the belief that they were being faithful to their inmost loyalty, their *engeres Vaterland,* their own Quebec. With passionate eloquence the orators evoked the picture of their devotion to their native land, where their forefathers had lived for three hundred years, where their own children had been born, the only country to which they owed allegiance and on which all their hopes, their ideals, and their ambitions were concentrated.[38] Furthermore, they were being true to their mystical faith in her destiny and to their dream of the civilizing rôle she was destined to play on the North American continent. They refused to believe that an all-wise providence which had brought French civilization to the shores of the St. Lawrence would allow it to perish.[39] Somehow a way could be found to preserve the fundamental rights of the French Canadians, their language, and their customs.[40] Although a few of the speakers in the Francoeur debate obviously felt that the resolution was opportune and that if English-speaking Canada felt that Quebec was a hindrance to the Dominion it would be wiser to separate, there could be no doubt that the great majority of the provincial delegates were opposed to

[36] *Ibid.,* Mr. Cannon.
[37] *Ibid.,* Mr. David.
[38] *Ibid.*
[39] *Ibid.,* Mr. David.
[40] *Ibid.,* Mr. Cannon.

any form of secession. It seemed preferable to them to be governed by a constitution whose defects they knew than to accept a new political system which might bring even greater evils in its train.[41]

The great ideal of the Fathers for a nation made up of different races which should work together for the common welfare without quarreling was invoked as a motto for the existing crisis.[42] The wish to withdraw because of the criticism of English-speaking fellow citizens was scored as being unworthy of Quebec's traditions as the senior partner of confederation. In an eloquent appeal to his countrymen, Sir Lomer Gouin, the Prime Minister, summed up the opinion of the majority that even though the French Canadians were justified in their feeling of injustice and resentment, to stay in the Confederation was their inevitable choice. The experiment of the Confederation of two different races in a single state had been going on for fifty years, and it was not right to say it had failed. The early fears of the French Canadians that they would be swallowed up had proved unjustified, and there had been progress in agriculture, in industry, and in the development of natural resources undreamed of by the founders. The results of secession, both spiritual and material, could not but work untold harm to Quebec. It was true that French Canada had been subjected to calumny and insult, but in spite of it the men of Quebec should try to preserve intact their field of action and to avoid even the thought of diminishing the work which it was their mission to accomplish.[43]

At the close of the Prime Minister's speech Mr. Francoeur rose to state that he was satisfied by the discussion of his motion and withdrew it, to the undoubted relief of the majority of his fellow members and of the province as a whole.[44] The reaction of the press of French Canada to the Francoeur debates was one of min-

[41] *Ibid.*, Mr. David.
[42] *Ibid.*, Mr. Cannon.
[43] *Ibid.*, Sir Lomer Gouin.
[44] *Ibid.*, Mr. Francoeur.

gled desire to air the grievances of Quebec and relief that her secession from the Confederation was not seriously under consideration. The *Presse* was of the opinion that the debate not only would serve to express the popular sentiments of Quebec but also would do a great deal to calm the spirits of those who had become over-excited as a result of recent events.[45] The final withdrawal of the motion and the speech of Sir Lomer Gouin were hailed with pleasure by the *Presse*, which added that in urging loyalty to the pact of Confederation the Prime Minister had spoken for the whole French Canadian race.[46] Laurier's organ, the *Canada*, added that a discussion of French Canadian wrongs would serve as an excellent means of letting off steam, provided that it did not go beyond the limits of calm dignity.[47] The *Patrie*, on January 18, praised the Francoeur debate for the frank confessions of loyalty it had produced and added that there was no doubt that political passion had considerably subsided in the month that had intervened since the election. The Conservative *Evénement* argued that the Francoeur debate had been nothing more nor less than an opportunity to make fine speeches. The *Devoir* took the attitude that the motion had never seriously contemplated secession.[48] The *Action catholique*, arguing that the motion had been not only inopportune but also puerile, believed that the debate had once more proven the urgency and wisdom of Quebec's remaining in the Confederation.[49] The rural press of Quebec was as emphatic in its disapproval of any project for secession as that of the cities. The Montmagny *Peuple* refused to consider the question seriously. The *Courrier de St. Hyacinthe*, on January 5, asserted that Quebec had no right to abandon the rôle of protector for the French Canadian minorities in the other provinces.

[45] *Presse*, January 18, 1918.
[46] *Ibid.*, January 24, 1918.
[47] *Canada*, January 19, 1918.
[48] *Devoir*, December 24, 1917, January 10, 15, 1918.
[49] *Action catholique*, January 25, 1918.

With the Francoeur debate the abscess of Quebec's discontent burst. It was as if the poison of her resentment and her feeling of injury at everything which English-speaking Canada thought of her had been released through the lancing effected by the Francoeur debate. It was obvious from the very beginning that there was not and could not be any serious intention of leaving the Confederation, in which the French province had always played so important a part.

IX

From Rioting to Conciliation, 1918

IN SPITE of some alleviation, evidenced in the Francoeur debate, the first few months of 1918 continued to show much dissatisfaction in the French Canadian province. The enforcement of the Military Service Act was meeting with difficulties, not the least of which was the almost wholesale scale in which exemptions had been granted throughout the Dominion. Of the 124,965 men of Class I who had registered under the act in Ontario, 116,092 had claimed exemption.[1] In Quebec out of a total of 115,602 registrants, 113,291 wished to be exempted.[2] In English-speaking Canada there were rumors of a steady stream of deserters from Quebec who were seeking refuge in the United States.[3] Sir Robert Borden, speaking in the Commons on February 13, stated that the large number of exemptions granted in Quebec was due to the fact that claims were on a particularly large scale and that the military authorities were bound to accept the decisions of the local boards.[4]

There was an uneasy feeling in Quebec that the authorities were determined to punish the province for her opposition to the law and that they sought every means to enforce the law as harshly as possible. When deserters were rounded up in Montreal, the

[1] Report of Director of Military Service Branch on operation of Military Service Act, pp. 42 *et seq.*

[2] It is interesting that the local exemption tribunals in Ontario refused 10.1 percent of the claims, while the corresponding tribunals in Quebec refused only 4.1 percent. Of the total number of cases handled by the local tribunals, the appeal tribunals, and the central appeal judge, the percentage of exemption claims refused in Quebec was 9.0 percent, while in Ontario it was 8.2 percent. See *Report of Director of Military Service Branch on Operation of Military Service Act*, pp. 42 *et seq.*

[3] *Chronicle*, February 23, 1918.

[4] *Ibid.*, February 14, 1918.

From Rioting to Conciliation, 1918

French Canadian press pointedly demanded whether the same zeal was being shown to apprehend the slackers in Ontario.[5] Throughout Canada there was a feeling that all was not well with the administration of the Military Service Act and a certain amount of chagrin that the percentage of exemptions was so high. Only 32,000 men had been obtained under the act by the spring of 1918, in spite of the fact that in May, 1917, the Prime Minister had urged the necessity of securing immediate reinforcements for the Canadian Expeditionary Forces.[6] The police authorities in the English-speaking provinces were co-operating with the military, and likewise the agents of the Department of Justice, but there were persistent rumors that in Quebec the local police were indifferent, to say the least. There were stories that bands of armed draft resisters were roaming the backwoods of the Laurentian Mountains and that at one point in Ontario a band of French Canadians had even entrenched themselves, run up the red flag, and threatened violence to anyone who might come to arrest them.[7]

When the old capital city of Quebec broke out into bloody antidraft riots on the Easter week end of 1918, they did not come as a surprise. The disturbances started innocently enough on the evening of March 29 with the detention by the Dominion Police of a French Canadian named Mercier who was unable to produce his exemption papers.[8] When Mercier was taken home and was able to show that his papers were in order, the police released him. But a crowd of several thousand had gathered by this time, who threatened the police and actually proceeded to burn the Dominion police station on the spot. At this point the Dominion police appealed to the military authorities for assistance, but they were

[5] *Presse*, March 23, 1918.
[6] *Chronicle*, April 20, 1918, Sir Robert Borden.
[7] Hansard, *Commons*, 1918, p. 632, Mr. Ethier quoting Ottawa *Citizen*, March 11, 1918.
[8] Hansard, *Commons*, 1918, p. 396, Sir Robert Borden.

referred in turn to the civil authorities of the city. The mayor of Quebec attempted to get the crowd to disperse, but to no avail. He was urged to read the Riot Act, but was so hesitant to do so and to call in the troops that matters soon got out of hand. The crowd singing "O Canada" and the "Marseillaise" marched to the offices of the Quebec *Chronicle* and the *Evénement,* which they sacked and looted. On the following evening, March 30, again a riotous mob gathered in the town and after dark attacked the office of the Registrar of the Military Service Act, where all papers in connection with the administration of the act were kept, and burned it to the ground. The Dominion police claimed that the police of the city of Quebec had in no way furnished adequate protection to the Registrar's office and had looked on passively while the mob attacked the building. On March 30 the military authorities had asked for reinforcements, and the government, with singular ineptitude, had sent a battalion of Toronto soldiers to help quell the riots in Quebec, thus bringing the racial question with all its passion into the forefront of the whole affair.

Easter Day, March 31, was marked by one long continuous riot, culminating in bloody outbreaks in the evening. The lower town of Quebec, the home of the poorer elements of the population, was in a ferment. The fact that the troops had charged a crowd with bayonets the evening before only increased the bad feeling. On March 31 the cavalry drove back the seething crowds with axe handles that had wrist thongs attached, while the mob did its best to interfere with the soldiers. The automobiles of the military authorities had difficulty in getting through the crowd, and there were cries of "Down with the officers—they're false as Judas." [9] By nightfall the situation had a decidedly ugly look. The civil and religious authorities were so alarmed that Cardinal Begin published an admonition to the population to refrain from violence saying that the Christian conscience disapproved of riots and that

[9] *Chronicle,* April 1, 1918.

From Rioting to Conciliation, 1918

the Church forbade them.[10] The press of the city was urging the citizens to remain at home and avoid joining in the riots at any cost.[11] On the evening of March 31 there was a curious attempt to dominate the mob by a person whom the press called "a certain individual" but who was generally acknowledged to be Armand Lavergne, to whom the civic authorities in their terror had appealed for help.[12] Lavergne addressed the crowds, claiming that he had an agreement with the military authorities and the Minister of Militia himself that the troops should be withdrawn if the rioters would disperse to their homes. General Landry, commanding the Quebec military district, denied this agreement at once,[13] and Lavergne only succeeded in further stirring up the passions of the mob by demanding the withdrawal of the troops and the use of reputable men to enforce the Military Service Act, which he claimed those who had arrested Mercier had not been. If the military authorities should remain adamant in what Lavergne termed their injustice to French Canadians, he promised to put himself at the head of the crowd and fight the authorities without mercy. Instead of quieting the mob Lavergne's demagoguery only aroused them the more, and they spent the evening in attacking the armories of the militia.

The evening of Easter Monday, April 1, saw the climax of the rioting. As darkness fell, a large crowd assembled; and from side streets, snow banks, and other places of concealment, the rioters opened fire on the troops. After several soldiers had been wounded, the troops returned the mob's fire with rifles and machine guns. The cavalry charged the mob with drawn swords, while the infantry picked off the snipers who were firing from the housetops and from the shelter of doorways. When the troops finally got the situation under control, it was found that five soldiers had been

---

[10] *Presse*, April 1, 1918.
[11] *Chronicle*, April 1; *Soleil*, April 1; *Action catholique*, March 30, 1918.
[12] *Chronicle*, April 1, 1918.
[13] *Ibid.*, April 1, 1918.

wounded while the civilian casualties had amounted to four killed and a considerable number wounded.

Although the city remained keyed to a high tension in the next few days, it was obvious that the military had the situation well in hand and that further resistance would be foolish in the extreme. On April 4 the government issued an order-in-council permitting the military authorities to hold prisoners without bail in spite of the provisions regarding habeas corpus. The order provoked much criticism in Quebec.[14] Furthermore, although there was much bitterness in Quebec over the killing of citizens, the population and the civil authorities were horrified at the outbreak of violence which went counter to the deepest and most pacific instincts of their race. The French Canadian had every intention of standing up for what he considered his just rights, but none whatsoever of turning revolutionary. The law remained the law, and the constituted authorities were there to be obeyed. Throughout the riots the press had counseled submission and calm although they insisted that the reasons for the disturbance were to be found in the stupid and brutal way in which the military authorities went after slackers and the complete lack of understanding for French Canadian feelings shown by the dispatch of a Toronto battalion to subjugate Quebec.[15] The population of Quebec was enjoined to show prudence and moderation and to beware of *agents provocateurs*.[16]

In circles favorable to the government it was frequently stated that the regrettable incidents had the approval of responsible elements in the population of Quebec, but it was felt by the provincial press that their very occurrence showed how exceedingly hostile was the feeling against the Military Service Act in that province. The federal authorities were called upon to realize that in so far as the act was applied by force it would be of problematic

---

[14] Hansard, *Commons*, 1918, p. 378.
[15] *Presse*, April 1, 1918.
[16] *Ibid.*, April 2, 1918.

From Rioting to Conciliation, 1918 231

assistance to the cause of the Allies.[17] The first duty of all citizens was to help in the re-establishment of public order,[18] while they were urged to discount the idea that the riots had been really representative of public feeling in Quebec or of very serious import.[19]

There was a decided feeling in Quebec, especially in the rural districts, that the disturbances had been due more to the maladministration of the Military Service Act than to dislike for the act itself, and the government was urged to take steps to remedy the unfortunate situation in the province.[20] The Church subscribed to this idea, but naturally it recommended that an immediate stop be put to any violence on the part of the population.[21] The faithful were sternly warned that, although the explosion of popular wrath in Quebec had been due largely to the deep indignation of French Canadians at the injustice done them in connection with the bilingual schools and the administration of the Military Service Act, they must beware of falling into the error of revolutionary individualism, which had been responsible for such acts as attacking the police and actual pillage and looting and must submit to constituted authority.[22]

On April 13 a Quebec jury, investigating the death of four citizens, put the French Canadians' viewpoint very plainly.[23] The blame for the outbreak of the riots was placed squarely on federal police in charge of the administration of the Military Service Act. It was said that their handling of the situation had been grossly tactless and unwise and that the result had been the death of four innocent bystanders. The Quebec jury was of the opinion that in consequence it was the duty of the federal government to atone

[17] *Patrie*, March 30, 1918.
[18] *Ibid.*, April 2, 1918.
[19] *Evénement*, April 1, 1918.
[20] *Avenir du nord*, April 5, 1918; *Canada*, April 4, 8, 1918.
[21] *Semaine religieuse de Quebec*, April 4, 1918.
[22] *Ibid.*, April 14, 1918.
[23] *Canadian Annual Review*, 1918, p. 463.

for the conduct of their employees as far as possible by an indemnification to the families of the victims and to all citizens who had suffered property damage. The considered opinion of the great mass of citizens of Quebec was that, while violence and armed revolt were certainly to be deprecated, the maladministration of the Military Service Act had undoubtedly called forth the riots of the Easter week end. English-speaking Canada was equally convinced that the riots were the direct outcome of Quebec's unwillingness to bear her part in Canada's war effort and of her resistance to the operations of the Military Service Act. Each race judged the question according to its firmly held prejudices and preoccupations. The truth seems to be between the two opinions. English-speaking Canada undoubtedly overestimated the degree of resistance to the act which Quebec would put up and underestimated the fundamental respect for law and order that animated French Canada as a whole, except for a small minority of extremists. It seems evident, also, that the Military Service Act had been tactlessly administered in Quebec and that hence the causes of the disturbances were much more local than they seemed at the time. The newspapers had been complaining for some time that the Dominion police were unnecessarily overbearing and brutal in their search for draft resisters. It was even claimed that the police contained notorious French-Canadian criminals, who were employed to act as *agents provocateurs*.[24] Quebec, for her part, put too much emphasis on the idea that the way the act had been administered and the methods by which the riots had been quelled were but further evidence of Anglo-Canadian tyranny and insult. However, as time went on and dissatisfaction with the Military Service Act, the cancellation of exemptions, and the so-called "order-in-council government" pervaded the Dominion and led to riots elsewhere, the Quebec riots took on much less of a distinctively French Canadian character

[24] *Chronicle*, March 6, 1918; *Canada*, April 8, 1918; *Presse*, March 21, 23, 24, 1918.

From Rioting to Conciliation, 1918

and were seen to be parts of a nation-wide movement of resistance to conscription.

The Quebec disturbances, which had caused an immense sensation in the whole of the Dominion, elicited much discussion in the Parliament at Ottawa. Speaking in the House of Commons on April 2 the Prime Minister stated that, while it was the duty of the government to see that the Military Service Act was enforced, the incidents in Quebec proved that some amendments to the act would be necessary, of which the first would be the automatic cancellation of the exemption of any man who openly resisted the enforcement of the act and his incorporation in the armed forces.[25] There were no two opinions on the necessity for submission to the law of the land. Sir Wilfrid Laurier echoed the Prime Minister's stern demand for submission and added that the law should be obeyed even by those who did not believe in its justice, simply because it was the law.[26]

The government did not waste any time in taking precautions to avoid any future outbreaks, for it, too, felt the imminent danger that there would be similar disturbances on an even larger scale in Montreal, with its turbulent population. By an order-in-council, April 5, the Governor General was empowered to declare martial law and to call out the troops regardless of any request by the civil authorities. The Quebec riots had shown that the civil power had a natural disinclination to call out the soldiers and that for that reason they had let the situation get out of hand. The government was determined that this should not be allowed to happen again. Doubtless it also felt that the threat of a declaration of martial law, with its accompanying suspension of habeas corpus and trial by civil courts, might act as a distinct deterrent.[27]

The parliamentary debates provided another chance for both English- and French-speaking Canadians to discuss the bitter racial

[25] Hansard, *Commons*, 1918, p. 236, Sir Robert Borden.
[26] *Ibid.*, p. 236, Sir Wilfrid Laurier.
[27] For order-in-council of April 5, 1918, Hansard, *Commons*, 1918, p. 378.

tension between them in the light of the recent unfortunate events at Quebec. The more extreme among the English Canadians advocated stern measures against Quebec, the internment of Bourassa and Lavergne, and the suppression of the *Devoir*.[28] Sir Sam Hughes, the ex-Minister of Militia, who in the past had always professed friendship for the French Canadians, took the occasion to unloose the vials of his wrath upon them. He rehearsed the old stories concerning French Canadian officers who had failed to raise battalions and units which once enlisted rapidly melted away by desertion. He openly accused the clergy of opposition to Canadian participation and even asserted that French Canada had been perverted by German propaganda. But it was striking that in spite of such outbursts among the English-speaking members there was a more conciliatory spirit toward French Canada than had been prevalent in the heat of the election campaign of 1917. Perhaps this could be traced to the fact that French Canadians were no longer the only ones who were resisting the Military Service Act. Throughout the English-speaking provinces, especially in the farming districts, there was growing opposition to the enforcement of conscription. Anglo-Canadian members who had Anglo-Canadian constituents opposed to military service were constrained to look more indulgently on similar opinions among French Canadians. There was criticism of the administration of the Military Service Act from both sides of the House, and, although English-speaking Canada felt that the number of exemptions which had been allowed in Quebec was quite beyond the bounds of reason, it was at least prepared to admit that the mass of the people of that province were still loyal, although they had been led astray by leaders who had preached passive defiance of the act.[29] Some of the English-speaking members from Quebec pointed out that one of the underlying causes of the disturbance

[28] *Ibid.*, 1918, p. 380, Mr. Currie.
[29] Hansard, *Commons*, 1918, p. 388, Mr. Stevens; p. 380, Mr. Currie; p. 418, Mr. Mackie.

lay in the fact that the province no longer was in the control of Laurier and the moderates but was swayed by the Nationalist extremists and the more fanatical of the clergy.[30]

Sir Wilfrid Laurier naturally spoke for his own countrymen.[31] He took the stand that the dissatisfaction with the Military Service Act lay in its administration and in the poor character of the officers selected to enforce it. In many cases these men had been of bad reputation and some were even notorious bullies. The old French Canadian leader hinted at what many of his compatriots believed, that the Quebec riots had been instigated by the enemies of French Canada as just another means of discrediting her war effort and making her liable to severe punishment. He pointed out that similar anti-conscription disturbances had taken place in Toronto and in Calgary without attracting so much attention, and he insisted that although the act was unpopular in Quebec his people wished to obey it. Laurier disclaimed for himself and his followers any connection with Bourassa, Lavergne, and their views. Speaking as the accredited representative of Quebec, he said that the people of that province were ready to accept the basic principles that the law must be obeyed, that property must be respected, and above all that peace must be preserved. Once more the old leader admitted that Quebec had not done her share for Canada's war effort, but he begged his fellow countrymen of English speech to realize that the only way to deal with French Canadians was not to coerce them but to appeal to their hearts and their imagination, and they would inevitably respond. In a final moving passage Laurier told his hearers and the country at large that all his life he had had to fight extremists, whether they were Anglo-Canadian jingoes or French Canadian Nationalists. Nevertheless he was still able to defend himself, and he still believed with all the faith in him that the only possible policy for

---
[30] *Ibid.*, 1918, pp. 422, 428, Messrs. Power and Edwards.
[31] *Ibid.*, 1918, p. 393, Sir Wilfrid Laurier.

Canada was one of conciliation and of appeal to the best elements in both races.

Most of the French Canadian members followed in the footsteps of their leader, criticizing the administration of the act and emphasizing the essential loyalty of Quebec in spite of her dissatisfaction with conscription. In some cases French Canadian Liberals openly blamed the Nationalists for the ferment then existing among the population of Quebec, but they defended the clergy from the charge frequently made by English-speaking members that they had done all in their power to sabotage the Military Service Act.[32] There were many members, English as well as French Canadians, who protested against the government's use of the order-in-council to enforce its wishes, especially in the administration of military service. There was considerable feeling that legislation by order-in-council constituted an abuse of the executive power, being no more nor less than government by ordinance issued by the federal cabinet.[33]

The Prime Minister, when he rose to uphold the government's mode of action in the Quebec riots, immediately defended the use of the order-in-council.[34] He stated that the right to use this form of legislation had been granted very extensively by the War Measures Act of 1914, that in the war emergencies it was often necessary to act quickly, and that the delay of an appeal to parliament might on occasion be disastrous. The rights of parliament were safeguarded by the fact that any legislation passed by the Governor-General-in-Council had to be given retroactive sanction by the legislature. Sir Robert Borden defended the administration of the Military Service Act and said that it had been enforced with like fairness in all parts of the country but that there could be no doubt that in Quebec exemptions had been granted on a

[32] Hansard, *Commons*, 1918, pp. 450-54, Messrs. Archambault, D'Anjou and Fournier.
[33] *Ibid.*, p. 394, Sir Wilfrid Laurier.
[34] *Ibid.*, p. 398, Sir Robert Borden.

From Rioting to Conciliation, 1918

wholesale basis by the tribunals of the first instance. The Prime Minister blamed the civil authorities of Quebec for inaction when the riots had first broken out and officially denied the widely made assertion that the authorities as a whole and the registrar of the Military Service Act in particular had asked Armand Lavergne to quiet the mob.

Before the country had recovered from the shock of the Quebec riots and the subsequent debate on the measures for the control of any further disturbances it was plunged into new excitement coincident with the government's cancellation of a large number of exemptions. On the very eve of the Quebec riots the Prime Minister of Great Britain had cabled an urgent request for more men to hold the battle lines so seriously endangered by the great German offensive of March, 1918. The Canadian troops had given of their best to help hold the front. General Currie, commanding the Canadian Corps, had even sent Canadian reinforcements to help British units, in spite of his strong conviction that Canadian troops should always be kept together.[85]

The number of recruits furnished by the Military Service Act in the first few months of 1918 was most inadequate, and it was obvious that something drastic must be done.[86] On April 17 the government took the course, unprecedented in Canada, of calling both Houses of Parliament into secret session for a statement on the measures to be taken in the crisis of the military situation which the German drive of the spring of 1918 had occasioned. On the following day the Prime Minister moved for approval of an order-in-council by which the exemptions of all men between the

---

[85] Lucas, *The Empire at War*, II, 209 *et seq.*

[86] In the course of 1918 the government was unable to send more than a total of 81,572 reinforcements overseas although as long ago as May, 1917, it had been stated that 100,000 were urgently needed. *Report of the Ministry of Overseas Military Forces of Canada*, London, 1919. The total number of men enlisted under the Military Service Act in all the provinces of Canada was 83,355 of whom 19,050 came from the province of Quebec. See *Sessional Paper 264, 1919, House of Commons*, in Library of Parliament, Ottawa.

ages of twenty and twenty-two who were eligible for military service should be automatically canceled in view of the gravity of the situation, notwithstanding the fact that an act of Parliament had specifically allowed the exemption of these men.[87] Furthermore, men aged nineteen years were to be added to those eligible under the original act of 1917. The Prime Minister openly and frankly admitted that the Military Service Act had not produced as many men as had been expected and that something had to be done at once to provide reinforcements for the hard-pressed troops at the front. In dealing with the difficulties of administering the act Sir Robert Borden insisted that the exemption tribunals had been attended with inequalities and occasional injustice and that in some parts of the country, on the other hand, the government had been forced to appeal 80 to 90 percent of the exemptions granted by the local boards. According to the report of the director of the Military Service Branch of the Ministry of Justice on the operation of the Military Service Act the percentage of those who had signed claims for exemption in Ontario was 92.9 percent, while in Quebec it had been 98 percent.[38] With regard to defaulters, the largest number had undoubtedly been in the province of Quebec where 40.83 percent of the total number of men ordered to report had failed to report, while in Ontario the ratio had been only 9.28 percent.

In combating the government motion Laurier was naturally the champion of all who opposed the somewhat highhanded procedure involved in the order-in-council form of legislation.[39] In his opinion it was a wide departure from the constitution and an encroachment by the executive on the rights of Parliament Laurier's theory was that an act of Parliament could only be amended by Parliament itself. Once again the old leader defended

[87] Hansard, *Commons*, 1918, p. 933, Sir Robert Borden.
[38] *Report of the Director of the Military Service Branch to the Hon. The Minister of Justice, on the Operations of the Military Service Act, 1917*, Ottawa, 1919.
[39] Hansard, *Commons*, 1918, p. 940, Sir Wilfrid Laurier.

his native province and disclaimed any desire on her part to dominate the rest of the country. He realized that people were saying that Quebec must be made to fight whether she wished or not, but in his opinion she had already shown how she could fight, and he thought that if the government would only stop coercing her all would be well.

When the Minister of Militia, General Mewburn, arose to explain the new military policy, it was soon evident that the government, alarmed by the strength of the opposition to the cancellation of exemptions, had thought it wise to be conciliatory, especially with regard to Quebec.[40] General Mewburn stated that when the conscripts between the ages of twenty and twenty-two were called out, those from the cities would be the first to be summoned, while farmers would be allowed to finish their seeding operations and would not be called until the last possible moment. The government undoubtedly hoped that this provision would dispose of the very vehement opposition to conscription which was prevalent among farmers, not only in Quebec, but also in Ontario, where a delegation of several thousand men marched to Ottawa and protested against the cancellation of exemptions.

In the course of May, 1918, the Minister of Militia was most friendly toward Quebec and spoke of the change of feeling in that province, which was evident in spite of the recent riots. The colleges and universities were now urging their students to enlist, and they had granted leave of absence to all who were liable under the Military Service Act. The Minister made it plain that he, for one, had never doubted the loyalty of Quebec, and that he was putting forth every effort to keep units together and would if possible see that friends enlisting at the same time should not be separated. General Mewburn even went so far in his conciliatory attitude toward Quebec as to assert that if Sir Sam Hughes had allowed the old militia units to go overseas and to act as recruiting

[40] Hansard, *Commons*, 1918, pp. 1935-36, Major General Mewburn.

units for reinforcements, the results might have been much better.

This new spirit of conciliation was hailed by French Canada in the person of Rodolphe Lemieux, who thanked the government for a welcome change in policy. But although the government evidently was anxious to conciliate Quebec, it did not seem able to grant one thing that might even then have brought Quebec into enthusiastic co-operation in the nation's war effort—the formation of a distinct French Canadian brigade. When a member from rural Quebec asked whether such a unit could not be formed and added that the whole province, from the Prime Minister to Henri Bourassa, was demanding a French Canadian brigade, the Prime Minister only answered in a vaguely friendly fashion.[41] Sir Robert Borden asserted that he would gladly do anything that he could to further the organization of such a brigade, but that the final decision lay not with him but with the military authorities. He had been in touch with General Currie, commanding the Canadian Corps in France, and the latter had suggested that reinforcements for battalions which contained many French Canadians should be recruited solely from soldiers of that nationality, and that in that manner exclusively French Canadian units might be built up. The Prime Minister concluded with the statement that in spite of everything the government was inclined to think that the mixing of the races in the army was a good thing.

It seems extraordinary that after nearly four years of experience with the French Canadians' passionate desire for the establishment of units made up exclusively of their compatriots the leaders of the government could still talk of the benefits of racial intermixture. In fairness, however, it must be remembered that the technical difficulties of forming a French Canadian brigade in the field in May, 1918, would have been insuperable. With armies crumbling before the desperate German onslaught, the

[41] Hansard, *Commons*, 1918, pp. 1194, 1927 *et seq.*, Mr. du Tremblay; p. 1933, Sir Robert Borden.

From Rioting to Conciliation, 1918

military authorities could hardly concentrate on soothing French Canadian susceptibilities. All this Sir Robert Borden could not explain in detail at the time, and he was driven to vague and halting replies. It was a blundering type of conciliation that the government was trying to adopt, but it was conciliation nevertheless, as was very evident when the Minister of Pensions went so far as to admit that, although Quebec had lagged behind in her enlistments, there could be no doubt but that in other parts of Canada there were thousands of men who had tried to evade military service by every possible means.[42]

From the moment when the exemptions were canceled, in April, conciliation was the order of the day as far as the government's policy toward Quebec was concerned. French Canada met this policy of conciliation with an equal degree of appreciation and the desire to improve the unfortunate state of feeling between the races. Perhaps Quebec's desire to co-operate was further increased by the widespread and genuine fear in March, 1918, that Germany was going to win the war in spite of all the Allied efforts. It shook all the Allied world and undoubtedly penetrated as far as Quebec. It must have sobered even Bourassa to realize that German victory had become a real possibility. If the German armies succeeded in reaching the Channel ports, what would it matter whether a French Canadian brigade were formed or whether every French Canadian child in Ontario enjoyed his full rights? It was obvious to all thoughtful people that the Allied cause was in the greatest danger and that if it were to be saved internal quarrels must be buried. During the summer of 1918 it was noticeable not only that Quebec co-operated willingly in the registration of all men and women over sixteen for possible war employment but also that enlistments from the province actually increased. The desire of Quebec for co-operation was noticed even among those who in the past had been her bitterest opponents.

[42] Hansard, *Commons*, 1918, p. 956, Hon. Mr. Carroll.

As early as April 30 the *Toronto Mail and Empire* commented on the gratifying way in which young men of Quebec were answering the call to arms issued under the new order-in-council.

Doubtless the extreme expressions of partisan spirit in the press which had marked the last two years were diminished by the application in April of a strict censorship which forbade any mention of military news without governmental approval. The French Canadian press accepted the news censorship regulations with calm and with the respect for the law of the land which is so characteristic of French Canada.[43] A final blast from the *Devoir* might have been expected, but none came. Did Bourassa feel, perhaps, that the time had passed when Nationalism could still be an active force? It was particularly striking that ever since the 1917 elections the *Devoir* had practically ceased its campaign of extreme opposition to the government. The Francoeur secession debates were sparingly commented on in its columns, while the Quebec riots called for little more than a strongly worded admonition to all classes of the population to keep cool. The tightening up of the censorship naturally served to restrain any extreme expression of opposition in the *Devoir*, but even news from the war seemed to take second place in its columns during the closing months of 1918.

As time passed there could be no doubt but that Quebec was quieting down. In the summer of 1917 it had seemed distinctly possible that there would be serious trouble in the province of Quebec. The huge anti-conscription meetings, with their attendant violence, the riotous street processions, the window smashings, and the stoning of troops, all seemed to point to the decided probability that Quebec would openly revolt if conscription became a reality. In spite of the seriousness of the situation, by midsummer of 1917 there were distinct signs that French Canada's innate sense

---

[43] This censorship was imposed by order-in-council under the War Measures Act of 1914.

From Rioting to Conciliation, 1918 243

for law and order was about to reassert itself. From Sir Wilfrid Laurier at one end of the political scale to Bourassa at the other, from the *Action catholique* to the *Devoir,* all the leaders of French Canadian opinion were cautioning their compatriots against "sterile violence." Even the 1917 election, with all its partisan propaganda, all its abuse and mud slinging, far from inflaming racial passions, served actually as a safety valve for passion and prejudice. When the Francoeur secession debates took place in January, 1918, it was clear that they aroused only an academic interest, for among the real leaders of the people there was no serious intention of leaving the Confederation. The very riots at Quebec, unfortunate and bloody as they proved to be, actually served as a steadying influence on Quebec's war attitude. The rioters expressed all Quebec's instinctive dislike for conscription, but the reaction against mob violence was almost universal. The Quebec riots pointed the lesson that the French Canadian nationality could not possibly gain by armed rebellion against constituted authority. It is true that to a certain degree passive resistance continued even after the riots of April, 1918. There were still hundreds, if not thousands, of French Canadians hiding from the draft officers. But events at Quebec had made French Canadian political leaders of all parties realize that unless they made some gesture of submission and indicated a willingness to co-operate in Canada's war effort, their people would be politically annihilated by the revenge of English-speaking Canada at the end of the war. It was clear that Quebec would never rise in rebellion. A truly nationalistic people subjected to the provocation that had been undoubtedly proffered Quebec might easily have done so. But Quebec was passively, not actively, nationalistic, and rebellion does not arise from a passive sense of nationality, no matter how strongly held that principle may be. All that Quebec wanted was to be left alone to work out her own salvation in her own particular way.

After the Quebec riots the government realized at last that it would be wise to leave Quebec alone. The effort to apprehend deserters was not entirely given up; and the execution of the order-in-council threatening all those who resisted with immediate incorporation in the army was not suspended in Quebec. But the government made no attempt to coerce Quebec, nor did it send armed forces of the crown to hunt down deserters in the trackless woods of the province. In August an amnesty was passed for defaulters in Class I, which was openly admitted to be an effort to bring in those French Canadians who were in hiding from the draft.[44] It was hoped that Quebec would react favorably to this conciliatory treatment, and to a certain degree it did. There was a sort of unwritten agreement that the Anglo-Canadians would not expect 100 percent war co-operation from Quebec and that the French Canadian leaders would do everything in their power to keep their province within the strict orbit of loyalty. Some of the gall and bitterness had gone out of the racial conflict. Men of both races had realized that for better or for worse they must go on living in the Canadian confederation and that it would be wise to make the best of it. Faced with the possibility of civil war, English-speaking Canada realized that it would be better to let Quebec go her own way than to seek to coerce her. French Canada, for her part, having expressed her passionate faith in what was due her separate "nationality," shrank from the ultimate test of armed resistance as few peoples who were actively instead of passively nationalistic would have done.

All these factors contributed to the improvement of the relationship between the two Canadian races in the closing months of the war. But the greatest of them all was the sudden emergence of confidence in victory after the break-through of the Allied armies at Amiens on August 8, 1918. From that day forward all Canada re-echoed to the amazing Crescendo of Canadian victories. The

---

[44] Regarding amnesty, see *The Canada Gazette Extra*, Ottawa, August 2, 1918.

From Rioting to Conciliation, 1918

Canadian Corps was constantly in action. Its losses were heavy, comprising more than 30,000 casualties between the end of August and the armistice, but its successes were constant.[45] The 22d French Canadians played a glorious part in the advance and in the accompanying sacrifices, for at one time all its officers were casualties.[46]

The resulting sorrowful pride in Quebec may be imagined. There was no longer any doubt in all Canada but that the French Canadians at the front were first-class fighting men. At the beginning of September Canadian troops assisted in the capture of the Hindenburg line, and the end of that month saw them again victorious in the battles around Cambrai. On October 9 the Canadians were the first to enter the city, and day by day saw their steady advance eastward. On November 2 the Canadian Corps took Valenciennes, and on November 11 it entered the historic city of Mons, where British troops had been bitterly defeated four years before. So ended the magnificent chapter of Canadian military achievement known as the "Hundred Days." From one end of the Dominion to the other there arose a paean of thanksgiving and joy in the achievement of Canada's sons. The bitterness of racial animosity was forgotten in the general atmosphere of jubilation. When the troops came home there were some who noticed that there were fewer flags and less cheering in rural Quebec than in Ontario, but that impression was wiped out by the triumphant reception accorded French and English Canadian troops alike in the streets of Quebec and Montreal.

As time wore on, however, and war enthusiasm subsided, thoughtful Canadians of both races realized that the racial problem remained the infinitely difficult question it had always been. The close of the war left the problem of Canadian unity still unsolved. The crises of the years between 1914 and 1918 had only

---

[45] *Soleil*, April 17, 1918; *Canada*, April 20, 1918; *Patrie*, April 17, 1918.
[46] Lucas, *The Empire at War*, II, 244.

served to emphasize the devotion of the French Canadian minority to their faith, their language, and their institutions; and, as in the days of Lord Durham, there were still "two nations warring within the bosom of a single state."

The events of 1917-18 showed once again that the French Canadian "nation" is content if it is left alone to work out its salvation in its own way. If its privileges or its religious rights are seriously interfered with, as they seemed to be to most French Canadians in those crucial years, it will rise to great heights in their defense; but if faced with the consequences of having to stand alone outside the Anglo-Canadian community its own impulse to rebellion and even secession will peter out. The closing years of the war proved that French Canada, at least for the time, was content to remain a nation within a nation. French Canadians have the strongest possible sense of the characteristics that differentiate them from their Anglo-Canadian neighbors, but they do not wish, nor have they ever wished, to impose them on other groups in the Dominion. In that essential characteristic lies all the difference between a sense of nationality and "nationalism." Only because that difference exists did the confederation of two races within the Dominion of Canada survive the bitter controversies of the War.

Appendix

THE NUMBER OF FRENCH CANADIANS IN THE CANADIAN EXPEDITIONARY FORCES

In estimating the number of French Canadians in the Army it is necessary to take several factors into consideration. From the very outset of the war no record was kept of the nationality—French or English—of recruits born within the Dominion. On enlistment, recruits were recorded as British-born, foreign-born, or Canadian-born. This statistical system lent itself to much misunderstanding and misstatement. Even an official of such high rank as Sir Sam Hughes asserted at one time that there were nearly 3,000 French Canadians in the first contingent,[1] but in 1917, the then Minister of Militia officially estimated that there had been only 1,217 French Canadians in that body. This contradiction was typical of the statements and counter-statements that prevailed on the subject. As the war progressed and racial feeling grew to unprecedented bitterness, the government became wary of giving out figures about what everyone knew was the inadequate part that Quebec was taking in recruiting.

However, there were statements in 1917 and 1918 from official sources that must be considered in arriving at a fairly accurate estimate. In reply to questions from a French Canadian member, the government announced in June, 1917, that until April 30, 1917, the total number of soldiers speaking the French language from all parts of Canada who had proceeded overseas was 14,100.[2] The Minister of Militia asserted that the greatest possible care had been taken in compiling the figures and that they were as approximately accurate as was possible. To an interrogator who raised the important question of how the government determined who was actually a French Canadian and whether it took into consideration that many men with English or

[1] Hansard, *Commons*, 1915, p. 1445, Sir Sam Hughes.
[2] Hansard, *Commons*, 1917, p. 2627, Sir E. Kemp; see also *Sessional Paper*, 143-B, 1917, in Library of Parliament, Ottawa.

248   The Canadian Expeditionary Forces

Scottish names were actually French-speaking, the Minister did not reply.

In March, 1918, in a statement to the Commons on the war effort, the Prime Minister estimated that according to figures furnished him by the Department of Militia and Defense there were 16,268 Canadians of French descent in the army.[3] As far as can be ascertained, this was the last government pronouncement on the number of French Canadians in the Canadian Expeditionary Forces.

After the war the government, in reply to a question from a French Canadian, stated that of the 549,359 men who had enlisted in the army, 228,751 had been British-born and 286,705 Canadian-born.[4] To further questions as to how many Canadian-born members of the army had been enlisted in each province and how many French Canadians had been enlisted in each province the Minister merely stated that to procure the information required it would be necessary to scrutinize the records of every individual in the Canadian Expeditionary Forces, which would be impracticable.

The attitude of the responsible authorities at the time of writing (1937) seems to be that for reasons of political expediency no accurate estimate of the number of French Canadians serving in the course of the war can be or should be made. Everyone admits that the French Canadians did not do very well, but Quebec is still an important political factor, and it is best to let sleeping dogs lie. It has proved impossible for the present writer to secure any exact estimate from the responsible authorities of the Ministry of National Defense or the Historian of the General Staff, despite the courtesy and willingness of these officials to co-operate in all other respects. The Ministry of National Defense, in a letter to the writer, has stated categorically that "there is not nor ever can be, any precise, accurate or authentic statement as to the number of French Canadians who served in the Canadian forces in the World War 1914-1919."[5]

It remains, therefore, to make as accurate a guess as is possible with the sources at hand. The government statement that there were 14,100

---

[3] *Ibid.*, 1918, p. 936, Sir Robert Borden.

[4] *Ibid.*, 1919, p. 614, Major General Mewburn; see also *Sessional Paper 198*, 1930, in Library of Parliament, Ottawa, which states that the total enlistments in the Canadian Expeditionary Force were 619,636.

[5] Letter to the writer from Hon. L. R. Laflèche, Deputy Minister of National Defense, November 30, 1935, No. 683-1-12.

The Canadian Expeditionary Forces 249

before the introduction of the draft in 1917 and 16,268 in March, 1918, must serve as the basis of discussion. A high authority connected with the Canadian section of the British General Headquarters believes that the estimate of about 15,000 French Canadians in France was substantially correct and that of these about 10,000 were serving in the combatant infantry battalions. The 22d French Canadians was the main depot for French Canadian reinforcements and about 6,000 men passed through their ranks, while the other four thousand were divided among other infantry battalions. The Royal 14th Montreal Battalion alone had one company of French Canadians. The remaining 5,000 were scattered among the Field Artillery, Cavalry, Army Service Corps, and so forth.

While most of the authorities agree that about 15,000 was the correct number of French Canadians at the front, it is more difficult to obtain an accurate estimate of the French Canadians enlisted under the Military Service Act. Of the total of 83,355 enlisted under the act in the whole of Canada, 19,050 came from the province of Quebec.[6] Not all of these were French Canadians, but, on the other hand, some French Canadian conscripts came from the provinces with an English-speaking majority. However, it may safely be assumed that 80 percent of the conscripts from the province of Quebec were French Canadians, and if the scattered French Canadians from the other provinces are added, the total number must have come close to 15,000 in the forces in training in Canada and in England.[7] To these must be added some four or five thousand French Canadians scattered among the naval forces of Britain and the Allies.[8]

As a result we arrive at an estimated total of between 32,000 and 35,000 French Canadians serving in the armed forces of the Allies. This is in substantial agreement with Colonel Wood's estimate in the Canadian Volume of the History of the British Empire, an estimate which he attributes to the Historical Section of the Canadian General

---

[6] *Sessional Paper No. 264*, 1919, in Library of Parliament, Ottawa.

[7] In 1911 the French Canadian population of Quebec was 1,605,339, and the total population of other origins was 314,997. See *Fifth Census of Canada*, Ottawa, 1911, II, 340.

[8] *Cambridge History of British Empire*, Cambridge, 1930, VI, 756. The writer of this chapter, Colonel Wood, is among the best known Anglo-Canadians in Quebec, long prominent in militia circles, author of many works on military history, war time member of the Canadian Special Mission in France.

Staff. It is also in agreement with the estimate of the distinguished officer who played a prominent part in the Canadian Section of British General Headquarters and may be taken as substantially accurate in the light of the information at hand at the time of writing.

To summarize French Canada's war effort, although she supplied two-fifths, or 40 percent of the total population of Canada, the estimated 32,000-35,000 French Canadian members of the Canadian Expeditionary Forces constituted roughly only 5 percent of the 600,000 soldiers furnished by the Dominion as a whole. But in considering this percentage, it must not be forgotten that approximately 228,751, or roughly 33⅓ percent, of the Canadian Expeditionary Forces were British-born; while the English-speaking Canadian-born population, which constituted about 60 percent of the total, contributed less than 50 percent of Canadian soldiers.[9] In estimating the number of French Canadians in the Army it must also be remembered that not all French Canadians came from the province of Quebec, for there was a total population of 225,451 of French stock in the other provinces.[10] There were many recruits from the Acadian population of the maritime provinces, and the western communities of French Canadians furnished their contingents before, as well as after, the introduction of conscription. In fact, of the total of 14,100 French Canadians serving on April 30, 1917, almost 50 percent were from other provinces than Quebec. As no statistics of French Canadian enlistments by provinces were consistently kept, it is impossible to estimate whether the final proportion of French Canadian enlistments was greater or less in Quebec than in the other provinces of Canada. However, it may be assumed that those communities of French Canadians, whether in the West or in the maritime provinces, who were further removed from the bilingual school agitation and other controversies that rocked Quebec in the war years were less affected by the anti-war feeling.

[9] Hansard, *Commons*, 1919, p. 614.
[10] *Fifth Census of Canada*, II, 340.

Bibliography

OFFICIAL GOVERNMENTAL AND ECCLESIASTICAL PUBLICATIONS

DEBATES

Debates, House of Commons of Canada, 4th-7th Sessions, 12th Parliament, Fifth George V, Ottawa, J. L. Taché, Kings Printer, 1914-17.
Ibid., 1st Session, 13th Parliament, Ottawa, 1918.
Ibid., 2d Session, 13th Parliament, Ottawa, 1919.
Ibid., Senate of Canada, 4th-7th Sessions, 12th Parliament, Ottawa, 1914-1917.
Ibid., Senate of Canada, 1st Session, 13th Parliament.
Quebec and Confederation, Record of the debates of the Legislative Assembly of Quebec, proposed by J. N. Francoeur, Quebec, 1918.

SESSIONAL PAPERS, HOUSE OF COMMONS
(in Library of Parliament, Ottawa)

Sessional Paper 35-A, 1913. Report of Inspector General of Militia.
Sessional Paper 18, 1911. (Drummond-Arthabaska Election)
Ibid., 35-A, 1915. Report of Militia Council.
Ibid., 231-A, 1916. Petition of Disallowance of Ontario Education Law.
Ibid., 271-A, 1916.
Ibid., 143-B, 1917.
Ibid., 264, 1919.   (*Re* Enlistments.)
Ibid., 161, 1921.
Ibid., 198, 1930.

ACTS AND PROCLAMATIONS

Acts of the Parliament of the Dominion of Canada, 5th George V, Fourth Session, Twelfth Parliament, Ottawa, 1914.
Proclamations and Orders in Council of the Governor-General Having Force of Law, Ottawa, *1915.* (*Re* Orders in Council of August-September, 1914.)

Copies of Proclamations, Orders in Council and Documents Relating to European War Compiled by Department of Secretary of State of Canada, Ottawa, 1915, with Supplements 1915–1918.
Canada Gazette, August 2, 1918. (*Re* Amnesty for Defaulters, Military Service Act.)

OFFICIAL ECCLESIASTICAL PUBLICATIONS

Lettre pastorale de NN ... SS. les archévêques et évêques des provinces ecclésiastiques de Québec, Montréal et Ottawa sur les devoirs des Catholiques dans la guerre actuelle, No. 86. (Official copy of this pastoral supplied to writer by Archivist of Archbishopric of Quebec.)
Circulars to Clergy of Archbishoprics of Montreal and Quebec. (Official copies furnished by Archivist of Archbishopric of Quebec.)

MISCELLANEOUS GOVERNMENT PUBLICATIONS

Report of Director of the Military Service Branch of the Ministry of Justice on the Operation of Military Service Act of 1917, Ottawa, 1919. (For enlistment statistics.)
Report of the Ministry of Overseas Military Forces of Canada, London, 1918.
Quarterly Militia List. Dominion of Canada, Ottawa, 1914.
Fifth Census of Canada. Vols. I-II, Ottawa, 1911.
Ontario Department of Education. *Regulations, Courses of Study, and so forth, of Public and Separate Schools,* Toronto, 1915.
Department of Public Information. *Canada's Part in the Great War,* Ottawa, 1919.

NEWSPAPERS
(July, 1914–November, 1918)

MONTREAL

Presse
Patrie
Devoir
Action sociale (after 1914 called *Action catholique*)
Canada
Gazette

Bibliography

QUEBEC

Evénement
Soleil
Chronicle

JOLIETTE, QUE.

Etoile du nord

ST. JEROME, QUE.

Avenir du nord

ST. HYACINTHE, QUE.

Courrier du St. Hyacinthe

THREE RIVERS, QUE.

Bien public

MONTMAGNY, QUE.

Peuple

TORONTO, ONT.

Mail and Empire, 1917-18

WINNIPEG, MAN.

Manitoba Free Press, 1917-18

MONCTON, N. B.

Evangeline

PERIODICALS

Canadian Annual Review of Public Affairs, edited by J. G. Hopkins, Montreal, 1914-19.
Canadian Magazine, Toronto, 1918. (For article attacking Quebec by H. G. Hocken, editor *Orange Sentinel.*)
Fairfax, J., *Canada's Forgotten Riots, Canadian Forum*...XV. November, 1935, 178.
Lanctot, G., *L'Histoire du Canada depuis 1900,* in *Revue de l'Université d'Ottawa,* II, 237, April, 1932.

Le Canada français, Université de Laval, Quebec, 1918-19.
Les Cloches de St. Boniface, 1914-18. (Organ of Archbishopric of St. Boniface, Manitoba.)
Le Pays laurentien, 1916.
Le Petit Canadien, Montreal, 1914-18. (Organ of Society of St. Jean Baptiste.)
Le Rosaire; revue dominicaine, St. Hyacinthe, 1914-18.
Le Semeur; organe de l'Association catholique de la jeunesse canadienne française, Montreal, 1914-18.
Revue canadienne (edited by group of Professors of Laval University), Montreal, 1914-18.
Semaine religieuse de Montréal, Montreal, 1914-18. (Published by authorization of the Archbishop of Montreal.)
Semaine religieuse de Québec et bulletin des œuvres sociales de l'action sociale catholique, Quebec, 1914-18.

PAMPHLETS

Asselin, O., *L'Action catholique, les évêques et la guerre*, Montreal, 1915.
—— *Pourquoi je m'enrôle*, Montreal, 1916.
Beauregard-Champagne, P. P. (Université de Montréal), *Album and Souvenir*, Montreal, 1931-32.
Borden, Sir R. L., *Canada at War*. Speeches, 1914-18. Privately printed.
—— *Canada and the Peace*. Speeches, 1919. Privately printed.
Bourassa, H., *Le Patriotisme canadien-français*, Montreal, 1902.
—— *Les Ecoles du nord-ouest*, Montreal, 1905.
—— *Le Projet de loi navale*, Montreal, 1911.
—— *Pour la justice*, Montreal, 1912.
—— *Le "Devoir," son origine, son passé, son avenir*, Montreal, 1915.
—— *Que devons-nous à l'Angleterre*, Montreal, 1915.
—— *The Duty of Canada at the Present Hour*, Montreal, 1915.
—— *La Langue française au Canada*, Montreal, 1915.
—— *Hier, aujourd'hui, et demain*, Montreal, 1916.
—— *Le "Devoir" et la guerre; le conflit des races*, Montreal, 1916.
—— *Independence or Imperial Partnership*, Montreal, 1916.
—— *Canadian Nationalism and the War*, Montreal, 1916.
—— *L'Intervention américaine*, Montreal, 1917.
—— *La Conscription*, Montreal, 1917.

Boyd, J., *Fair Play for Quebec*, Montreal, 1917.
Bruchesi, Mgr., *Le Problème des races au Canada*, in *Proceedings and Transactions of Royal Society of Canada*, third series, Vol. IX, Ottawa, May, 1915.
Desjardins, L. C., *England, Canada and the Great War*, Quebec, 1918.
Landry, P., *Le Désaveu*, Quebec, 1916. (*Re* Disallowance of Ontario Education Law.)
La Presse (newspaper), *Our Volunteer Army; Facts and Figures.* Montreal, 1916.
"Patriote," *Ou allons-nous? Le Nationalisme canadien.* Montreal, 1916.
Roy, F., *L'Appel aux armes et la réponse canadienne-française*, Quebec, 1917.
Skelton, O. D., *The Language Issue in Canada* in *Bulletin of Departments of History, Political and Economic Science*, Kingston, Ont., No. 23, April, 1917.
"Jean Vindex," *Halte-là, "Patriote," que penser de notre école politico-théologique, de l'impérialisme qu'elle professe, du nationalisme qu'elle censure*, Rimouski, 1917.

BOOKS

BACKGROUND, 1763-1914

Arnould, L., *Nos amis, les Canadiens*, Paris, 1913.
Belisle, H., *Histoire de la presse franco-américaine*, Worcester, Mass., 1911.
Borden, Sir R. L., *Canadian Constitutional Studies*. Revised ed., Toronto, 1929.
Bourinot, J. G., *Canada under British Rule, 1760-1900*, Cambridge, 1900.
Bovey, W., *Canadien; a Study of the French Canadians*, Toronto, 1933.
Bracq, J. C., *Evolution of French Canada*, New York, 1924.
Brebner, J. B., *New England's Outpost*, New York, 1927.
Burt, A. L., *The Old Province of Quebec*, Toronto, 1933.
Cambridge History of the British Empire, Vol. VI, *Canada*, Cambridge, 1930.
Decelles, A. D., *The "Patriotes" of '37. "Chronicles of Canada,"* Vol. XXV, Toronto, 1914-16.
Derosiers, Abbé A., and Bertrand C., *Histoire du Canada*, Montreal, 1925. (School text.)

Durham, Earl of, *Report*, London, 4th edition, 1930. (Editor Sir C. Lucas.)

Egerton, H. L., *Federations and Unions within the British Empire*, Oxford, 1924.

Ewart, J. S., *The Kingdom Papers*, Vol. II, Ottawa, 1912.

Faucher de St. Maurice, *Le Canada et les Canadiens. Français pendant la guerre. Franco-Prussiene*, Quebec, 1888.

Frechette, L., *Feuilles volantes*, Montreal, 1891.

Gagnon, E., *Chansons populaires du Canada*, Quebec, 1865.

Groulx, L., *La Confédération canadienne*, Montreal, 1918.

Hawks, A., *The Birthright; a Search for the Canadian Canadian*, Toronto, 1919.

Hémon, L., *Maria Chapdelaine*, New York, 1921.

Kennedy, W. P. M., *Statutes, Treaties and Documents of the Canadian Constitution*, 2d edition, Oxford, 1930.

Laurier, W., *Discours au Canada*, Montreal, 1909.

Lionnet, J., *Chez les Français du Canada*, Paris, 1910.

Prior, G. T., *The French Canadians in New England; Thesis submitted for Degree of M.A. in History in Graduate School of Brown University*, 1932.

Prunne, J. J. de, *Les Canadiens-français à New York*, Montreal, n. d.

Riddell, W. R., *Constitution of Canada*, New Haven, Conn., 1917.

Robert, E., *Voyages au Canada français*, Paris, 1919.

Rutché and Forget, *Précis d'histoire du Canada*, Montreal, 1932. (School text.)

Shortt, A., and A. G. Doughty, *Public Archives of Canada; Documents Relating to the Constitutional History of Canada*, Ottawa, 1918.

―――― *Canada and Its Provinces*, Toronto, 1914.

Siegfried, A., *Les Deux Races au Canada*, Paris, 1907.

Skelton, O. D., *Life and Letters of Sir Wilfrid Laurier*, New York, 1922.

Trotter, R. G., *Canadian Federation*, London & Toronto, 1924.

Vattier, G., *Essai sur la mentalité canadienne-française*, Paris, 1928.

Viator, C. S., *Histoire du Canada, cours élémentaire—1917; cours intermédiaire—1915;* published by "Les Clercs de St. Viateur," Montreal. (Texts used in Quebec church schools.)

Bibliography

Whitelaw, W. M., *The Maritimes and Canada before Confederation*, Toronto, 1934.
Wittke, C., *A History of Canada*, New York, 1933.

THE WAR PERIOD, 1914-18

A., H. J., *Les Poilus canadiens; le roman du 22 bataillon canadien français*, Quebec, 1918.
Aitken, Sir Max, *Official Story of the Canadian Expeditionary Forces*, Vols. I & II. London, 1916-18. Vol. III is by C. G. D. Roberts.
Duguid, A. Fortesque, *Canadians in Battle, 1915-18*, in Canadian Historical Association Report of Annual Meeting, Toronto, 1935.
Fetherstonhaugh, R. C., *The Royal Montreal Regiment; 14th Battalion C. E. F., Montreal, 1927.*
H. J. A., *see* A., H. J.
Hopkins, J. G., *Canada at War*, New York, 1919.
Kerr, W. B., *Historical Literature on Canada's Participation in the Great War*, in *Canadian Historical Review*, Vols. XIV-XV, December, 1933, and June, 1934.
Lucas, Sir C., *The Empire at War*, Vol. II, Oxford, 1923. (Contains section by Underhill, F. H., on *The Canadian Forces in the War*.)
Winter, C. F., *Lieutenant General Sir Sam Hughes*, Toronto, 1931.

Index

Acadians: loyalty of, 191; recruits, 250
Action catholique, 43, 66, 111, 149; defends Ontario minority, 98; controversy with Olivar Asselin, 114 ff.; attitude toward participation in war, 117, 171 n; silence on recruiting situation, 134; on Encyclical Letter of Pope, 158; on Military Service bill, 194; on isolation of Quebec, 205, 211; against secession, 210; controversy with Bourassa, 213; on Francoeur debate, 224
Action sociale, 61, 66
Allies: desperate situation in 1917, 172; men, the paramount need of, 195; cause in danger, 241
American Revolution, brings Loyalists to Canada, 6
Amiens, result of victory at, 244
Anglo-Canadians: French Canadian attitude toward, 81, 190 n; distrustful of French Canadian loyalty, 159; in Canadian Expeditionary Forces, 190 n, 248; accused of blind devotion to Empire, 221; *see also* Race problem
Anticlericalism, French Canadian dislike for, 38, 47
Anti-conscription, *see* Conscription
Appropriation for defense, 64
Army, *see* Canadian Expeditionary Force
Artistic expression, French Canadian's love of, 45
Asselin, Olivar: attacks on hierarchy, 94, 115, 212; controversy with *Action catholique*, 114 ff.; 163d Battalion raised by, 130, 135; belief in voluntary participation of individual, 131, 135; efforts not appreciated by public, 135
Assembly, French Canadian, struggle with government for control, 10
Atholstane, Lord, plot to blow up residence of, 198

Autonomy, Canadian, advocated by Bourassa, 114, 145
Avenir du nord, 71, 76, 100, 109; opposition to conscription, 195, 206

Barré, Hercule, 83
Begin, Cardinal, 73; quoted, 98; criticized by Asselin, 115; signs petition for federal disallowance of Ontario school law, 155; approval of National Service scheme, 163; on Military Service bill, 194; admonition against violence, 228
Belcourt, Senator, 83
Benedict XV, Pope, Encyclical Letter on bilingual-school issue, 157
Bennett, R. B., 161; chairman of National Service Board, 124, 125
Bien Public (Three Rivers), 75, 107, 133; on conscription, 206
Bilingual controversy, 91 ff., 152 ff., 188; effect upon enlistments, 76; grant to bilingual schools stopped, 94; ferment over Ontario schools, 131 ff.; becomes a federal question, 153; Papal Encyclical on, 157; Britain's promise to safeguard, broken, 213
Bishops sign petition for federal disallowance of Ontario school law, 155
"Bleus," 19
Blondin, P. E., 30, 32, 87; appointed deputy speaker of Commons, 86; urges compatriots to enlist, 110, 166; in cabinet, 203
Bonne Entente movement, 152, 175
Borden, Sir Robert: substitute for Naval Act of 1910, 32, 33; war government, 86 f.; admitted to Committee of Imperial Defense: invited to sit with British cabinet, 101; on British Empire, 114; attitude toward overseas War Office and Sir Sam Hughes, 127; stand on bilingual question, 153; visit to England, 163; seated

Borden, Sir Robert, *continued*
in Imperial War Conference: attitude toward imperial cabinet and co-operation of Dominions, 164; plan for the reorganization of Canada's war effort, 172; states the government's intention of introducing conscription, 173; Military Service bill introduced by, 182; attacked by press, 194, 195; attempts to bring about coalition, 175, 200; leadership of Union government, 203; suggests need of amendments to Military Service Act, 233; defends use of order-in-council, 236; on difficulties of administering Military Service Act, 238; demand for French Canadian brigade, 240

Borden naval bill, 32, 33

Bourassa, Henri, 47, 52, 74, 135; opposition to government war policy, 26; Nationalist movement under guidance of, 27; rumor of portfolio offer, 32; attacks *Action sociale*, 62; *Devoir* founded by, 66; attitude toward war, 76 ff., 88, 89, 101, 112, 113, 140, 142; conservative gains owing to, 86; part in bilingual school controversy, 92, 94, 96; extreme views of, opposed by rural press, 109; *Que devons-nous à l'Angleterre*, 113; advocates Dominion autonomy, 114, 145; influence upon recruiting, 131; Captain Papineau's appeal to, 137; clarifies attitude against war participation, 138; personality, 143; viewpoint analyzed, 144; attack upon England, 146; solution of Canadian problem, 147; opposes annexation to United States, 148; opposition of French Canadians to, 149; solutions of Canadian problem refuted by D'Amours, 150; mistakes, 170; clergy influenced by, 171; attempt to calm compatriots: opposition to conscription, 180; stand on Military Service bill, 195, 197; article on "Sterile Violence," 197; counsel against violence, 198; effort to defeat Union government, 205; attitude toward isolation, 211; analysis of racial question, 212; controversy with *Action catholique*, 213; backed by lower clergy in anti-British campaign, 218; blamed for isolation of Quebec, 221; internment of, demanded, 234; Laurier disclaims connection with, 235; demand for French Canadian brigade, 240; ceases campaign of extreme opposition to government, 242

Boycott of British goods, 11
Briand, Bishop, Pastoral Mandement, 6
Britain, *see* Great Britain
British-born Canadians in army, 81, 190 n
British Defense of the Realm Act, 65
British General Headquarters in France, Canadian section established, 81
British North America Act, 16, 48, 113, 153; clause guaranteeing rights and privileges to Roman Catholics, 155; Section 93, 157
British North American federation discussed, 15
Brown, George, 15
Bruchesi, Archbishop, quoted, 58, 95, 134; defends Ontario minority, 98; approval of National Service scheme, 163; attitude toward conscription, 181; resents conscription issue, 215
Byng, Sir Julian, troops under, 125

Cabinet, British, Borden invited to sit with, 101, 164
Cabinets, Imperial and War, distinction between, 164
Cambrai, Canadian troops victorious in battles around, 245
Canada: ceded to British, 1, 3; Upper and Lower Canada, division into, 8; reunion, 10, 13; Dominion of Canada formed by British North America Act, 16; annexation to United States, 48, 148, 150; urged to look to her own defense, 63; autonomy advocated by Bourassa, 114, 145; Dominions represented in Imperial War Cabinet, 164; status of French Canada in Dominion, 213

Canada, 66, 67; estimate of French Canadian enlistments, 128; on recruiting situation, 133; on conscription, 177; on Military Service bill, 194; on isolation of Quebec, 205; against secession of Quebec, 210; on Francoeur debate, 224
Canadian Army Corps: formed, 102; Sir Arthur Currie takes command, 199; re-

inforces British units, 237; casualties: successes, 245
Canadian Expeditionary Force: in process of organization, 65; plan for organizing, 80; first contingent sails: British-born recruits, 81, 103; native-born recruits: Second Division organized, 82; French Canadian unit, desire for, 83; in 1915, 90; winning laurels, 101; First Division at Ypres and St. Julien, 102; Second Division lands in France, 102; British military control of, 103; dissatisfaction of French Canadian units with inaction, 105; Ministry of Overseas Forces of Canada established to control, 127; troops attacked in Quebec, 167; numbers in France; exploits, 199; women relatives of members given franchise, 201; French Canadians' desire for units made up of their compatriots, 240; triumphant reception of troops, 245; number of French Canadians in, 247 ff.
Canadian Patriotic Fund, 66, 89
Canadians: disenfranchisement of naturalized, 202; *see also* Anglo-Canadians; French Canadians
Canadienisme of French Canadians, 108, 152
Captain of militia, position of, 2
Carleton, Sir Guy, 7
Cartier, George, 15
Casgrain, T. Chase, 85, 86, 125; urges Canadian participation, 110
Catholic Church, *see* Roman Catholic Church
"Catholic Program," 20
Censorship of military news, 242
Chamberlain, Joseph, 25
Charlottetown, Prince Edward Island, conference, 15
Château Clique, 10
Chronicle office looted, 228
Church, *see* Roman Catholic Church
Civil law, French, preserved under Confederation, 16
Civil war, possibility of, 244
Clergy: recruited from habitants, 2; interference with voting, 20; influence of, 40; loyalty, 61; alarmed by Nationalists' anti-war propaganda, 150; dislike for anticlerical France: reason for siding with Bourassa, 170; attitude on conscription, 218; *see also* Roman Catholic Church
Coalition government: proposed too late, 87; advantages, 88; Borden's attempts to form, 175, 200; Laurier's attitude toward, 175
Colleges, urge students to enlist, 239
Colonial Conference, 25
Commission of Inquiry, 11
Committee of Imperial Defense: "War Book" prepared in co-operation with, 54; Sir Robert Borden admitted to, 101
Compulsion, French Canadians' dislike for, 187
Compulsory service, *see* Conscription
Confederation: security of Quebec under, 16; the new Dominion, 18; Abbé Groulx lectures on origins of, 213; results of, 214; position of Quebec in, 221; no serious intention of Quebec's leaving, 243
Confederation Pact of 1867, proposal to break, 220 n
Connaught, Duke of, 89
Conscientious objectors, excused from service, 183
Conscription: rumor, 110, 114; riots, 111; attitude of press, 111, 177 ff.; anticonscription demonstrations, 111, 174, 178 ff., 196, 227 ff.; feared, 123; conflict of 1917, 161 ff.; compulsory selective, proposed, 173; opposition of Laurier, 176; of French Canada, 177 ff.; debates on, 184 ff., 192; divinity students not exempt from, 189, 193, 218; conscripts summoned to report, 200; government's *volte face* on issue resented by churchmen, 215; growing opposition to enforcement of, 234; *see also* Military Service Act
Conservatives: birth of the party, 19; supported by clergy, 20; form alliance with Nationalists, 31; gain in Quebec, 86; stand on bilingual question, 153; French-speaking, oppose conscription: English-speaking, support conscription, 182; vote for Military Service bill, 193
Constitution, violated by military legislation, 221

Constitutional Act of 1791, 7, 113
Courrier de St. Hyacinthe, 72, 100; on conscription, 206; against secession of Quebec, 211; on Francoeur debate, 224
Cremazié, quoted, 48
Croix, 66, 182
Currie, Sir Arthur: in command of Canadian Corps, 199; sends reinforcements to help British units, 237; suggestion for building up French Canadian units, 240

Dafoe, J. W., attacks on Laurier and Quebec, 208
Daily News (Toronto), attack on Quebec, 207
D'Amours, Abbé: Nationalistic condemnation forces retirement, 62 n; called instigator of anti-national attitude of hierarchy, 115; refutation of Bourassa's anti-war theories, 149; view of Nationalism, 150; solution of problems vexing French Canadian opinion, 151; "Jean Vindex'" reply to, 216 ff.; attacked by "Jean Vindex," 217
Dandurand, Senator, 64, 171; on school controversy, 188
Defaulters, 238; amnesty for, 244
Derby Scheme of registration, 122
Desertion, Quebec battalions accused of, 106, 226
Devoir, 66, 67, 68, 89, 158; Nationalist program, 27; attitude toward the war, 76; bilingual controversy, 96, 97, 153, 154; attack upon Britain and Ontario, 109; on conscription, 111, 179, 195; Bourassa's anti-war propaganda, 140, 142; opposition to recruiting, 141; article on "Sterile Violence," 197; supports anti-government electoral campaign, 205; controversy with *Action catholique*, 213; on Francoeur debate, 224; suppression demanded, 234; ceases campaign of extreme opposition to government, 242
Diamond Jubilee Conference, 25
Divinity students refused exemption, 189, 193, 218
Doherty, Mr., Minister of Justice, defends conscription, 192

Dominion formed by British North America Act, 16
Dominions, voice in control of Empire's policy, 101
Dorion, Antoine, 15
Draft, selective, *see* Conscription
Drummond-Arthabaska election, 30, 31
Durham, Lord, 204; report on affairs in British North America, 13

Ecole des Hautes Etudes Commerciales, 40
Economic depression of 1837, 11
Economic field, progress in, retarded, 44
Educational system, Quebec, 39; *see also* Bilingual controversy
Election of 1917, 199 ff.
Elgin, Lord, 14
Encyclicals, Papal, 24, 157
England, *see* Great Britain
English-French Separate School Board, 94
English-speaking Canadians, *see* Anglo-Canadians
Enlistments: mismanagement of, 76; appeal for 500,000 men, 120, 124; analysis of figures, 121, 128; Laurier's opposition to compulsory, 142, 161, 176, 178; French Canadians in army in 1917, 189, 190 n; no record of nationality, 247
Etoile du nord, 69, 70; attitude toward war, 70; supports referendum on conscription, 195; counsel against violence, 198; against secession of Quebec, 211
Evénement, 66, 67; on conscription, 110, 111, 177; attitude on Canada's war effort, 131, 132, 134; on recruiting situation, 131, 133, 134; on Military Service bill, 194; on Francoeur debate, 224; office looted, 228
Exemptions: number demanded, 200; dissatisfaction with administration of, 201; in Quebec, 226, 234; government's cancellation of, 237; government alarmed by strength of opposition to cancellation, 239
Expeditionary Force, *see* Canadian Expeditionary Force

Farmers, opposition to conscription, 239
Federation movement, 14

Feudal tenure of land maintained, 5
57th Battalion (CEF), 103
Foreign entanglements: French Canadians desire to avoid, 26, 31; instinctive recoil from, 63, 132, 138
Foreign policy, imperial, Canada's lack of control over, 108
Forestry Corps (CEF), 199
Forget, Sir Rodolphe, 57
41st Battalion (CEF), 103
14th Battalion (CEF), Royal Montreal Regiment, 103, 249
France, French Canadian's feeling for, 2, 45 ff.
Francoeur, J. N.: secession resolution, 209, 220 n; withdraws motion, 220, 223: secession debates, 223, 243
Frechette, L., quoted, 46 n
Free Press (Manitoba): attacks on Laurier and Quebec, 208; on isolation of Quebec, 209
French Canada: annexation to United States suggested, 11, 48, 148, 150; status in Dominion, 213; *see also* Canada; Montreal; Quebec
French Canadian nationality: birth, 1; Loyalists as menace to, 6; new weapons for preservation of, 8; idea defeated, 12; deprived of active nationalistic character, 12; effect of Lord Durham's report upon, 13; trials, 18 ff.; devotion to sense of, 108, 152, 220; crises of war emphasized, 120, 245 f.; aversion to interference with sense of, 219
French Canadians: religion jeopardized; ability to hold office removed, 3; faith in British justice, 4; attempt of British government to dominate, 10; dissatisfaction over lack of self-government, 11; rebellion against constituted authority abhorrent to, 12; become keystone of government, 14; aversion to participation in foreign wars, 24, 92, 107, 219; sense of belonging to superior nationality, 40; characteristics, 42 ff.; attitude toward Britain and toward English-speaking Canadians, 50; antipathy to Irish coreligionists, 51; exclusive attachment to native land, 63, 108, 152, 180, 187, 212; in Canadian Expeditionary Force, 83, 105, 247 ff.

(*see also* Canadian Expeditionary Force); platonic attachment to France, 91; relegated to minor posts in World War, 104; recruiting efforts considered inadequate, 128; war efforts belittled, 149; determination to defend native land, 180; dislike for compulsion, 187
French language: dominance of, maintained in Quebec, 5; defeat of attempts to oust, 9; dispute over, in schools of Manitoba, 22; French Canadians' devotion to, 42; *see also* Bilingual controversy
French Revolution, reaction of French Canada to, 8

Galt, A. T., 15
Garneau, Sir George, 171
Gauthier, Mgr., 175
Gazette (Montreal), 43, 111; on conscription, 177, 179; on Military Service bill, 193
George, David, *see* Lloyd George, David
Gouin, Sir Lomer, 85, 97, 219; leader of provincial Liberal government, 154; against isolation of Quebec, 223
Governor-General-in-Council, legislation passed by, 236
Governors, British, friendly to French Canadians, 4
Great Britain: attempt to dominate French Canadians, 3, 10; demand for active help in defense of Empire, 27; entry into World War, 55; Canadian troops under control of British war office, 81; Sir Robert Borden seated with cabinet and war councils, 101, 164; military control of Canadian troops, 103; Bourassa's attack upon, 146; attitude of Canadian Church toward, 152; cry for help, 164; British War Cabinet, 165
Groulx, Abbé, lectures on origins of Canadian Confederation, 213
Guibeault, Abbé, 134

Habitants: adjustment to alien allegiance, 1; clergy recruited from, 2; dissatisfaction with Quebec Act, 5; sympathy with cause of American Revolution, 6
Halte-là, "Patriote," 216 ff.

Hawks, Arthur, 175
Hindenburg line, Canadian troops assist in capture of, 245
Home Defense Force, attempt to raise, 165, 168
Hudson's Bay Company, revolt of half-breeds over taking of territory from, 19
Hughes, Sir Sam, 54, 80, 239, 247; accused of anti-French and anti-Catholic prejudices, 104; evasive answer on French Canadian contingent, 106; member of Orange Order, 107; overzealous conduct: asked to resign, 127; accusation against French Canadians and the clergy, 234
Hull (Quebec), anti-conscription meeting, 179
"Hundred Days," 245

Immigration, European menace to Canadian nationality, 214
Imperial Defense, Committee of, 54
Imperial War Conference, 164
Imperial Wars, *see* Wars
Industries, war, 121, 122; men engaged in, excused from service, 182
Institutions, French Canadians' devotion to, 42, 52
Isolationism, 9, 53, 152, 209, 222

"Jean Vindex," *see* "Vindex, Jean"
Joliette, Quebec, 69, 71

Lacoste, Sir Alexander, attempt to swing French Canada over to more active participation, 135
Laflèche, L. R., quoted, 248 n
Lalande, Père Hermas, 216 n
Lalumière, Elie: resistance to conscription, 196; arrest, 198
Lamarche, P. E., 57
Lanctot, Gustave: appeal to compatriots, 139, 140; attack upon Bourassa, 149
Landry, General, 104; devotes himself to cause of Ontario minority, 155; on recruiting policies of government, 187; refusal to withdraw troops in Quebec riots, 229
Language, French, *see* French language
Language question, *see* Bilingual controversy

Lapointe, Ernest, resolution on bilingual question, 153
Laurier, Sir Wilfrid: assumes leadership of Liberal Party, 20; opposes Remedial Bill, 23; war policy, 26, 56; opposed by Bourassa, 28 ff.; naval policy attacked, 29; swept out of power, 31; assertion that Britain's war is Canada's war, 68; approves separate war units for French Canadians, 83; appeal for party truce, 99; advocacy of war supplies, 99, 100; refusal to co-operate with National Service Board, 124; move for parliamentary inquiry into purchase of war material: opposition to compulsory enlistment, 142; stand on bilingual question, 153; support of Lapointe resolution, 154; opposition to conscription, 161, 176, 178; on Sir Robert Borden's sitting with War Cabinet, 164; invited to assist in creating coalition cabinet: declines, 175, 200; reply to the government on Military Service bill, 183; proposes amendment to the Military Service bill, 184; accused of responsibility for Quebec's anti-British bias, 185; Liberal reaction to his stand for a referendum, 186; questions enlistment figures, 191; final appeal against conscription, 192; his amendment to Military Service bill voted down, 193; criticized by *Devoir*, 196; dissatisfaction of Liberals with, 202; Winnipeg convention votes confidence in, 203; loyalty of French Canadians, 204; attacked in election campaign, 207; demand for submission to law, 233; explanation of dissatisfaction with conscription: plea for conciliation, 235; opposition to order-in-council form of legislation, 238
Laurier-Greenway Agreement, 23
Laurier naval bill, 28 ff.
Laval University, 39, 61
Lavergne, Armand, 31, 73, 74, 135; rumor that portfolio had been offered to, 32; stand on language question, 96; command of battalion offered to, 107; and refused, 108; influence upon recruiting, 131, 132; against war participation, 140; reaction to Roy's appeal, 171; against conscription, 179; at-

tempt to dominate mob, 229; internment of, demanded, 234; Laurier disclaims connection with, 235; asked to quiet mob, 237
Law: French civil law preserved under Confederation, 16; French Canadian respect for force of, 157
Lemieux, Rodolphe, 57, 83, 85, 240; advocates participation in war, 110; recruiting estimate, 128, 129; defense of Quebec's war effort, 134
Lessard, General, 73, 104, 166
Lessard-Blondin recruiting mission, 166, 167
Liberals: Church's attitude toward, 19; French Canadians' support of, 20; swept out of power, 31; control in Quebec throughout war, 88; part in racial conflict of 1915, 98 ff.; attitude toward conscription, 142, 182, 186; stand on bilingual question, 153; accused of interference with recruiting in Quebec, 185; vote on Military Service bill, 193; opposition to coalition, 200; dissatisfaction with Laurier's leadership: resent disenfranchisement of enemy-alien voters, 202; majority in Quebec election, 1916, 208; defeat in 1917 election, 212
Ligue Nationaliste, 27
Literature, French Canadian, 44
Lloyd George, David, proposals for imperial co-operation, 164, 165
Lougheed, Senator, 64
"Louis Romain," *see* "Romain, Louis"
Lower Canada: establishment of, 8; proposal to reunite with Upper Canada, 10; reunion with Upper Canada, 13
Loyalists: immigration of, a menace to French Canadian nationality, 6; conflict with, the beginning of racial struggle, 7

Macdonald, Sir John A.: 15; policy of conciliation, 18, 22; ideal to see Canada independent, 147
Mail and Empire (Toronto): on Laurier's refusal to enter a coalition government, 177; on conscription, 180; attacks on Quebec, 207; on Quebec enlistments, 242

Maistre, de, cited, 151
Male population of Canada, classification of, 162
Mandements of Catholic hierarchy, 6, 59, 62
Manitoba: French Canadians emigrate to, 22; school system kept intact, 23
Manpower, inventory of, opposed, 123; classification of, 162
Maritime provinces, loyalty of Acadians from, 191
Maritime union, considered: French Canadian opposition: solution, 15; *see also* Confederation
Martial law, Governor General empowered to declare, 233
Mason, General, enlistment figures, 121, 128, 190
Medical Corps (CEF), 199
Meighen, Arthur, 79; would bankrupt Canada to save Empire, 113
Merchant Report of 1912, 92
Mewburn, General, explanation of new military policy, 239
Migneault, Arthur, 70, 83
Military-boot scandal, 100
Military service, compulsory, *see* Conscription
Military Service Act: put into force, 200; mandate for enforcement of, 209; French Canadian opposition to, 211; Quebec riots against enforcement of, 220; violation of constitution, 221; difficulties of enforcement, 226; office of Registrar burned, 228; Quebec riots due to maladministration, 231; opposed in English-speaking provinces, 234; administration of, defended, 236; total number of men enlisted under, 237 n; French Canadians enlisted under, 249
Military Service bill, 174, 175, 178; debates in Dominion Parliament, 182; provisions, 182; proposed amendment to, 184; attitude toward, of ex-Nationalists, 185; support by Liberals, 186; Laurier's amendment for a referendum voted down: bill becomes law, 193; attitude of press, 193 ff.
Military supplies, scandals over, 99
Military Voters bill, 202

Index

Militia, Minister of, friction with military authorities overseas, 127
Militia Acts, 113, 183
Militia and Defense, Department of, enlistment figures, 248
Ministry of Overseas Forces of Canada, 81
Monk, Mr., 30
Mons, Canadian Corps enters, 245
Montmagny (Quebec), 73
Montreal: French element strongest, 35; recruiting meetings, 85, 141; anti-conscription meetings, 111, 178; industrial population opposed to war, 133; in 1917, 174; opposition of municipal council to conscription, 181; danger of disturbances, 233
Montréal, Université de, 39
Montreal Recruiting Association, attempt to swing French Canada over to more active participation, 135
Motion pictures, influence of clergy, 41
Munitions factories, 121
Murray, Governor, conciliatory policy toward French Canadians, 4

Nantel, W. P., 32, 86
Napoleonic wars, reaction of French Canada to, 9
National Defense, Ministry of, 248
Nationalism opposes imperial patriotism, 27
Nationaliste, 27, 143
Nationalists: form alliance with Conservatives, 32; disclaim desire to form separate party, 42; criticize ultra loyalism of hierarchy, 62; attacked by press, 74; position toward war, 77; use language controversy to embarrass government, 93; opposition to government war policy, 105; stand on participation in Imperial wars, 107; extreme views opposed by rural press, 109; use conscription rumor in anti-British campaign, 110; espouse cause of Ontario minority, 112; feel that Canada should concentrate on war supplies, 122; oppose inventory of man power, 123; denounce recruiting effort, 135; anti-war propaganda, 140, 142; attitude of ex-Nationalists on conscription, 185; effort to defeat Union government, 205; attitude toward isolation of Quebec, 211; defended by "Jean Vindex," 217; accused of agitation against cause of Allies, 222; blamed for ferment in Quebec, 236
National Service: inventory of man power, 123; registration of population for: meetings, 125; approved by Church, 163; vagueness and compromise over, 163
National Service Board, 162; composition predominantly Conservative, 123
National Unity Congress, Montreal, 175
Naval Service Bill of 1910, 28 ff.; Borden's substitute for, 32
Navy, Canadian building of, opposed, 27
New Brunswick: Acadians in battalions of, 191; racial harmony in, 192
New England, French Canadians in, 44
New France, religious tenor of, 36
"New School of Imperialists," 217
Newspapers, *see* Press
Ninety-two Resolutions, 11

"O Canada," 111
163d Battalion (CEF): dispatched to Bermuda, 130; raised to war strength, 135
165th Battalion (CEF), 191
Ontario: language controversy, 76, 91 ff.; attempt to pass anti-French laws, 96 ff.; recruiting situation, 136; recruiting efforts of Quebec and Ontario compared, 162 n, 190 n; exemptions, 201, 226 n; press attacks Quebec, 207; opposition to conscription, 239
Ontario Department of Education, Regulation Seventeen, 92, 93, 153, 156
Ontario minority, 112; wrongs endured, 131 ff.; concession to, opposed by West, 154
Ontario School Law: considered violation of confederation pact, 156; constitutionality of, upheld, 157
Order-in-council: permits military authorities to hold prisoners, 230; protest against government's use of, 236
Order-in-council government, 65; dissatisfaction with, 232

Ottawa schools, legislation creating a government commission to control, declared unconstitutional, 157
Overseas Military Council, Sir Sam Hughes' attempt to establish, 127
Overseas Military Forces of Canada: Ministry of, 199; established, 127

Paaschendaele-Ypres salient, Canadian victory in, 199
Pacquet, Mr., resignation, 181
Papal Encyclical: urged acceptance of Laurier-Greenway Agreement, 24; on bilingual-school issue, 157
Papineau, Louis Joseph, 137; elected speaker of assembly, 10; Ninety-two Resolutions: flees at outbreak of 1837 rebellion, 11
Papineau, Captain Talbot, appeal to compatriots, 137, 139, 140
Paquet, Mgr., 215 n
Parc LaFontaine, anti-conscription meeting, 111, 178
Parc Sohmer, Montreal, recruiting meeting, 85
Parliament (Dominion): war measures approved, 63; divided on racial lines, 182; discussion elicited by Quebec riots, 233; both Houses called into secret session, 237
Pastoral letters, 59 ff., 74, 115, 144, 212, 214
Pastoral Mandement of 1914, 59; *Action sociale* follows lead of, 62
Patenaude, E., 86, 87, 125; resignation, 181; disapproval of conscription bill, 185
Patricia, *see* Princess Patricia
Patrie (Montreal), 66, 67, 98, 110, 149; deplores Nationalist accusations, 112; bilingual controversy, 153, 154; attitude on conscription, 177; on Military Service bill, 194; against secession of Quebec, 210; on Francoeur debate, 224
Patriotism: imperial, opposed by nationalism, 27; two concepts of Canadian, 212
Pelletier, L. J., 32, 73, 86, 104
Periodicals, Catholic, 61
Petit canadien, 61; defends Ontario minority, 98

Peuple (Montmagny), 73; attack upon Bourassa, 110; on conscription, 195, 206; counsel against violence, 198; against secession of Quebec, 211; on Francoeur debate, 224
Police, behavior in Quebec riots, 227, 232
Politics: clerical interference in, 41; French Canadian's passion for, 42 ff.; revival of partisan, during war, 98
Population, proportion of British-born to Canadian-born, 103
Press: critical of government's war policy, 26; influence of clergy on, 41; preoccupation with politics, 43; patriotism of French Canadian, 66 ff.; slow to appreciate significance of crisis, 67; champions cause of Ontario minority, 97; efforts to stimulate recruiting, 108; attitude toward conscription, 110, 111, 174, 177 ff., 204; attitude toward enlistment, 131 ff.; attitude toward National Service scheme, 162; on Military Service bill, 193; counsel against violence, 198; on isolation of Quebec, 209; reaction to Francoeur debate, 223; acceptance of censorship regulations, 242
Press, Catholic, 61
Press, metropolitan: efforts to maintain attitude of loyalty, 109
Press, rural: enthusiasm for cause of Britain and France, 69; attitude toward war, 70 ff., 109; reaction to war-supplies scandals, 100; opposes extreme views of Nationalists, 109; of Quebec opposition to conscription, 195; on election issuse, 206; attacks on Quebec, 207; against secession of Quebec, 211
Presse (Montreal), 66, 67, 68, 84, 98; on conscription, 111, 177; deplores Nationalist accusations, 112; estimate o French Canadian enlistments, 128; on recruiting situation, 132; recruiting pamphlet, 135; bilingual controversy 153; on compulsory service, 167; on Military Service bill, 194; on exemptions, 201; supports Liberal cause alarmed by Quebec's isolation, 204 against secession of Quebec, 210; on Francoeur debate, 224

268　　　　　　　　　　*Index*

Princess Patricia's Canadian Light Infantry, 81

Privy Council, London, Judicial Committee, decision on Ontario School Law, 156

Quebec (province): dominance of French language maintained, 5; isolation, 9, 53, 204 ff.; conference to consider maritime union: solution arrived at, 15; special rights preserved under Confederation: becomes pivot of Dominion, 16; war policy, 28; opposes 1910 naval bill, 30, 33; a state within a state, 35; educational system, 39 (*see also* Bilingual controversy); allegiance to, 52; attitude toward the war, 55, 138; early war enthusiasm, 56, 106; loyalty of rural press, 72; recruiting situation, 112, 120 ff.; dislike for the war, 138; solidarity shown by return of provincial Liberal government, 154; recruiting efforts compared with those of Ontario, 162 n, 190 n; reasons for apparent recruiting failure, 170, 184; opposition to conscription, 181, 197, 239; possibility of secession from Confederation, 182; Laurier held responsible for anti-British bias, of, 185; exemptions problem, 189, 193, 201, 218, 226 n; against Union government, 203; attacked by press in Ontario and the West, 207; election campaign: returns anti-government delegation, 208; Francoeur secession resolution and debates, 209, 220, 223, 243; anti-war feeling in 1917, 218; reaction of provincial legislators toward isolation, 222; essential loyalty, 236; Laurier's defense of, 238; General Mewburn's conciliatory attitude toward, 239; demand for French Canadian brigade, 240; co-operation in registration of men and women, 241; fears German victory, 241; innate sense of law and order, 242 f.; passively nationalistic, 243; French Canadian population, 249 n

Quebec Act, 1, 4; habitants dissatisfied with, 5

Quebec riots: attributed to persecutions, 188; election riots, 208; riots against Military Service Act, 220; anti-draft riots, 227 ff.; Toronto battalion sent to subdue, 230; jury investigation, 231; instigated by enemies of French Canada, 235; results, 243

Que devons-nous à l'Angleterre, 113

Race problem: conflict between French Canadians and Loyalists, 7; racial antipathy, 49; interracial relationship, 50; revived, 90; animosity extended to Britain, 91; Bourassa's view of, 144; hatred increased, 150; *Bonne Entente* movement, 152, 175; Parliament divided on racial lines, 182; cleavage of country on racial rather than party lines, 186, 193; harmony in New Brunswick, 192; Bourassa's analysis of, 212; menace of European immigration, 214; Toronto soldiers sent to Quebec inflame passion, 228, 230; tension discussed in Parliament, 233 f.; improvement of relationship at close of war, 244; problem of unity unsolved, 245; unprecedented bitterness fostered by war, 247

Railway troops (CEF), 199

Rainville, Mr., resignation, 181

Rebellion of 1837, 11; defeat at Lacolle, 12

Recruiting situation, 120 ff.; Montreal meetings, 85, 141; analysis of figures, 121, 128; difficulty of, in 1916, 129; French Canadian reaction to, 134, 159; no record of nationality of recruits, 247

Registration of population for National Service, 125, 162

Regulation Seventeen, Ontario Department of Education, 92, 93, 153, 156

Religion, *see* Roman Catholic Church

Religious orders, French, 38

Remedial bill, 23

Revue canadienne, 61

Revue dominicaine, 61, 72

Riel, Louis, 19

Riot, conscription: Parc Lafontaine, Montreal, 111; *see also* Quebec riots

"Romain, Louis," article on doctrinal aspects of Canadian participation in the war, 214; probable identity, 215 n

Roman Catholic Church: French Canadian's relations with, 2; Britain grants new subjects liberty of Catholic religion, 3; right to collect tithes, 5, 38; control of tithes, 7; influence over education in Quebec, 16; Jesuit estates returned: attitude toward Liberal Party, 19; opposes Laurier, 23; Papal Encyclicals on bilingual controversy, 24, 157; in Canada, 36 ff.; organization, 38; hostility to French freethinking, 45, 47; Canadian Church in the United States, 51; attitude toward war, 58; Pastoral Letters and *Mandements*, 59 ff.; publications, 61; school taxes, 91 n; charged with disloyalty to cause of Canadian participation in war, 105; Asselin's attacks upon Canadian hierarchy, 114; accused of exceeding its powers, 115; attitude toward Canada's war effort, 134; anti-Catholic feeling increased, 150; attitude toward Britain, 152; bishops petition for federal disallowance of Ontario school law, 155; bad feeling between Irish and French Canadian Catholics, 158 n; approval of National Service scheme, 163; clergy influenced by Bourassa, 171; attitude toward conscription, 181; aroused by proposal to deny exemption to divinity students, 189; division of opinion on war policy, 212; guarantee of religious rights to, not upheld, 213; attitude on participation in war, 214; disunion within, 215; clergy resent conscription issue, 215; "Jean Vindex" criticizes hierarchy, 216; *see also* Clergy; Ontario minority

Roy, Ferdinand: appeal to compatriots, 168 ff.; reaction to appeal, 171

Roy, Paul Eugène, 115

St. Hyacinthe (Quebec), religious setting, 71

St. Jean, training quarters, 84

St. Jean Baptiste Society, 61; defends Ontario minority, 98

St. Jerome (Quebec), 71; anti-conscription parade, 179

St. Julien, First Canadian division at, 102

Scandals over war-supplies, 99

School controversy, *see* Bilingual controversy

Schools, clerical dominance of, 39

Secession resolution and debates, 209, 220, 223, 243

Seigneurs, relation to habitants, 2, 3; loyalty to Britain, 5

Semaine religieuse, defends Ontario minority, 98

Separate School Board (Ontario), 157

Separate School System, Ontario, 94

Sevigny, Alfred, 30, 57, 86; in cabinet, 166, 203; upholds conscription, 185

Shaughnessy, Lord, on recruiting for war and industry, 122

Shell Committee, 142

Sifton, Sir Clifford, leader of anti-Laurier Liberals, 202

61st Militia Regiment, 73

69th Battalion (CEF), 103

Soldiers' vote to uphold government, 209

Soleil, 66

South African war, 25, 80

Students of divinity refused exemption, 189, 193, 218

Taché, Etienne, 15

Tarte family, *Patrie* owned by, 67

Tellier, J. M., 83, 85

Test Act, French Canadians required to subscribe to, 4

Theater, influence of clergy, 41

Three Rivers (Quebec), 74

Tithes: right of church to collect, 5, 38; church control of, 7

Toronto, war policy, 28

Toronto battalion sent to subjugate Quebec, 228, 230

Treaty of Paris of 1763, 3

Troops, Canadian, *see* Canadian Expeditionary Force

22d (French Canadian) Battalion (CEF), 89, 102, 103, 140, 249; formation authorized, 84; in victory at Courcelette, 126; part played by, 200, 245

206th Battalion (CEF), 130

Union government: Sifton's plan for, 202; support of Liberals, 203; triumphant return of, 208

United States: question of annexation to, 11, 48, 148, 150; French Canadian atti-

270   Index

United States (Cont'd)
  tude toward, 50; French Catholic communities in, 51
Université de Montréal, 39
Universities urge students to enlist, 239
Upper Canada: occupied by Loyalists, 8; proposal to reunite with Lower Canada, 10; reunion with Lower Canada, 13

Valcartier (Quebec), military camp, 81, 82
Valenciennes, Canadian Corps captures, 245
Verité, article on doctrinal aspects of Canadian participation in the war, 214
Vimy Ridge, captured by Canadian troops, 199
"Vindex, Jean," *Halte-là, "Patriote,"* 216 ff.

War Book, 33, 54
War industries, 121, 122; men engaged in, excused from service, 182
War measures, large number enacted in 1916, 142
War Measures Act, 1914, 65
War policy of Canadian hierarchy attacked by Asselin, 114
Wars, imperial, participation in: agitation against, 24; Bourassa's views, 92; attitude of Nationalists, 107; not an obligation of Canadians, 216
War-supplies scandals, 99

War Time Election Act, 1917, 201, 203; violation of constitution, 221
West: opposes concession to Ontario minority, 154; in favor of conscription, 203, 208
Winnipeg convention of western Liberals, 203
Women, enfranchisement of, 202
Wood, Colonel, 249
World War: Quebec's reluctance to take active part in, 9; Canada's preparation for, 54 ff.; entry of Britain and Canada, 55; attitude toward, 66 ff.; French Canadian recruiting, 79; Canadian military effort, 80; high watermark of enthusiasm for participation in, 85; cooling off of ardor, 87; battles in which Canadians took prominent part, 102, 125, 199; accurate estimate of French Canadian enlistments difficult to make, 103, 106; French Canadians relegated to minor posts in, 104; opposition among industrial population of Montreal, 133; hostility to Dominion's war effort, 166; Canadian participation in, 214 ff.

Ypres, First Canadian division at, 102

Zouaves, Papal, French Canadians enlist in ranks of, 25

NOTE ON THE AUTHOR

It perhaps appears curious that such an important Canadian study as *Crisis of Quebec, 1914-1918* was written by an American, but Elizabeth Armstrong's background suited her for the task. She was born in New York City of a fairly well-to-do Episcopalian family. In 1920 she graduated from Bernard College, one of the best liberal art colleges in the United States. She travelled in Europe many times, acquired a fluent knowledge of French and attended University of Zurich in 1927. The surging tides of nationalism then rising in Europe must have made a deep impression on her in those years. Her brother, George Alexander Armstrong, was an American career diplomat and Elizabeth spent some years in such parts as Warsaw and Lisbon. In the middle thirties she entered a doctoral program at Columbia University, where she probably studied under Carleton Hayes, a great American authority on nationalism. However, it was Professor John Bubner who suggested that she write the thesis on French-Canadian nationalism which was later published in 1937 under the title of this book. During the forties she entered the American diplomatic service as a representative of the United States on the United Nations commitees that dealt with non-self-governing territories and Carribean matters. In 1951 she joined the Brookings Institute from which she retired in 1953. She died in 1957.*

* The biographical notes were supplied by James Frederick Green who was a friend of Elizabeth Armstrong as well as one of her colleagues in the American diplomatic service.

SUGGESTIONS FOR FURTHER READING

Miss Armstrong included an extensive bibliography in her book. But since 1937, the year in which the *Crisis of Quebec* appeared, a considerable literature has been added to the history of the period. A good, general review of the events of the war, seen from French Canada, is to be found in Mason Wade's *The French Canadians, 1760-1945* (Toronto, 1955). His interpretation is similar to that of Miss Armstrong but he has incorporated material not used by her in his work.

Miss Armstrong's view of Laurier was based on the powerful biography of the Liberal leader by O. D. Skelton, *Life and Letters of Sir Wilfrid Laurier*, 2 vols. (Toronto, 1921, re-issued in the Carleton Library series, Toronto, 1965). A pertinent contemporary article by Skelton, not to be found in Miss Armstrong's bibliography, is "Conscription," *Queen's Quarterly*, Vol. 25, No. 2, (1918). Skelton, who considered Laurier to be the "noblest and most unselfish man" he ever knew, believed that the Conservatives were responsible for the breakdown of national unity. Most historians writing since have been sympathetic to this point of view. Joseph Schull's biography of Laurier (*Laurier: The First Canadian*, Toronto, 1965) continues this line of argument. But perhaps the most convincing defence of Laurier is to be found in the last chapter of H. B. Neatby's book, *Laurier and a Liberal Quebec: A Study in Political Management* (The Carleton Library, No. 63, McClelland and Stewart Limited, 1973). Neatby has also written a perceptive article on Laurier's view of imperialism in "Laurier and Imperialism," *Canadian Historical Association Report*, 1955. James A. Crowley argues that political expediency and Imperial influences were the main reasons for the introduction of conscription. (James A. Crowley, Borden: Conscription and Union Government, unpublished Ph.D. thesis, University of Ottawa, 1958). See also Paul Stevens' "Wilfrid Laurier: Politician," in Marcel Hamelin, ed., *The Political Ideas of the Prime Ministers of Canada* (Ottawa, 1969).

In 1922 John Dafoe published his trenchant criticism of Laurier's actions during the conscription crisis – *Laurier: A Study in Canadian Politics* (Toronto, 1922, later reprinted in the Carleton Library Series, No. 3, 1963). A contemporary scholar who finds fault with Laurier is D. G. Creighton in his book, *Canada's First Century* (Toronto, 1970). G. R. Cook presents the most judicious discussion of the claims of both Laurier and Dafoe supporters in his very important article, "Dafoe, Laurier and the Formation of Union Government" (*Canadian Historical Review*, XLII(3) September, 1961).

In her bibliography, Miss Armstrong omitted two important pamphlets by Henri Bourassa: *Win the War and Lose Canada* (Montreal, 1917) and *Le Pape, arbitre de la paix* (Montreal, 1918). Bourassa's views and action during the war are vividly described by one of his great admirers, Robert Rumilly, in his *Henri Bourassa: la vie publique d'un grand Canadien* (Montreal, 1953). On the other hand, M. P. O'Connell attacks the Nationalist leader's war time attitudes: (Henri Bourassa and Canadian Nationalism, unpublished Ph.D. thesis, University of Toronto, 1954). P. E. Smith also disapproves of Bourassa: (Henri Bourassa and Sir Wilfrid Laurier, unpublished M. A. thesis, University of Toronto, 1948). There is a chapter on Bourassa in war time in C. Morrow, *Henri Bourassa and French-Canadian Nationalism: Opposition to Empire* (Montreal, 1968). Rene Durocher throws a considerable light on Bourass'a relations with the Catholic Church during the war in his article, "Henri Bourassa, les évêques et la guerre de 1914-1918," to appear in the forthcoming issue of the *Canadian Historical Association Report*. The reader should also consult Joseph Levitt's; *Henri Bourassa and the Golden Calf: The Social Program of the Nationalists of Quebec* (Ottawa, 1969) and his collection of Bourassa's writings and statements, *Henri*

Bourassa on Imperialism and Biculturalism 1900-1918 (Toronto, 1970). Oliver Asselin's complex attitude towards Canadian participation is discussed in the second volume of Marcel A. Gagnon's *La Vie Orageuse d'Oliver Asselin* (Montreal, 1962). An important article by A. R. M. Lower, not used by Miss Armstrong is "In Unknown Quebec," *U.T.Q.*, Vol. 6, no. 1 (1936-7), pp. 89-102.

The most important contributions to appear on the subject since the publication of Miss Armstrong's book have been a number of excellent biographies of English-speaking participants: W. R. Graham, *Arthur Meighen: The Door of Opportunity* (Toronto, 1960); M. Donnelly, *Dafoe of the Free Press*, (Toronto, 1968); G. R. Cook, *The Politics of John W. Dafoe and the Free Press* (Toronto, 1963), and M. Prang, The Political Career of Newton W. Rowell (unpublished Ph.D. thesis, University of Toronto, 1959). Four important articles, all drawn from *The Canadian Historical Review*, have been brought together, with Carl Berger's stimulating introduction, in *Conscription 1917* (Toronto, n.d., Canadian Historical Readings, No. 8). In addition to the essay by Ramsay Cook already referred to ("Dafoe, Laurier and the Formation of Union Government"), the collection comprises: O. M. Bliss, "The Methodist Church and World War I," demonstrates how Methodist opinion was mobilized for conscription; M. Robin, "Registration, Conscription, and Independent Labour Politics, 1916-1917" shows how complicated was Labor's reaction towards conscription, and A. M. Willm's provides a stout defence of Borden's conscription policies in "Conscription 1917: A Brief for the Defense."

Of primary value on the Ontario School Question there are F. A. Walker, *Catholic Education and Politics in Ontario* (Toronto, 1964); M. Prang, "Clerics, Politicians and the Bilingual School Issue in Ontario, 1910-1917" in *The Canadian Historical Review*, XLI (4) December, 1960; and M. Barber, "The Ontario Bilingual Schools Issue: Sources of Conflict," *Canadian Historical Review*, XLVII (3) September, 1966. A more informative source is P. Ferraro, "English Canada and the Election of 1917," (unpublished M.A. thesis, McGill University, 1971). Desmond Morton examines recruiting in French Canada from a different perspective in "French Canada and War, 1868-1917: the Military background to the Conscription

Crisis of 1917," a chapter in J. L. Granatstein and R. D. Cuff, *War and Society in North America* (Toronto, 1971). There are two excellent recent histories of the Canadian participation in the war: Col. G. W. L. Nicholson, *Canadian Expeditionary Force 1914-1918* (Ottawa, 1962) and J. Swettenham, *To Seize the Victory: The Canadian Corps in World War I* (Toronto, 1965) – Nicholson's volume has a most useful appendix on enlistments and casualties.* There is a good short description of the election of 1917 in J. M. Beck, *Pendulum of Power: Canada's Federal Elections* (Toronto, 1968) and in the *Canadian Annual Review of 1917* (Toronto, 1918), two chapters of which were published separately by the editor, J. C. Hopkins, under the title of *The Union Government*. In view of his later importance, on Mackenzie King's reaction to the conscription crisis see R. MacGregor Dawson, *William Lyon Mackenzie King: A Political Biography 1874-1923* (Toronto, 1958), F. A. MacGregor, *The Fall and Rise of Mackenzie King* (Toronto, 1962) and an article by H. S. Ferns and G. Ostry "Mackenzie King and the First World War," *Canadian Historical Review*, XXXVI (2) June 1955.

---

* It is to be noted that Armstrong did not make use of L. G. Dejardin's *L'Angleterre, le Canada et la grande guerre* (Quebec, 1918).

NOTE ON THE AUTHOR OF
THE INTRODUCTION

Joseph Levitt is Associate Professor of History at the University of Ottawa. He is the author of *Henri Bourassa and the Golden Calf: The Social Program of the Nationalists of Quebec, 1900-1914.*